Governing by Design

Culture, Politics,
and the Built Environment

Dianne Harris, Editor

GOVERNING BY DESIGN

Architecture, Economy, and Politics
in the Twentieth Century

AGGREGATE

University of Pittsburgh Press

Published by the University of Pittsburgh Press, Pittsburgh, Pa., 15260
Copyright © 2012, University of Pittsburgh Press
All rights reserved
Manufactured in the United States of America
Printed on acid-free paper

10 9 8 7 6 5 4 3 2 1

Library of Congress Cataloging-in-Publication Data

Aggregate (Group), author.
Governing by design : architecture, economy, and politics in the twentieth century /
Aggregate.
pages cm — (Culture, politics, and the built environment)
ISBN 978-0-8229-6178-9 (pbk.)
1. Architecture and society—History—20th century. 2. Design—Social aspects—
History—20th century. I. Hyde, Timothy, author, editor. II. Title.
NA2543.S6A395 2012
724'6—dc23   2011048864

Contents

PART III Engineering and Culture

Introduction

■

DANIEL M. ABRAMSON, ARINDAM DUTTA, TIMOTHY HYDE, AND JONATHAN MASSEY FOR AGGREGATE

HOW does change happen? This question underlies the chapters collected in *Governing by Design*. From this basic query arise new accounts of the twentieth-century built environment that pursue a set of corollary questions: Who authors design? How does architecture participate in modernization? How does architecture govern?

Governing by design, this book suggests, is not simply a matter of monumental symbolism and space, state power and authority, imposed control and surveillance. This book instead sets architecture in relation to mundane matters: food, bodies, housing, markets, cities, and culture. How do we regulate basic aspects of our lives through design, such as the consumption of food and shelter? How do we manage the risks of modernization to our bodies and environments? How is culture produced by politics, planning, and architecture? How are we fashioned as citizens by our homes, cities, and heritage? Examining how issues of risk, regulation, consumption, and citizenship have played themselves out in architectural practices and projects from the 1880s up to the present in the Americas, Africa, Europe, and Asia, these chapters may help change the way we look at architecture and its history globally.

What links this book's contributions together is the idea of architecture governing conduct—mediating power—through networks and norms, frames of action and possibility that flow through all scales from the body to the home to the city to the globe, at the hands of not just the state but also individuals and institutions. The chapters are linked, in other words, by an engagement with "governmentality," the concept that the philosopher Michel Foucault developed to describe the combination of protocols, rules, structures, and institutions through which our desire to be governed is cultivated and channeled. Rather than frame governance only through the activities of the state, Foucault and others have mapped an array of mechanisms that mediate power to regulate our conduct, encompassing everyday practices and mind-sets along with administrative protocols and organizational procedures.

Foucault developed his conception of governmentality through studies of eighteenth- and nineteenth-century Europe, where states and nongovernmental institutions aggregated data to constitute knowledge frameworks and expertise profiles capable of managing populations by regulating their demographics, health, housing, environmental conditions, employment, social lives, and culture. This "administration of life" constituted a biopolitics that the sociologist Mitchell Dean has described as being "aimed at enhancing the lives of a population through the application of a norm."[1] For Foucault, Dean, and others the goal of governmentality, and the raison d'être of the modern state, is to provide security to the processes of life—to tame risk, be it through social insurance schemes, food regulation, or housing norms.

Governmentality works less by the application of raw state power than through a multiplicity of heterogeneous public and private agencies, standards, forms of knowledge, effects, outcomes, and consequences that Dean has described as "mobile, changing, and contingent assemblages" continually "constructed, assembled, contested, and transformed."[2] It operates not in the register of high culture, politics, and history, but rather in what the anthropologist Paul Rabinow, writing about French planning practices, has characterized as "a middle ground where social technicians were articulating a normative, or middling modernism . . . pragmatic technicians seeking to find scientific and practical solutions to public problems in times of crisis."[3]

For this book's contributors, architecture is coextensive with the assemblage that is governmentality; we recognize it not only in the edifices that house and facilitate modern institutions but also in the organizational logics, processes, and systems that call them forth. This edited volume explores the complex and dynamic ways that forms of knowledge and regimes of practice emerge, are institutionalized, and are transformed. Take the concept of home. It can seem self-evident, something to be taken for granted. Conversely, it can be explained through totalizing theories of modernization and progress. Several of the chapters that follow address "home," treating it instead as a multiple, mutable concept produced and reproduced in a range of contexts by specific agents, practices, ideas, and events.

For residents of the United States, citizenship and social standing have been intimately bound up with the forms of self-regulation built into norms of "home" shaped and contested by government policy, by the markets in credit, insurance, and other services as well as by the shelter press and other cultural media. For midcentury Iranians, domestic choices engaged in complex contestations among international Cold War politics, Western consumerism, traditional architectural morphologies, local leftist politicians, and the religious views of Shiite clerics. In Pakistan, meanwhile, "home" was conceived as a place where the state's management of the built environment would be as ceaseless as the citizenry's transition to modernity.

An analytics of governmentality calls for methods of historical research and interpretation that often diverge from those that predominate in existing histories of twentieth-century architecture. The best recent compendiums on the subject are still today self-confessedly "largely a history of the masters" focused on famous "landmarks as emblematic of larger tendencies" in architectural culture.[4] In those accounts the goal of theorizing architectural modernism too often separates design from the process of modernization, treating modernity as a preexisting framework that design either exemplifies, confronts agonistically, or compensates for in the mode of a "coping mechanism."[5]

The chapters in this edited volume take a different tack. To reconstruct the ways architecture has participated in modern governmentality, they explore complex concepts of authorship and agency, focus on events and the contingency that characterizes them, and attend to the diverse projects and practices through which architecture has contributed to the formation of liberal power. To be sure, in reading through this book, you will encounter figures familiar from other accounts of twentieth-century architecture, including Louis Sullivan, José Luis Sert, and Buckminster Fuller. But you will also meet figures and subjects little discussed in previous architectural histories—from the Quincy Market Cold Storage Company, the American Public Health Association, and the Karachi Housing Authority to the economist John Maynard Keynes, the Ayatollah Khomeini, and the housing reformer Constance Bartlett Crane of Kalamazoo, Michigan. This reflects the authors' shared conviction that agency is complex; that authorship of the built environment is dispersed across multiple registers comprising not only architects and designers but also many other kinds of producers and consumers, along with a multitude of associations, institutions, and bureaucracies.

Complementing this expanded field of agents, or architectural subjects, is a revised conception of architectural objects. Rather than focus on singular buildings, monuments, and landmarks, these chapters develop close readings of architectural events—moments when architecture and design participated integrally in managing the changes associated with modernization. The salvage of Nile River Valley temples threatened by the Aswan Dam, the replanning of Havana, the relocation of food markets from central Paris to its suburbs—these and other events are moments of transition when architecture was called forth as the solution to a crisis induced by the process of modernization. By focusing on events, the book's chapters shift our attention from the avant-garde, and the many varieties of modernism that its members promoted, to the architectures that facilitated and emerged from broader social transformations.

Disaggregating architecture's subjects and objects in this way highlights not only the complexity of agency but also its fundamental contingency. Rather than affirming the continuity from architect's intention to realization in the completed building, or confirming master narratives of progress or conflict, these chapters emphasize the degree to which intention and outcome are separated by accidental confluences, redirected intentions, and unforeseen outcomes. Several contributions, in fact, address failures, points in the historical record when projects went unrealized. They suggest that plans, schemes, books, journals, objects, buildings, and technologies often emerge less from pure intentionality as out of negotiation with the radical indeterminacy of a given situation. These various designs are contingent assemblages through which the apparatuses of power take on architectural figure.

This edited volume, including the introduction, has been collaboratively developed by ten scholars trained in the history and theory of architecture. Although the ten chapters are individually authored, and by and large reflect research trajectories already under way at the collection's inception, they reflect a multiyear process of mutual interrogation and assistance. Coming together in intermittent symposia and working sessions, we helped one another to frame our subjects, present our findings, coordinate our questions, and rethink our results. Like the architectural events they analyze, each of the chapters that follow results from successive episodes of conversation and conceptualization, critique and revision. Collectively the chapters provide a view of the twentieth century from the perspective of architectural history—not an architectural history of static objects, individual designers, and disciplinary autonomy, but rather an account of how architecture participated in the political, economic, and cultural management of change.

What then can a collection of architectural histories spanning from the 1880s to the present teach us about modernization in general? Historical accounts of the past century identify certain unifying themes: great catastrophes along with intense, intermingled hopes and fears for the future; capitalism's confrontation with socialism, plus its golden age in the twentieth century's third quarter; increasing government control over economic life; the loss of cultural memory; and urbanization and globalization.[6] Tracing broad chronological and geographical arcs, the chapters in *Governing by Design* feature a diversity of material intersecting these themes.

In part one, "Food, Shelter, and the Body," four chapters, presenting material from the first four decades of the twentieth century, show how basic aspects of human life came under various regulatory practices and regimes, produced symbiotically between states and other social and economic groupings. Michael Osman gives us the pioneering cold storage facilities of turn-of-the-twentieth-century Chicago and Boston, which helped produce new habits of buying and assessing the risks of modern, commodified food. Jonathan Massey presents a history of American domestic design through the lens of evolving mortgage practices, how architects and promoters since the 1920s have adapted plans, technology, styling, and financing to the expectations and limitations of mortgaged home ownership. Daniel M. Abramson's chapter on obsolescence traces the concept's development from 1920s office buildings to 1930s cities as a dominant public health and planning paradigm for comprehending and managing change in the built environment. The obsolescence paradigm resulted in postwar urban renewal projects like the infamous demolition of Boston's West End neighborhood. John Harwood's chapter shows how the 1930s invention of ergonomics designed the human body's relationship to modern machine environments—on the factory floor, in wartime, and in space. This resulted not only in today's commonplace architectural design standards but also in the governance of ourselves as always and everywhere in need of protection from environmental risk, or "man as target" in the industrial designer Ernst Neufert's apt, chilling phrase for our age of carpal tunnel and sick building syndromes.

In these chapters by Osman, Massey, Abramson, and Harwood, architecture's role was not to create monumental objects symbolizing order and stability but to research and design norms for food, shelter, community, and bodies. Design would help govern conduct not primarily through representation but by engaging a whole range of subjects—businessmen, architects, policy makers, and citizens—in forms of knowledge formation and lived practices whose ultimate goal was the mitigation of risk in a modernizing society. In other words, what takes place in the events revealed in these chapters was the recognition, assessment, and management of risk. In them we see various actors facing up to the fearful consequences of modernization and using design in attempts to control the future.

These techniques, norms, and practices of design, all adumbrated by 1940, were thus set to be implemented and expanded in post–World War II reconstruction efforts, creating a framework for the long period of stability and prosperity in the capitalist West that stretched roughly from midcentury into the 1970s. What this book's history of architecture from 1900 to 1950 shows us in detail—and thus how architecture teaches history—are the manifest ways that regulations of risk were complexly produced, selected, and adapted from the levels of state and economy down to the intimate scales of body and home, where history is directly lived. The regimes of risk regulation that emerged to propel and stabilize the postwar period emerged out of a whole range of contingent circumstances in the previous forty years. The implicit argument in these chapters is that you can't understand postwar stability without comprehending the prewar history of governing by design, through the regulations of risk in cold storage food warehouses, mortgaged home ownership, urban obsolescence, and bodily ergonomics.

In part two, "Global States and Citizens," chapters by Timothy Hyde, Pamela Karimi, and M. Ijlal Muzaffar explore how governance by design worked variously in the period between 1940 and 1960 outside of the leading capitalist nation-states. Hyde explains how links between midcentury Cuba's constitution writing and cultural debates found expression in urban planning, so that a Harvard law professor's proposal for Cuba of "an impermanent constitution" helps explicate the traditionalism of José Luis Sert's modernist Plan for Havana. Within this plan, gridded streets and courtyard houses constituted a kind of built constitutional framework—urban planning tools for governing citizenship. In Karachi, Pakistan, as Muzaffar's chapter explains, the state forcefully intertwined design and governance, producing with foreign expert assistance standardized housing schemes to acculturate refugees to modern urban living.

At the same time, the state projected these urban plans as deliberately open-ended so as to ensure the state's own long-term role coordinating the population's cultural identity conceived of as permanently in transition, permanently modernizing, and so in permanent need of active state planning and governance. The top-down governance through design of culture in transition also features in Karimi's chapter on postwar Iranian domesticity. Here, significantly, a bottom-up history emerges of resistance and redirection by Iranian leftists, Shiite clerics, and everyday citizens toward officially sanctioned American modernization. This demonstrates that governing by design can be a two-way street, that local actors can within an overarching field of action still make choices and produce alternatives for the design and governance of their cultural identities and conduct.

In examining midcentury constitutional urbanism in Cuba, domestic design in Iran from the 1950s on, and refugee housing in Pakistan circa 1960, these chapters trace ways that European and American design norms interacted with local political, cultural, and social circumstances. From these close studies, what emerges is the agency and particularity of the local. Whether it is Cubans in the 1940s constructing their own intermingled cultural, urban, and political identities; or Iranians of various political and religious stripes producing complexly hybrid domestic paradigms; or the Pakistani state deploying Western planning tactics for immediate political purposes, the overarching impression is of local actors carving out distinctive options and solutions within and yet independent from the larger, international Cold War framework. What architectural history teaches here is the malleability of ostensibly universal norms, the contingency of local outcomes when it came to governing by design at the level of the city and the home, and therefore the weakness of totalizing explanations of the Cold War period, seen from the high altitude of international superpower relations.

What also starts to emerge from these chapters on the midcentury is the primacy of culture as a category of governance by design, transmitted globally by European-American expertise, coming into contact with strongly defined local, national situations. In each instance—Cuba, Iran, and Pakistan—the historians' theme of the twentieth century's loss of cultural memory figures importantly. Design is called upon to mediate between past, present, and future, whether in the form of the Cuban *cuadra*, the Iranian living room, or the permanently transitional Pakistani housing estate. What these specific architectural histories teach history—that twentieth-century historiography perhaps overlooks—is that memory was never actually lost, but rather constantly and dynamically being reworked and rewoven, by various actors with conflicting agendas, into designed formations that strove to hold the present in symbolic and symbiotic relationships with the past and future. These contributions suggest that this intensive governance by design of culture may be both the result and the cause of broadly felt anxieties about cultural memory loss. The processes of reworking cultural memory, through various composite design strategies, in and of itself produced distance rather than proximity with the past.

The dynamic play mediated by design between culture, memory, and identity in the postwar period was not only localized in so-called developing nations like Cuba, Iran, and Pakistan. It also figured prominently at the international scale and within the Western metropole. These are the themes proposed in part three, "Engineering and Culture," in chapters by Lucia Allais, Meredith TenHoor, and Arindam Dutta that carry the story into the 1960s and 1970s and toward the present. Allais's account of UNESCO's salvage operation of twenty-two ancient Nile Valley Nubian temples threatened by the Aswan High Dam shows how a multinational technocratic design operation internationalized local cultural memory into politically neutral museum spaces of decontextualized monumental objects. Allais's chapter discusses universal heritage designed as antidote for global modernization and the sharp edge, it might be argued, of later United Nations–sanctioned interventions on nation-state sovereignty, from Serbia to Libya, in the name of universal human values and international community cohesion. TenHoor's chapter returns to the theme of food in her account of the midcentury Paris market rebuilding campaign. She adds the extra ingredient of cultural memory, so the loss of the old monumental Les Halles wholesale market, exported to the imageless, hi-tech, network structures at suburban Rungis was felt as profound trauma on the city's identity: food not merely as biological necessity or capitalized commodity but as cultural memory.

That the Les Halles neighborhood would be compensated with the Centre Pompidou cultural palace, designed as a spectacle of hi-tech infrastructural architecture, and the old market itself replaced by a shopping mall are ironies hardly lost on TenHoor.

Allais's and TenHoor's chapters use architectural history to teach history how the traumatic effects of modernization—be they urban or hydroelectric—could be ameliorated in design by compensatory monumental objects produced not crudely by brute, symbolic state power but more or less consensually through technocracy and culture. Thus by the 1970s, honed techniques of regulation and governance by design had achieved new levels of competence and conciliation, capable of using architecture to ameliorate at the levels of culture and consumerism the consequences of modernization and commodification. In this manner, "soft" governance by design arguably helped maintain stability and security, at local and international levels, as the world entered a period of economic crisis after 1973.

Arindam Dutta's chapter on the economist John Maynard Keynes, the engineer Ove Arup, and contemporary architectural spectacle brings the story up to the present. Dutta shows how the current neoliberal world order represents a fulfillment of Keynes's aesthetic-economic vision of the 1930s in which thrift and scarcity are superseded by pleasure, freedom, and risk. This is embodied architecturally by the consumerist Arup-engineered spectacles worldwide—from the Sydney Opera House to London's South Bank. The achievement of Dutta's far-ranging chapter is to show how design can be entangled within political economy, made to offer up culture in the service of capitalist urban redevelopment, and how such duties govern the professional identities of architects and engineers.

What does this collection of architectural histories say about the twenty-first century? Dutta's contribution implicitly argues that globalization in economics and architecture is not an inevitable stage of capitalist development but rather one produced in theory and practice across multiple disciplines. By showing us the historical construction—the design—of such basic architectures as food, home, culture, and the body, not to mention the broader built environment, *Governing by Design* points to the fundamental contingency not only of history but also of the present and future. Recognizing that modernization has not been the ironclad product of authorial intention or historical inevitability or totalizing theories of modernism but the contingent consequence of entangled agencies, we recognize the future, too, as not ironbound but rather like the past, open to accident, manipulation, and reconfiguration.

Notes

1. Mitchell Dean, *Governmentality: Power and Rule in Modern Society* (London: Sage, 1999), 99, 102.

2. Dean, *Governmentality*, 26.

3. Paul Rabinow, *French Modern: Norms and Forms of the Social Environment* (Cambridge: MIT Press, 1989; reprinted, Chicago: University of Chicago Press, 1995), 13, 16. For architecture and governmentality, also see Stephen Legg, *Spaces of Colonialism: Delhi's Urban Governmentalities* (Malden, Mass.: Blackwell, 2007).

4. Alan Colquhoun, *Oxford History of Art: Modern Architecture* (Oxford: Oxford University Press, 2002), 9; and Elizabeth A. T. Smith, "Re-examining Architecture and Its History at the End of the Century," in *At the End of the Century: One Hundred Years of Architecture*, edited by Russell Ferguson (Los Angeles: Museum of Contemporary Art, 1998), 23.

5. Sarah Williams Goldhagen, "Coda: Reconceptualizing the Modern," in *Anxious Modernisms*, edited by Sarah Williams Goldhagen and Réjean Legault (Cambridge: MIT Press, 2000), 302.

6. Eric Hobsbawm, *The Age of Extremes: A History of the World, 1914–1991* (New York: Pantheon, 1994); Michael Howard and Wm. Roger Louis, eds., *The Oxford History of the Twentieth Century* (Oxford: Oxford University Press, 1998); A. G. Hopkins, ed., *Global History: Interactions between the Universal and the Local* (New York: Palgrave Macmillan, 2006); and Jeremy Black, *The World in the Twentieth Century* (London: Longman, 2002).

PART ONE

Food, Shelter, and the Body

I

Preserved Assets

■

MICHAEL OSMAN

E DWARD BELLAMY's novel *Looking Backward,* written in 1887, begins
with a description of the main character, Julian West, refurbishing the
basement of his Boston home. Regulating the environment in this underground space, he believed, would make it possible to maintain the vitality of his
body through an extended period of uninterrupted sleep. After inviting a professor of animal magnetism to entrance him into a deep slumber, West awoke
more than a century later in the year 2000, perfectly preserved. This death-
defying feat was apparently made possible by the combination of a unique hyp-
notic method and a well-crafted piece of architecture. The conditions in West's
basement were fully considered: cool fresh air was regularly fed in, while stale
air was pushed out. Wandering through the new millennium, West gradually
discovered that all the economic and political problems plaguing the nation in
1887 had been decidedly resolved. Technological progress in all domains of life
had made it possible to regulate an uncertain future into a perfectly coordinated
mechanical utopia.[1]

The success of *Looking Backward* is well known—it sold nearly half a million
copies in the first year of its publication. Bellamy continued his trope of hyp-
notized time travel in *Equality,* a sequel that he published in 1897. A reviewer
of this second novel referred to the already famous sleeping chamber as Julian
West's "cold storage house." This was no ordinary technical description. In the
ten years that had passed between Bellamy's first and second novels on the
adventures of Julian West in the year 2000, cold storage had become a topic
in every major newspaper in the nation and the professed solution to the economic crises that were constant during the 1890s.[2]

Cold storage warehouses were devoted to preserving the lives of things over time and were regulated by the types of machines that populated Bellamy's futuristic novels. Newly invented mechanical services controlled the environmental conditions around perishable produce to protect these commodities from the effects of bacterial decay as well as the instabilities of economic demand. Indeed, the proliferation of these buildings at the end of the nineteenth century was driven by capital investment from entrepreneurs who aimed to extend the speculative activities that had developed at midcentury from grain to perishables. This chapter explores some of the discontinuities that this new architectural typology registered in a broad shift in economic thinking in the United States—from laissez-faire ideas based in classic political economy to those involving greater governmental regulation. In particular, the history of two significant investments in warehouse design in Chicago and Boston demonstrate the challenge that cold storage presented to the profession of architecture, revealing the necessity to define the place of both technology and the regulatory state in the design of buildings.

The attempts made by the architects to address "the public" through the design of cold storage warehouses expose a number of different paths through which power was formulated at this time as it gradually shifted from small groups of entrepreneurs to corporations and governmental agencies. The diverging methods for making a building public, in turn, speak directly to competing models within architectural practice during the period—models based in some combination of art, service, and expertise that continue to this day. In Chicago the construction of an enormous civic monument for cold storage required commissioning the city's most famous architectural partnership, Dankmar Adler and Louis Sullivan. In Boston, on the other hand, the architect William Gibbons Preston was hired to design multiple modest buildings by a local storage firm that over time established the nation's largest network of public storage space.

Scale and style were thus critical variables in locating these institutions within their respective cities and in relation to transformations in governmental power. Traditional uses of architectural form and urban design, despite their necessity for bringing new technology into the city, were being brought under question through this emerging urban function. As agencies sought to control and expand American commerce through the development of the cold storage system, architects began to absorb numerous forms of technical expertise to assure investors as well as the broader public of predictable results. While debates over the correct approach to introducing new technology into buildings were often indirect, the history of this modern building type reveals a major turning point in the way that architects managed the change brought about by increasing demands on their knowledge of technical and legal matters.

Until the 1880s, cold storage warehouses were cooled with harvested ice.

Expensive to transport and nearly impossible to maintain a regular supply during the summer months, ice was far from a perfect cooling agent. Most large-scale cooling facilities found in cities were built as infrastructural support for the transport and storage of meat. First Gustavus Swift and then the rest of the "Big Four" meat companies discovered the significant advantages offered by refrigerated railroad cars around midcentury. The key benefit offered by these cars was the capacity to transport slaughtered meat rather than live cattle, eliminating both the time delays associated with feeding along the journey and the additional investment in terminal slaughterhouses. Ice-cars, essentially moving refrigerators, centralized the meat packing operation and established a network of cooled terminal buildings at major distribution centers. Swift insisted that "reefer cars"—cooled by the newly available technology of compressed ammonia—could further expand his network. Cooling without ice, he insisted, would allow the company to extend its sales to even more distant markets. As added benefits, mechanical refrigeration could make cold year-round and also free up valuable space in the railroad car for more meat.[3] The development of cooling technology thus moved from ice-cooled buildings to cooled railroad cars and then returned from the mechanically cooled reefer car to machines large enough to cool entire storage warehouses.

Investors in public cold storage facilities sought to use these systems for cooling a variety of perishables other than meat by hiring the engineers who had designed the reefer-lines for Swift and the other meat packers to develop these systems for buildings. Their long-term aim was to establish a reserve in commodities like dairy, poultry, vegetables, and fruit that could support speculation through futures contracts analogous to those used for grain at the Board of Trade. The remaining impediment to fulfilling their goal was the size and dependability of the available storage facilities: they were too small and not technically adequate for maintaining a constant reserve requisite for issuing futures contracts. By scaling up the technology of the compressed ammonia system, made up of huge assemblies of coiled expansion pipes that absorbed heat wherever needed, refrigeration engineers believed they could increase the scale and dependability of cooled storage to establish the needed space for housing such a reserve. As they experimented, they found that regulating the quantities of ammonia flowing through pipe work could establish exact temperatures in each storeroom based on the unique needs of the commodity stored there.[4] Scientific efforts were thus initiated to find a temperature range for storing eggs as opposed to apples. Investigators were asked to calculate how much humidity was tolerable or even desirable to maintain the produce in its "original" state. In the early days of cold storage, there was simply no data to assess how long a fruit or vegetable could be kept on such life support systems. All this research was part of an effort to make the technology of the system reliable and predictable enough so that the architecture could be responsive to the perishable market as seasons changed and demand fluctuated.

In Chicago a significant attempt to employ this technology on a large scale was led by the engineer J. Ensign Fuller, president of the New York Consolidated Refrigeration Company. To prove that his apparatus could work on an architectural scale, Fuller installed a refrigeration plant within an old warehouse and invited more than a hundred potential investors to experience the power of the ammonia-based system. According to a reporter for the *Chicago Daily Tribune*, the temperature in the storage rooms could be fixed anywhere between 45 degrees above zero and 35 degrees below zero and remained miraculously stable, thanks to a novel thermostatic mechanism.[5]

Fuller, together with the real estate magnate Joseph L. Lathrop, began to organize a team of shareholders to found a company called the Chicago Cold Storage Exchange. Hoping to convince others to invest in "the world's largest cold storage facility," located on the shore of the Chicago River, they published their plans in the summer of 1890. By November, enough capital had been raised to begin construction, and a cornerstone ceremony featured a speech by the city's mayor. A supporter of the project at the ceremony called the planners "a company of wizards," expressing his fascination with the systems that miraculously produced the exact temperatures desired to store any perishable product imaginable. But his closing and most laudatory comments were reserved for the company's selection of the famed architects Adler and Sullivan. The supporter noted that this famous architectural partnership will "pass from planning and building that superb temple—the Auditorium Building—devoted to the culture of our great city, to the design and construction of this eminently useful structure that is destined to contribute much to the health and comfort and employment of life of our whole community, rich and poor."[6]

Why would the Chicago Cold Storage Exchange have chosen these architects? From the newspaper stories that followed the cornerstone ceremony, it is clear that this choice was a large part of the business strategy. Immediately the notoriety gained would bring further investment into a scheme that was still far from solvent. Even more far-reaching, however, was the impression that the company hoped to deliver to the city by planning a civic monument. The proposal they published was intended to make the structure read to any Chicagoan as "public architecture" (figure 1.1). Far more than just the exterior pomp of wide Romanesque arches and a tall dentil cornice, the heterogeneous program included within the buildings would combine storage with a glass shopping arcade spanning between the two ten-story warehouses from Lake to Randolph Streets.

This promenade was planned to hover over the existing railroad tracks that served both to deliver goods for storage and to pick them up upon demand.

Figure 1.1. Adler and Sullivan's rendering of the two warehouses and arcade on West Water Street. *Source:* From "Chicago Cold Storage Exchange," *The Inland Architect and News Record* 16, no. 3 (1890).

The arcade would be lined on either side by a total of thirty-five storefronts for the produce trade. In addition, the entire level above the street within the warehouse buildings was configured to house ninety offices for commission merchants and an expansive room for the daily operations of the Cold Storage Exchange.[7] Indeed, Adler and Sullivan's fame was uniquely attractive to the organizers precisely because they had just completed another equally heterogeneous project at the Auditorium Building, a building that combined a theater and hotel in one dense square block on the southeastern corner of the elevated train "loop." If the aim was to make this new structure on the northwestern corner of the loop, as obviously public and successful a venture, the firm was not only a practical but also an obvious choice.

Carl Condit, the historian of building technology, called this warehouse "a study in texture and geometric purism," but he remained strikingly silent regarding the novelty of the mechanical systems and the programmatic mixture of storage, shopping, and office space.[8] In most histories dedicated to Adler and Sullivan, in fact, discussions of program are devoted entirely to their work on the Auditorium Building and tall office buildings like the Wainwright Building in Saint Louis. Office buildings were the focus of Sullivan's now famous jingle, "form ever follows function"—an argument that he made as a "final solution" to the architectural needs brought on by changes in modern work.[9] As for the functionality of the cold storage warehouse, historians leave us with only a few words regarding its "fortress-like" character that might be spun as "functioning" to protect perishables from seasonal inclemency, thus giving the architecture some semblance of iconographic power. Putting aside any correspondence of form to function, however, and reading Sullivan's legendary chapter on "The Tall Office Building Artistically Considered" against the views held by Dankmar Adler, a latent rupture in the partnership is noticeable. This fissure was emblematic of a deeper crisis in the profession as a whole.[10]

By the time Sullivan's essay had been published, the partnership with Adler had been fully dissolved. After only a few months Adler responded to his former partner's aphorism at the thirtieth annual convention of the American Institute of Architects with a corrective. Recognizing that Sullivan had based his "law" on "observations of nature," Adler argued that this scientific perspective had not been taken far enough. Form and function were related indeed, but as evolutionary science had recently shown, it was "an ever changing environment" that produced differences between species. This dynamic and unpredictable assembly of natural forces would, Adler noted, continue to affect the development of ever-new forms of life. Therefore, if "form follows function," it does not follow in a straight line, nor in accordance with a simple mathematical formula, but along lines of curves whose elements are always changing and never alike. And if the lines of development and growth of vegetable and animal organisms are infinitely differentiated, the processes of untrammeled human thought and human emotions are even more subtle in the differences and shadings of their manifestations. The natural variations in conditions of human environment are as great as those that influence the developments of form in the lower organisms. Human work is further modified by necessary artificial conditions and circumstances.[11]

Replacing Sullivan's relation of form to function through "straight lines" with "lines of curves" and then curves with shades of difference, Adler's comments proposed a deeper complexity in the relation between architectural style and the ambitions of its occupants and makers. Environmental changes—among which he included new technologies, new working habits, new social beliefs—were fundamental in the determination of any emerging architectural style. In fact, style would have far more nuanced responses to such demands in their accumulation through history. Adler proposed that Sullivan's "law" thus be revised to: "function and environment determine form." Rather than claim to have overcome style with final solutions, Adler proposed that the profession, as part of its natural evolution, absorb historical discontinuities of whatever sort. For him, change was inevitable and socially dispersed; it could not be localized within a single mind. In turn, style was a social force that held form, function, and the environment in a momentary, if fleeting, historical unity.

The design of the Chicago Cold Storage Exchange preceded this discussion but instantiates the difficulty of embracing stylistic change as a quasi-natural process. The numerous so-called environmental changes housed within the buildings were fully integrated within this single massive project. Yet despite the novelty of the program and the technology that controlled the conditions within the storerooms, Adler and Sullivan's architectural response unified the design of the project to give it a strong civic presence; no exterior indication was given of the systems that were housed inside. Indeed, the two huge signs that hung on the Water Street façades were necessary additions for announcing the functions offered by the buildings. Trains were routed beneath the arcade, and the cargo boats loaded and unloaded along the river dock kept the fluctuations of supply and demand almost entirely concealed from public view; the appearance of the buildings from the street was thus ostensibly unified. No view revealed the mechanics buried in the basements, no gap disclosed the cooling apparatus that rose up through the wall cavities, and all the changes in supply and demand negotiated by the commission merchants at the Cold Storage Exchange were hidden deep inside the warehouse mass. All in all, the dynamic and heterogeneous systems that made this place so unique were kept fully internalized while the exterior style produced the image of a civic monument. If Adler's proposal implied that style could absorb historical discontinuities through a process analogous to biological variation, the sheer scale and unity of the Chicago Cold Storage Exchange would not allow for such variation. It was ultimately very much in keeping with a Sullivan-like "final solution."

When the global economic downturn of 1893 tested the resilience of this new institution, it revealed that neither three hundred thousand cubic feet of cooled reserves nor the investment in the unified monumental architecture could hold off the effects of the crisis. In 1898 the Exchange claimed bankruptcy, and only three years later the buildings were demolished. Thus the argument between Alder and Sullivan that revealed a growing rift in the profession was concurrent with a shift in the way that public institutions distributed urban services to the population. This shift rendered any investment in civic appearance largely irrelevant to a cold storage company's longevity and effectiveness. While "public" once meant large, unified, and monumental, an increasingly systematic relationship between technology, capital, and law served to reformulate this concept. Enacting techniques of regulatory power that were more infrastructural directed the reach of governance through the extension of networks, both physical and abstract, that ensured continuous and predictable delivery of the services to the modern city. The cold storage network established between 1882 and 1915 by the Quincy Market Cold Storage Company in Boston offers a revealing alternative to the Exchange in Chicago by relating form and function through a far looser fit. Here, many of the mechanical systems were physically separated from the architecture of the warehouse. Rather than integrating architecture into a monumental urban presence, the mechanics of cold storage were considered on an urban scale, requiring the attention of architecture on an occasional basis.

In 1882, when the Quincy Market Cold Storage Company first approached the architect William Gibbons Preston to design a warehouse, he was known mostly for his bungalows on Cape Cod and the Rogers Building at the Massachusetts Institute of Technology. The proposal he presented to the company for its new warehouse on Commercial Street in Boston was a relatively understated building when compared with the pomp and scale of the Chicago Cold Storage Exchange. While a public shopping arcade had been planned to be open to street traffic in Chicago, here the entry arches led to the company's receiving room and the manager's office. There was nearly no investment in advertising the project in the newspapers, and the lone published image reflects a building that was traditional from both architectural and technical points of view (figure 1.2). The scene surrounding the building in Preston's rendering was stripped of the busy life of the market district. This illustrated that its performance as an urban monument was not valued in the same way as it was in the building designed by Adler and Sullivan.

A cross section through the warehouse reveals that the storerooms were originally cooled with blocks of ice stored in the fifth floor "ice-loft." The chilled air from the loft was forced to the floors below through a system of ducts that ran along an interior corridor cutting through the center of the entire structure lengthwise. Raised floors that contained "a very large quantity of one-inch-

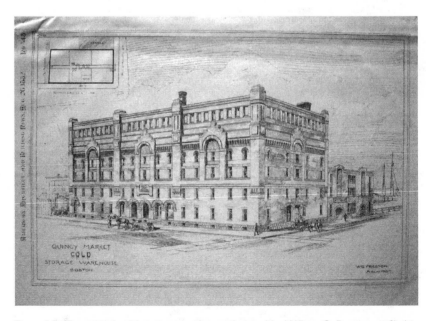

Figure 1.2. The original cold storage warehouse designed by William G. Preston profiled in *American Architect and Building News* on August 22, 1882.

thick hair-felt" insulated each floor from those above and below.[12] Without any means for precise temperature calibration, however, the warehouse could only maintain a roughly graduated interior climate from the top to the bottom, with the highest floor closest to freezing and the bottom floor the closest to the outside temperature.

After ten modest years of operation in this building, a merger with the Faneuil Hall Cooling Co., and a significant increase in demand for cooled storage space in the city, the company set out to acquire a plot of land behind the original warehouse facing the adjacent street. The company directors aimed to use this newly acquired land to construct a second warehouse and approached Preston again to design the structure that would be cooled with a variation on the newly available refrigeration technology used in the Chicago warehouse. Rather than sacrificing any space within the warehouse for the mechanical systems, Preston chose to attach an engine and boiler house to the rear to power a refrigeration machine with the capacity to cool the combined storage space in both warehouses (figure 1.3). At a height of twenty-four feet and a length of forty-five feet, "the largest refrigerating machine ever built" was by far the company's greatest investment.[13] This two-hundred-ton "Boyle machine," stationed within its own Beaux-Arts structure, was lit from above by skylights and surrounded on all sides by catwalks and ladders to allow for engineers to maintain the machine. Instead of investing in the world's largest warehouse, the company chose to spend most of its capital in commissioning the construction of this gargantuan compression engine.

The expansion of ammonia compressed by this machine was no longer circulated directly into the warehouses; rather, it cooled brine that was then pushed through insulated pipes to a final destination in the neighboring structures. Within a year the company's head engineer, George H. Stoddard, was able to convince the directors that a second machine of the same scale, powered by additional steam boilers, should be added to make it possible for the company to continue its growth. With two engines in place, Stoddard calculated, the company could produce the equivalent effect of 860 tons of ice melting every twenty-four hours, a quantity of cooling power that would far outmatch the sum total of all the space designed for cooled storage in the entire city. Focused on the task of cooling a network of buildings, Stoddard initiated a project that by 1915 would deliver cold brine to seventeen nearby warehouses, several market companies, and as many as five hundred independent concerns.[14]

A permit to lay and operate the pipeline throughout the market district issued by Boston's municipal agencies was crucial to pursuing this plan. It was filed in 1895 and the company immediately began to install the cooled brine system underground. The network's growth was aided by the intimate scale and nature of the perishables market in Boston. The president of the cold storage

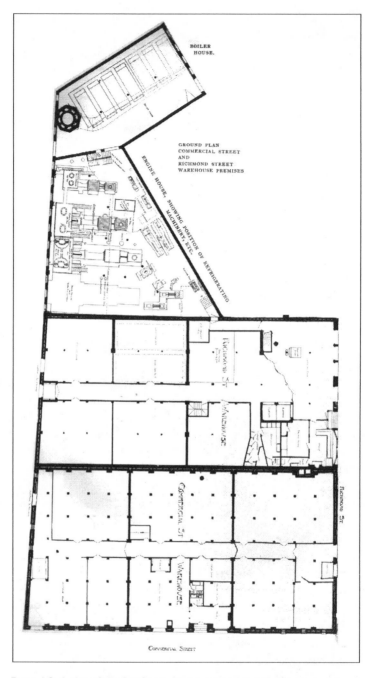

Figure 1.3. A plan of the first floor of the warehouses, including the engine and boiler houses. *Source*: From "Boston's Cold Corner," *Ice and Refrigeration* 9, no. 6 (December 1895): 375–76.

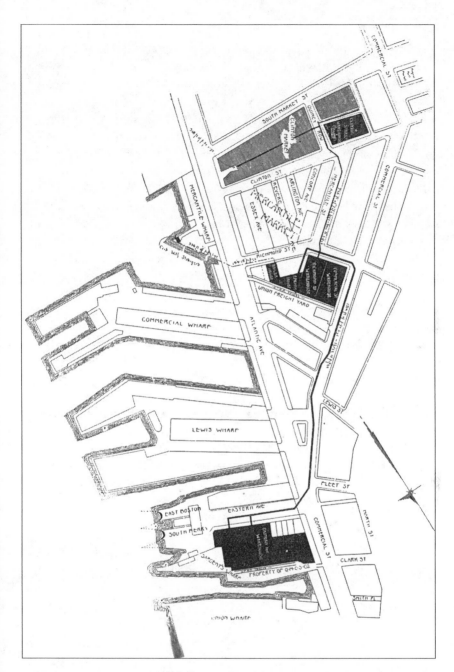

Figure 1.4. Plat showing property owned by the Quincy Market Cold Storage Company in 1895. The solid black hatch is the property owned by the company, the shaded black hatch is property cooled by the company, the black line is brine pipe, and the dotted line is water pipe. *Source*: From "Boston's Cold Corner," *Ice and Refrigeration* 9, no. 6 (December 1895): 376.

company, J. V. Fletcher, was also a longstanding occupant of Faneuil Hall, and James C. Melvin, the treasurer, was the director of the Clinton Market Co., the company that owned the nation's largest meat market. So it is no surprise that the first pipeline built by the company was designated to connect the cooling apparatus in the engine house to Clinton Market (figure 1.4). Running in the opposite direction, up Richmond and along Commercial Streets, another long trench was dug to connect to the company's new million-cubic-foot warehouse on Eastern Avenue. According to one observer's description, digging for the pipeline exposed the accumulation of utilities that were increasingly being buried beneath the city streets: "The trench for the pipe line was seven feet wide, and at places nine feet deep, and the pipe line had to dodge sewers, gas, and water pipes, telephone, telegraph, electric light and electric power conduits and manholes of every description."[15]

A photograph taken during construction shows the long gash in the market district with three white conduits of brine running along the bottom of the trench under temporary bridges that connected one side of the street to the other. The length of the brine conduit that had been laid from the engine house to surrounding buildings was pushing beyond the capacity of the engineers to guarantee a temperature at some distance away. How would Stoddard know if the third floor of the warehouse on Eastern Avenue, for instance, was properly cooled if he was sitting as far away as his office on Richmond Street? In matters of preservation, even one degree of inaccuracy could be the cause of massive spoilage. It was not enough to install a thermostat in each storeroom that might malfunction; control required that the system be brought under the guiding eye of single trustworthy human.

As a solution, the company installed a surveillance instrument called a "thermophone" in their engine house. The name, a combination of the Greek words for "heat" and "voice," evokes the function of this novel technology. By "speaking the temperature," the thermophone transformed an unknown environmental condition into an utterance of meaningful data that could be continuously governed. The journal Ice and Refrigeration described the apparatus: "We illustrate herewith the recently invented Thermophone, an instrument which seems to come into general use in large modern refrigerating plants. For a long time there has been a call for some form of apparatus, which should enable the engineer or manager of a cold storage warehouse to instantly inform himself of the temperature of individual rooms or of circulating pipes and ducts in distant or inaccessible parts of the building" (figure 1.5).[16]

The thermophone at the Quincy Market Cold Storage Company was made up of a network of forty sensitive coils. Each coil was situated in one of the company's storerooms and linked back to a brass button on a switchboard that hung in the engine room behind the Richmond Street warehouse. The

Figure 1.5. The thermophone at the Quincy Market Cold Storage Company, hanging on the wall of the engine room. *Source*: From "The Thermophone Installation of the Quincy Market Cold Storage Co.," *Ice and Refrigeration* 12, no. 1 (January 1897): 34.

coils transferred electrical impulses that could be translated into a temperature reading of the distant location by bringing a small rubber handle attached to the indicator into contact with buttons linked to one of the sensing coils. Listening to a tone that modulated as the dial on the indicator was tuned made it possible to detect the temperature of a distant storeroom within a matter of seconds. At the moment that the tone was no longer audible, the exact temperature of a location was known and could be immediately brought under control. The switchboard could contain as many as a hundred such connections, all gathered within one man's arm length, thus bringing together "the temperature of air ducts in the seventh story of the building, of pipes under floors and on high ceilings, and of others in deep and dark brine tanks."[17]

While six miles of brine pipeline physically connected the compression engines to the surrounding warehouses, the thermophone created a secondary regulatory apparatus that unified the system through the oversight of a single observer. Imagine George H. Stoddard standing beside this switchboard: here he occupied the center of the network in which change was constant and the danger of spoilage was always imminent. All the commission merchants in Boston relied on the correct functioning of his refrigeration machines, of his pipeline, and of his thermophone to ensure that their assets would be properly preserved. The city as a whole was tied to the proper functioning and coordination of these systems. Indeed, as the Quincy Market Cold Storage Company expanded its network incrementally, it became the only source of temperature-controlled space in Boston. By 1910 the total cubic volume of warehouse space available through the company came to be understood throughout Boston as one of a growing number of the city's public utilities—in other words, another buried network.[18]

If the Chicago warehouses were made public through monumental architecture, a glass-enclosed shopping arcade and the notoriety of a signature firm, Boston's system absorbed the architecture of cold storage in a piecemeal fashion—fulfilling Adler's evolutionary metaphor—as if it were gradually learning to take on the form, scale, and demand of the city. Architects at the time did not have the internal procedures for adapting to such complex assemblies of buildings, machines, and pipelines. This became all the more obvious once city, state, and federal regulators added an additional level of complexity to the design of cold storage warehouses in the form of legal stipulations that aimed to unify the system into a national reserve. Soon experts in cold storage design and construction began to occupy the pages of trade journals like *Ice and Refrigeration* with advertisements of their specialized knowledge. Titles like Hans Peter Henschien's reference book, *Packing House and Cold Storage Construction*, were emblematic of this shift toward expertise: "A general reference work on the planning, construction, and equipment of modern American meat packing plants with special reference to the requirements of the United States Government and a complete treatise on the design of cold storage plants including refrigeration insulation and cost data. Fully Illustrated."[19]

These claims to expert knowledge in the construction, environmental technology, and legal regulation of warehouse architecture were responding to new forms of resistance in the system's expansion. A cartoon published in the magazine *Puck* in 1910 illustrates a spreading suspicion of the unspoken ambitions of a national cold storage system. It depicts a food speculator as a masked bandit holding two loaded guns that are each labeled "cold storage" (figure 1.6).[20] One gun is aimed at the producer—the farmer carrying butter, milk, eggs, and a slaughtered pig on his back; the other is aimed at the consumer—an urbanite who is clenching his money from the fear of this unanticipated interruption in his trip to the market. The three characters have been assembled on the "road of supply and demand," where they are now stuck at a violent impasse. The cartoon's caption, "Double Hold-Up," gives two possible interpretations: the first is that we are watching a theft in which money is being stolen by the imposing bandit, an uninvited third party unwelcome in a proper transaction; the second is that the event is a stoppage in time, a delay in the meeting of the buyer and the seller. It was the food speculator who "held up" the movement of food from its origin to its destination—in other words, of finding its place into the urbanite's empty basket. Critics of the expansion of the cold storage system claimed that through manipulations of time—time banditry—food

Figure 1.6. *Source:* "A Double Hold-Up," *Puck* (October 6, 1910): 8–9.

speculators hoodwinked a naive public, raising prices and delivering spoiled goods to boot.

One advocate of the "pure food movement," a butcher named Herman Hirschauer, noted the troubling possibility of "cases of poultry yet in stock that were killed and packed more than two years ago." Within these forgotten bodies, he imagined a "nasty, greenish mess" of rotting entrails that could only be cleaned by certain radical measures such as the use of "chemicals and dopes" that only further compromised the wholesomeness of the product.[21] Yet the *Puck* cartoon contained a second caption, more hopeful in tone: "Good Guns, Bad Hands." It was not the cold storage system itself that had caused these problems; it was the abuses of the system by greedy speculators.

With this rise of pressure from an increasingly alarmed public, the U.S. Senate prepared hearings to discuss the quality of foods held in cold storage and to assess the effects of speculation on their price. Dr. Harvey W. Wiley, chief of the Bureau of Chemistry in the Department of Agriculture, opened the proceedings with his findings on the proper storage time and the range of suitable conditions for holding poultry and eggs. The lengthy hearings centered almost entirely on technically defining terms that would traditionally be qualitative: "wholesomeness" of food and its possible "adulteration" transformed into chemically specifiable conditions. Establishing strict guidelines to govern the management of cold storage, the senators believed, would regularize the system, making it more reliable and thereby transform consumer suspicion into public trust.[22] States with significant cold storage holdings initiated inspections of their largest refrigerated warehouses. The House of Representatives of Massachusetts, for example, appointed five inspectors to collect data about the preserved holdings in the state, report on the effect that speculative practices were having on the quality of food, and, more urgently, calculate if they were the cause of the recent increase in the cost of living.[23]

They found that speculation in futures contracts had coincided with rising costs but on the whole had also stabilized prices. A Harvard economics professor, F. W. Taussig, explained the phenomenon: "The influence of speculation is to lessen fluctuations in price and promote 'the expedient rate of consumption.'" In other words, extending the field of speculation to include perishable food products stabilized the distribution of supply. "Fruit, meat, fish, eggs," he wrote, "no longer come on the market in spasmodic and irregular amounts. Supplies that are heavy at one time are brought by dealers, put in storage, and held for sale at a later period of scantier supply. Prices are more equable, and on the whole the profits of the dealers are probably less. There is less risk to them, and the community gets its supplies at a smaller charge for their services as middlemen."[24]

As warehouses built for preserving assets produced new markets for speculators to run risks under controlled conditions, the process of constructing the system itself was strewn with contingencies that forced the architectural profession to confront some basic working assumptions. Networks of buildings regulated through new technology and legislative guidance had moved the traditionally public domain of architectural attention from the buildings' exterior façades to their interior environments. Although modernists like Adolf Loos had already begun to focus their attention on the interior as the site for urban luxury, controlling the interior of the refrigerated storeroom established a new form of expertise in cladding that brought the principle of material honesty to a point of total quantification. With volumes of refrigerated space expanding and becoming ever more specifically regulated by the law, statisticians who studied the quality of food and its price advised engineers and architects on ways to fine-tune the coordination of their insulated envelopes with the cooling power of refrigeration machinery to maximize the longevity of their contents. The interior of the storeroom became a space where the tabulations that aimed to predict prices could perform within a fixed range of acceptable deviations.

As a way of legally unifying the system, the American Warehousemen's Association framed the Uniform Warehouse Receipts Act (1906) to shift the administrative power over warehouse conditions from isolated groups of merchants and business associations to federal regulatory agencies.[25] The hope was to make it possible for those who stored their goods in public warehouses to receive "uniform receipts" that could become nationally recognized instruments of exchange. In his treatise on *Public Warehousing*, the professor of business administration John H. Frederick explained how the law was envisioned: "The fundamental purpose of the Uniform Warehouse Receipts Act was to increase the integrity of all types of public warehouse receipts in order that they might be more highly regarded by storers as evidence of their ownership of the goods deposited, and by bankers as collateral for loans. Uniformity of rules and regulations governing the issuing of public warehouse receipts and the responsibilities of public warehousemen for the storage and delivery of goods in their custody was necessary in order that the receipts of a warehouse in one state, or section of the country, may be acceptable as collateral or as delivery of the goods in another part of the country."[26]

The uniform receipt became a legally binding negotiable instrument (that is, a contract available for transfer or sale) allowing for a complete separation of an object's utility in storage from its relative value on the market. To guarantee the receipt as negotiable, the warehouseman was required to print a statement on it that he was responsible for the safe delivery of the goods in his custody. Thus the act also established the uniform receipt as yet another regulatory apparatus that protected speculative traders from unwelcome risks like theft, loss, or damage to the goods they were trading. The passage of this first uniform law brought every public warehouse in the nation under the authority of government.

Deemed safe from the unpredictable risks that could destroy their value, perishables held in storage were integrated into a standardized receipt system. However, only a few cold storage companies conformed to the stipulations set by the Uniform Warehouse Receipts Act. Receipts from these companies still did not gain that status of a negotiable instrument. Thus in 1914, Congress proposed a Uniform Cold Storage Act that forcibly brought the industry under one legal code. The law stipulated that all cold storage owners were required to receive licenses from the Department of Agriculture and annually renew them to ensure that their warehouses were kept in sanitary conditions and were properly managed to avoid hoarding by "profiteers." In addition, the law required that all "foods branded, stamped, or marked in some conspicuous place, upon the receipt thereof, with the day, month, and year when the same was received for storage or refrigerating."[27]

This was the origin of what we know in contemporary life as the "sell-by date." After 1914 a central authority regulated the amount of time that any item of food could be held in storage. At the very moment that most of the food consumed in America was spending time in storage, an anxiety emerged about its freshness. What did this term mean? Would anything be fresh again? Until cold storage had become a universal reality, food was either fresh or not fresh. With the integration of a national system, representatives of the industry aimed to extend the time associated with the concept of freshness to include any and all the time a product was held in storage. The position held by one warehouseman in the hearings surprised some inquiring congressmen: "The word 'fresh' is not as an offset against cold storage, but it is as against preserving by other processes. That is the meaning of the word 'fresh,' in my judgment." Anything that was not pickled or frozen was now legally understood to be "fresh," including a vegetable picked months ago, even an egg laid a year ago.[28]

In the development of the cold storage system, an interior environment defined by temperature, humidity, and technical dependability produced spaces in which commodities could retain their identity through time. These spaces were formed simultaneously with a limited number of socially acceptable price ranges for those very things. By 1920 every object in storage—or to be more accurate, every population of objects, animal or vegetable, chicken or egg—was given an acceptable range in which it could continue to exist as both a consumable commodity and a negotiable instrument. Limiting the risk of an object's unanticipated decay was, in other words, essential to constraining its effect on the unpredictability of market forces. This form of regulation depended on the new approach being formulated to make architecture public. As monuments to civic modernity proved to be ineffective tools for economic and environmental regulation, the profession responded with designs that embraced novel forms of service and expertise. This was not strictly a struggle within architecture; it was part of a gradual reconstitution of modern life through regulatory instruments that today are all too easily taken for granted.

Notes

1. Edward Bellamy, *Looking Backward* (Boston: Houghton Mifflin, 1889), 30–31. For more on the context in which the novel was written, see John F. Kasson, *Civilizing the Machine: Technology and Republican Values in America, 1776–1900* (New York: Penguin Books, 1984), 191–202.

2. "Editor's Study," *Harper's New Monthly Magazine* 95, no. 569 (October 1897): 798.

3. Mary Yeager Kujovich, "The Refrigerator Car and the Growth of the American Dressed Beef Industry," *Business History Review* 44, no. 4 (Winter 1970): 460–82. Kujovich wrote her dissertation on the meat packing industry under Alfred Chandler, "The Dynamics of Oligopoly in the Meat Packing Industry: A Historical Analysis, 1875–1912" (PhD dissertation, Johns Hopkins University, 1973). It was published as *Competition and Regulation: The Development of Oligopoly in the Meat Packing Industry* (Greenwich, Conn.: JAI Press, 1981). Chandler's book makes some reference to Kujovich's early research; see Chandler, *The Visible Hand: The Managerial Revolution in American Business* (Cambridge: Belknap Press of Harvard University Press, 1977), 299–302; 391–402.

4. For a more technical treatment of the ammonia system, see Oscar Edward Anderson Jr., *Refrigeration in America* (Princeton: Princeton University Press, 1953).

5. "Artificial Cold on Tap," *Chicago Daily Tribune* (November 1, 1888), 7.

6. "The Great Cold-Storage Plant," *Chicago Daily Tribune* (July 7, 1891), 4.

7. Frank M. Lester, *Handbook of Chicago Stocks and Bonds* (Chicago: Jameson & Morse Co., 1891), 65.

8. Carl Condit, *The Chicago School of Architecture* (Chicago: University of Chicago Press, 1964), 135. Or see also Hugh Morrison: "It is in reality architecture reduced to the most elemental terms of volumes and plane surfaces, and suggests, a generation ahead of its time, 'Die neue Sächlichkeit' of modern German architecture," from his *Louis Sullivan: Profit of Modern Architecture* (New York: W. W. Norton & Company, 1935), 126.

9. Louis Sullivan, "The Tall Office Building Artistically Considered," in his *Kindergarten Chats and Other Writings* (New York: Dover Books, 1979), 206. Originally published in *Lippincott's* 57 (March 1896): 403–9.

10. Thomas Leslie, "Dankmar Adler's Response to Louis Sullivan's 'The Tall Office Building Artistically Considered': Architecture and the 'Four Causes,'" *Journal of Architectural Education* 64 (September 2010): 83–93.

11. Dankmar Adler, "Function and Environment," in *Roots of Contemporary American Architecture*, edited by Lewis Mumford (New York: Grove Press, 1972), 244. Originally published with the title "The Influence of Steel Construction and Plate Glass upon Style," in *The Proceedings of the Thirtieth Annual Convention of American Institute of Architects* (1896), 58–64.

12. "Quincy Market Cold Storage Warehouse in Boston, Mass.," *American Architect and Building News* 12, no. 348 (August 26, 1882): 98.

13. "Boston's Cold Corner," *Ice and Refrigeration* 9, no. 6 (December 1895): 374, 384.

14. "Boston's Biggest Ice Chest," *Boston Daily Globe* (January 17, 1915): 45.

15. "Boston's Cold Corner," 394. For more on the tunnel construction and insulation of the pipeline, see Madison Cooper, *Practical Cold Storage* (Chicago: Nickerson & Collins Co., 1905), 105.

16. "The Thermophone Installation of the Quincy Market Cold Storage Co.," *Ice and Refrigeration* 12, no. 1 (January 1897).

17. Ibid. For more on the thermophone, see Louis M. Schmidt, *Principles and Practice of Artificial Ice-Making and Refrigeration* (Philadelphia: Philadelphia Book Co., 1908), 398–400.

18. The president of the company in 1910 boasted that "at the present time we cool more space than any other company in this country, and this means more than any company in the world." At that point they controlled 9.5 million cubic feet of cooled space. Senate Committee on Manufactures, *Foods Held in Cold Storage*, 61st Cong., 3rd sess., 1911, 140.

19. Hans Peter Henschien, *Packing House and Cold Storage Construction* (Chicago: Nickerson and Collins Co., 1915).

20. "A Double Hold-Up," *Puck*, October 6, 1910, pp. 8–9.

21. Herman Hirschauer, *The Dark Side of the Beef Trust: A Treatise Concerning the "Canner" Cow, the Cold Storage Fowl, the Diseased Meats, the Dopes and Preservatives* (Jamestown, N.Y.: Theodore Z. Root, 1905), 92–93. Compare to Upton Sinclair, *The Jungle* (New York: Doubleday, Page & Company, 1906). In June 1906, President Theodore Roosevelt signed the Food and Drug Act, or the "Wiley Act." See Oscar E. Anderson Jr., "The Pure-Food Issue: A Republican Dilemma, 1906–1912," *American Historical Review* 61, no. 3 (April 1956): 550–73.

22. Senate Committee on Manufactures, *Foods Held in Cold Storage,* 61st Cong., 3rd sess., 1911.

23. Eric Rauchway, "The High Cost of Living in the Progressives' Economy," *Journal of American History* 88, no. 3 (December 2001): 898–924.

24. F. W. Taussig as quoted in House No. 1733, the Commonwealth of Massachusetts, *Report of the Commission to Investigate the Subject of the Cold Storage of Food and of Food Products Kept in Cold Storage* (Boston: Wright & Potter Printing Co., 1912), 93.

25. For the legal statues of each state up until 1903, see Barry Mohun, *A Compilation of Warehouse Laws and Decisions: Containing the Statutes of Each of the States and Territories Pertaining to Warehousemen: Together with a Digest of the Decisions of the State and Federal Courts, in All Cases Affecting Warehousemen* (New York: Banks Law Publishing Co., 1904). A draft of the Uniform Warehouse Receipts Act was published by the National Conference of Commissioners on Uniform State Laws as *Draft of an Act To Make Uniform the Law of Warehouse Receipts* (Cincinnati: Gibson & Perin Co., 1906). For legal reviews of the issue, see Francis Bacon James, "Practical Suggestions on Codifying the Law of Warehouse Receipts," *Michigan Law Review* 3, no. 4 (February 1905); and Barry Mohun, "The Effect of the Uniform Warehouse Receipts Act," *Columbia Law Review* 13, no. 3 (March 1913): 202–12.

26. John H. Frederick, *Public Warehousing, Its Organization, Economic Services, and Legal Aspects* (New York: Ronald Press Company, 1940), 144.

27. This is Section 3 of the bill, as quoted by Chester Morrill, Assistant to the Solicitor, Department of Agriculture in House Committee on Agriculture, *Cold Storage Legislation,* 66th Cong., 1st sess., 1919, 6.

28. The issue of "freshness" in the hearings is discussed throughout; for a few exchanges, see *Cold Storage Legislation,* 125, 181, 384.

Selected Bibliography

Banham, Reyner. *The Architecture of the Well-Tempered Environment.* Chicago: University of Chicago Press, 1969.

Chandler, Alfred. *The Visible Hand: The Managerial Revolution in American Business.* Cambridge: Belknap Press of Harvard University Press, 1977.

Cowan, Ruth Schwartz. "How the Refrigerator Got Its Hum." In *The Social Shaping of Technology.* Edited by Donald MacKenzie and Judy Wajcman, 202–18. Berkshire, UK: Open University Press, 1985.

Cronon, William. *Nature's Metropolis: Chicago and the Great West.* New York: W. W. Norton, 1991.

Freidberg, Susanne. *Fresh: A Perishable History.* Cambridge: Belknap Press of Harvard University Press, 2009.

2

Risk and Regulation in the Financial Architecture of American Houses

■

JONATHAN MASSEY

W HAT is a house? Among other things, it is an instrument for dis-
tributing economic risk and opportunity among individuals and
institutions. In the United States, two of three owner-occupied
houses serve as collateral for the mortgage loan that made the house purchase
possible. Through the financial structures that organize homeownership, American houses mediate our relation to state and market—they are instruments of
governmentality.

Although it is often seen as a stable foundation for home life and household
finance, the house is equally an unstable commodity affording its owners the
opportunity for profit and the risk of loss. While many borrowers think of the
mortgage loan as an instrument allowing them to buy the house they want, it is
also—as some borrowers recognize—a vehicle for speculating in the real estate
market on credit. From the perspective of investors in the credit market, the
house is merely an instrument through which to sell consumers debt. Financing
a house purchase with a mortgage entails participation in global credit markets
beyond the scope of everyday awareness and in disciplines that shape homeowner conduct.

Because housing is central to the national economy, it is among the most
regulated of industries, and this regulation serves as an instrument of social
policy. House design and construction are governed by zoning codes and building codes, of course, but they are also regulated by tax codes and institutional
practices that encourage some kinds of consumption and discourage others by
assessing them at different rates. Expenditures on housing are subject to this
kind of sumptuary regulation through tax provisions such as the mortgage interest deduction and institutional supports, including the mortgage insurance pro-

vided by the Federal Housing Administration. The lending, underwriting, and insurance assessment practices of FHA, other bureaucracies, and banks affect the balances between risk and opportunity in homeownership and between convention and innovation in house design. In shaping the ways we consume our houses, such sumptuary regimes also shape subjectivity. The disciplines of the monthly mortgage payment and the credit score are among the mechanisms of self-regulation that constitute liberal governmentality in this era that philosopher Gilles Deleuze called the control society.[1]

The sumptuary regime governing the consumption of houses has evolved significantly over the past century, and this modernization of housing finance has affected both the design and the social meaning of houses in ways that have changed with time. This chapter examines the changing role of the house over the past century or so as a financial instrument drawing its consumers into distinctive relations with state and market. By assembling an overview of lending practices and correlating that history with changes in residential development and design, I suggest a framework for further research into the financial architecture of American houses.

This history has four major periods, linked to cycles of boom and bust in the real estate market and the larger economy. As the twentieth century began, the laissez-faire state provided little support for homeownership apart from the homesteading provisions in land policy, and credit markets were small and localized. After World War I, collaboration between the state and real estate interests during the economic surge of the 1920s forged an "associational state" that expanded access to credit and began to integrate the mortgage finance market at a national scale. The interventionist state that emerged from the Depression and the New Deal established a highly regulated, state-supported national mortgage market that shaped American houses, neighborhoods, and land-use patterns up to the oil shock of the early 1970s. From the mid-1970s through the first few years of the twenty-first century, market innovations and the globalization of finance combined to outpace and undermine the existing regulatory regime as Keynesianism yielded to neoliberalism as a prevalent political ideology. Following years of rapid appreciation in the housing market, falling prices during the mid-2000s eroded confidence in an inflated mortgage market, triggering a worldwide credit contraction that soon expanded into a global financial crisis.[2] During each of these periods, new lending institutions and practices have reshaped the role of the house in mediating among individual, state, and market so as to manage the changing needs of an evolving capitalist economy.

The Laissez-Faire State

The mortgage loan is a legal and financial device that provides property owners—borrowers—with financing, liquidity, and capital. It was fundamental to the expansion of the American middle class in the twentieth century, and, as historians Michael Doucet and John Weaver have observed, it has a significance in shaping cities and their buildings comparable to those of the subdivided lot and the balloon frame. A mortgage is a loan secured by real property in which the buyer transfers all or part of his or her interest in the property to the lender as collateral on the condition that this interest be returned to the owner when the terms of the loan have been met. Mortgage lending practices and laws have established a system that negotiates the risks and opportunities of both lenders and borrowers by governing the respective rights and liabilities of each party to the transaction. Although the mortgage has served since antiquity as a legal instrument for financing homeownership, its terms have varied in both time and space. While the legal terms of American mortgage finance had largely stabilized by the mid-nineteenth century, there has continued to be much change in its financial structure.[3]

In the late nineteenth century, the residential development process in the United States was decentralized, barely regulated, and poorly coordinated. For most purchasers buying a house required complex and uncertain credit arrangements. Housing was largely custom-built, and families often built their own homes. Those who couldn't turned for assistance to small-scale operative builders who rarely completed more than a few houses per year. Homeownership was often precarious and was typically achieved incrementally by tapping local networks organized through personal and ethnic affiliation. Capital for individuals and families wishing to purchase or build houses was very limited, and it came usually from individuals, as banks limited their risk exposure by focusing on short-term loans to commercial concerns such as traders and wholesalers. Potential buyers had to accumulate large sums to make the high down payments needed to purchase a house. Most people lived in rented housing, with the homeownership rate at 46 percent in 1900.[4] For many owner-borrowers, the employment stability and savings pattern necessary to pay off a mortgage were elusive.

The development of a house usually began with its future occupant's purchase of a building lot, either from savings or through short-term financing, such as a one- to five-year mortgage from a family member, friend, or—less often—from a life insurance company or bank. Most loans were "balloon loans," in which the borrower made interest-only payments annually or semiannually, with the full principal of the loan—the balloon—due at the end of the term. The borrower could then repeat the process at a larger scale, offering the property as collateral on another balloon mortgage for the funds with which to build a house. Individual mortgage loans typically constituted no more than 30 to 40 percent of the assessed property value, with loan terms rarely exceeding five or six years. Buyers with limited capital frequently resorted to higher-interest second and third mortgages, or "junior" mortgages, to bridge whatever funding gap remained once their primary loan and down payment were factored in.[5]

Ideally, the borrower accumulated enough savings during the term of a balloon loan to pay off the mortgage when it came due. In practice, however, this was difficult, and loan renewals were the norm. While this system worked well during boom times, when confidence was high and holders of capital were eager to lend, it tended to intensify downturns and financial panics, as lenders called in their loans at term's end. The scarcity of capital and the complexity of assembling large-scale financing in this era meant that real estate developers found it difficult to develop large subdivisions complete with houses, so speculators usually divided land into lots, cut streets, and then began to sell off house lots in small batches to families and operative builders.

There was no national mortgage market in this era. Instead, credit was furnished through hundreds of local markets, with varying lending policies, interest rates, and regulation by different state laws. Since the 1830s, entrepreneurs and civic leaders had begun forming mutual savings banks that pooled member savings for mortgage investment. But with demand for capital higher than these fledgling institutions could supply, the larger cities evolved mortgage markets made up of thousands of small investors, lending in small quantities for short terms. Mortgage brokers and real estate agents linked these small investors and borrowers through webs of personal acquaintance and informal market knowledge. Accordingly, credit was differentially available to consumers based in part on their race, ethnic origin, and gender. Polish American residents of Milwaukee, for instance, like members of other immigrant ethnic communities in the industrial cities, supplemented their savings with loans from local, ethnically based lending circles. In Polish neighborhoods these were known as *skarbi*, or "treasuries." Members of such communities frequently built houses room-by-room through additions and expansions as families struggled to finance construction within stringent lending terms.[6]

The localization of finance, design, and construction created disparities in availability of capital that limited housing production in emerging economies such as those of Western frontier settlements, and it fostered the emergence of regionally distinctive housing vernaculars. Despite its broad diffusion of agency, this development system produced a high degree of architectural consistency within regional and local housing markets through what the historian Sam Bass Warner has called market-driven "regulation without laws." The late-nineteenth-century suburban neighborhoods of Boston that formed the basis of Warner's research were made up of lots and blocks developed and built out by different owners and investors, creating mixed and variable urban fabrics. These patches were integrated by gridded street planning, however—and also by adherence to traditional and popular patterns in the planning and design of houses, chosen by the many homeowners and small investors betting all or most of their capital on the construction of a house. Disciplined by risk to make conservative choices, these housebuilders imitated one another in their decisions about type, size, siting, and style. At the same time, the small scale of decision making and construction yielded extensive variety in the specific elaboration and detailing of those familiar forms.[7]

The Associational State

World War I prompted the first direct interventions in the housing market by the federal government, as part of the broader placement of some parts of the economy under wartime command economy provisions. These command provisions severely limited housing construction during the war, and a postwar recession exacerbated the freeze rather than ameliorating it. Real estate interests identified a shortage of housing as the problem, and they organized to stimulate both production and consumption of houses. In response to this perception of a housing shortage, real estate agents launched national campaigns to promote homeownership and construction of single-family detached houses. In 1914 real estate groups had initiated a nationwide campaign of advertising, publications, and exhibitions urging consumers to "Buy a Home." This initiative had been curtailed two years later by the widening impact of the war, but in 1918 the National Association of Real Estate Brokers joined with the Department of Labor and lumber companies to sponsor an even more ambitious campaign with the slogan "Own Your Own Home." These campaigns promoted the idea that the house was a special kind of commodity, one worth the risk attendant upon investing a substantial down payment and going into debt. They were part of a process that historian Jeffrey Hornstein has called "dreaming the American home," through which the house became "a sustained focus of scientific, technical, reformist, political, and business discourse," in the process coming to symbolize ideals of family life and citizenship.[8]

As commerce secretary in the 1920s, then as president during the early 1930s, Herbert Hoover attended closely to promoting a moral economy of the home that centered on the house as both an artifact and a site of consumption. Shortly after becoming secretary of commerce in 1921, Hoover incorporated national housing policy coordination into the Commerce Department purview, and he applied to the field of housing his conviction that the proper role of the state was to promote cooperation among private entities. He founded the Division of Building and Housing to promote standardization and efficiency in the housing industry. Among the areas of standardization and simplification of practice that the division tackled, in collaboration with industry groups, were those of building codes, real estate contracts, and zoning. After Mrs. W. B. Melony, the editor of *Delineator* magazine, launched a national campaign to promote better houses, Hoover embraced her movement as a counterpart to his own antiwaste campaigns, and he helped to formalize Melony's Better Homes in America (BHA) initiative as an educational foundation with professional leadership and headquarters in Washington, D.C.[9]

Modernizing housing finance was a significant component of the housing initiatives of both Hoover and the Better Homes organization. "We have mobilized the commercial capital of the country through the Federal Reserve Banks," Hoover explained to President Warren G. Harding in 1922. "We have mobilized the farm mortgage capital through the Farm Loan Bureau. . . . The country badly needs a mobilization of the home building capital based upon our building and loan associations, insurance companies, and savings banks." Hoover's Commerce Department promoted homeownership through pamphlets and other publications. Among the major goals of BHA, meanwhile, was "to encourage thrift for home ownership, and to spread knowledge of methods of financing the purchase or building of a home." The organization sponsored lectures and pamphlets on such topics as "How to Own Your Home" and "Financing the Small Home."[10]

Changes in the sources and terms of loan funds that gradually displaced the older forms of familial lending and ethnic association spurred an expansion of mortgage lending in the 1920s. Building and loan associations—since the 1930s called savings and loan associations—had emerged in the 1880s, and by the 1920s they had become a significant source of capital for homebuilders and homebuyers. These institutions pooled the savings of individuals, then lent these savings funds to member-investors who were buying or building a house. They epitomized Hoover's vision of the "associational state," in which economic sectors would be rationalized and regulated through voluntary cooperation among trade associations rather than by the state.

Building and loan associations introduced more generous lending practices, such as eleven- and twelve-year loan terms, as well as amortization, under which the borrower made monthly payments that blended interest charges with partial principal payments and sometimes even tax and insurance payments. In this way principal was paid off incrementally, reducing the risk of default by inculcating in homeowners a strict month-to-month fiscal discipline. Blended-payment amortization helped to instantiate savings practices that had proven difficult for many purchasers when left up to their own devices. It constituted a fiscal discipline that helped make homeownership a savings practice. Although they typically charged slightly higher interest rates than did conventional banks, building and loan associations also lent a higher proportion of the cost—60 to 75 percent of the assessed home value, as opposed to the 50 percent common among lending banks. This increase in the loan-to-value ratio meant that a home loan required a smaller down payment and the homeowner was less likely to need additional mortgage loans at higher rates. Building and loans were also more willing than other lenders to extend capital for the risky process of house construction.[11]

The lending terms of building and loan associations made mortgages both more accessible to borrowers and more stable for investors. A Census Bureau study conducted in 1923 showed that while the homeownership rate had remained steady over the preceding decades, the terms of ownership had changed markedly: between 1890 and 1920 the percentage of homes mortgaged had increased by more than a third, from 28 to 38 percent, and the ratio of debt to home value had risen as borrowers increasingly tapped institutional rather than individual lending sources. Aggregate mortgage debt had risen sixfold, to a total of six billion dollars. "Today the building and loan association is the working man's way par excellence of achieving a home," wrote Robert S. Lynd and Helen Merrell Lynd, authors of the 1929 sociological study *Middletown*. In Muncie, Indiana, which the Lynds studied as a typical middle-American city, four building and loan associations together financed an estimated 75 to 80 percent of new houses in the peak year of 1925.[12]

These new financing mechanisms combined with changes in design and construction to engender a new way of consuming the house, which became by the mid-1920s a consumer durable accessible to a wider range of buyers through normalized, liberalized credit. The 1910s and 1920s saw the rise of the smaller yet more intensively serviced house, reformatted to control price in an age of rising costs in construction and land as well as to reflect declining family size. While houses were smaller, with fewer rooms overall and fewer special-purpose rooms (such as a library and a parlor), they were more likely to be equipped with modern services and equipment: central heating, automatic heating with thermostatic control, electricity, automatic refrigeration, running water, and modern plumbing. As the nation's economy shifted from an agricultural toward an industrial and corporate base, home production of food, clothing, and other goods yielded to consumption of factory-made and store-bought items—and something similar happened with the house itself. Rather than being built and equipped incrementally by enterprising owners, it was more often built all at once or purchased as a finished artifact. While a century earlier the attainment of homeownership had possessed radical overtones through its role in helping working men gain the franchise, by the 1920s homeownership had become substantially more commodified.[13]

These changes were thematized in the demonstration houses built and exhibited by local Better Homes chapters from 1923 into the mid-1930s (figure 2.1). One of the major BHA activities was the staging every spring of national Better Homes Week, an intensive campaign during which local chapters orchestrated a battery of programs promoting homeownership. The focus of

Dover

26 ft. x 36 ft. over all
6 Rooms and Bath

The Dover is a splendid example of how the all-on-one-floor bungalow home can luxuriously and comfortably house a large family.

In appearance, this home is ideally balanced. Graceful roof lines blend into its shingled sides. Porch pillars carry through the idea of substantiality. Overhanging eaves give the final touch to the bungalow theme.

Let us analyze the Dover from the viewpoint of solid comfort. The twenty-six foot porch promises plenty of outdoor comfort and air. The living room provides space for not only the whole family but several guests in addition. The dining room is large enough to accommodate a holiday dinner party. In case of large entertainments, the two rooms can practically be opened into one. The three bedrooms suffice for a family of five or six—or with less people, a guest room is available.

There's a kitchen ample for all needs. You may have noticed where you can build a fireplace in the living room. That bay in the dining room you can plan for flowers and plants, or just a cozy cushioned seat. You have made a note of that celebrated step-saver, the kitchen cabinet. Did you see the closets for each sleeping room?

If it's a bungalow home that meets your fondest wishes, and the Dover satisfies your needs, then we can assure you that it will be ideal.

SPECIFICATIONS

Ceiling height first floor approximately 9 ft.
Girders 6 in. x 8 in.
First floor joists 2 in. x 8 in.
Ceiling joists 2 in. x 4 in. Rafters 2 in. x 6 in.
Ceiling joists plan B 2 in. x 6 in.
Front door—special design, 3 ft. x 6 ft. 8 in. and
    1¾ in. thick, glazed.
French doors between living room and dining room.
Our kitchen cupboard No. 2 and medicine cabinet
    included in the selling price. *See pages 36-37.*
Attic stairs and flooring included in the selling price
    of plan B.

See pages 8-9 for general specifications.

50

Figure 2.1. Bennett Homes catalog page featuring the Dover, a compact three-bedroom, one-bath bungalow sold as a kit of prefabricated parts for on-site construction by a local builder, 1920. *Source:* Ray H. Bennett Lumber Co., Inc., *Bennett Homes: Better-Built Ready-Cut*, catalog #18 (1920).

these events was usually the showcasing of houses built or renovated to serve
as examples of good house design and home culture. During the first national
campaign, in 1923, local chapters in at least fifty-seven cities and towns built
such demonstration houses, some constructing more than one, so that at least
seventy-eight houses were on show that year. In the 1929 campaign, of the
nearly 6,000 committees participating, 269 reported showing a total of 532
houses, including extant, remodeled, and new houses. In 1934, Better Homes
built an unusually prominent demonstration house at the intersection of Thirty-
Ninth Street and Park Avenue in Manhattan, which had the lowest homeownership rate in the nation—a mere 2.1 percent as of 1920. A collaboration with
Columbia Broadcasting Studio, "America's Little House" incorporated a radio
studio from which CBS broadcast special Better Homes Week programming
(figure 2.2).[14]

An especially well-documented case is that of Everyman's House, a compact yet carefully worked-out demonstration house built in 1924 by the Kal-

Figure 2.2. Richard Averill Smith, photograph of America's Little House,
New York, 1934. *Source*: Better Homes in America, *America's Little
House* (New York: Better Homes in America, 1934).

amazoo, Michigan, chapter of BHA (figure 2.3). Designed by Caroline Bartlett Crane, a doctor's wife who had organized local and statewide home-ownership initiatives, and detailed for construction by architect Gilbert Worden, Everyman's House adapted a traditional American house form—the colonial revival cottage—to the changing needs of middle- and working-class families as well as to the availability of longer-term amortized loans from building and loan associations (figure 2.4). The purpose of this demonstration house, open to the public during National Better Homes Week and subsequently sold to a local family, was to promote homeownership by showing "the best possibilities in home-building and home-equipment at a cost within the reach of a large number of non-home-owning people," estimated at around five thousand dollars.[15] By publishing a book on the subject of the house, Crane spread its fame well beyond Kalamazoo and provided insight into the ideological dimensions of Better Homes Week (figure 2.5).

Everyman's House incorporated many of the features of the smaller, better-serviced house, such as a living room with built-in dining alcove and an

Figure 2.3. Caroline Bartlett Crane with Gilbert Worden, Everyman's House, Kalamazoo, Michigan, 1924; view from the street. *Source:* Western Michigan University Libraries, Archives and Regional History Collections, Caroline Bartlett Crane "Everyman's House" Collection.

Figure 2.4. Caroline Bartlett Crane with Gilbert Worden, Everyman's House, Kalamazoo, Michigan, 1924; promotional photograph of the Everymans at dinner. *Source*: Western Michigan University Libraries, Archives and Regional History Collections, Caroline Bartlett Crane "Everyman's House" Collection.

efficiently planned kitchen with built-in fixtures and appliances. But an equally significant dimension of its modernity was its highlighting of the new possibilities in home finance. Echoing Hoover and other Better Homes advocates, Crane pointed out that the high cost and geographical fixity of housing had the value of stabilizing workers and bringing them into the middle-class social and political imaginary. Crane saw the role of her demonstration house as that of reducing political dissatisfaction with America's capitalist economy by increasing the proportion of Americans who owned property and so had a stake in maintaining the existing social order. By helping a man "achieve a home," she explained in her book, the house promised to give him "a vital stake in government." Along with the "sense of dignity in belonging to the social order" that came with homeownership, Everyman would acquire "respect for organized industry and for the law-regulated institutions of finance which furnish him the employment and insurance and credit necessary for the building of that home. Home-owning and Bolshevism," Crane concluded, "are just naturally strangers." Crane echoed the rhetoric of Hoover and the many other proponents of homeownership who saw it as the basis of good citizenship or even, as the slogan of the United

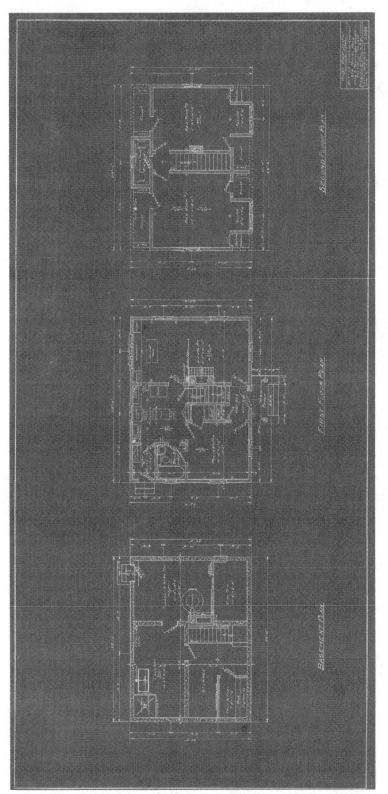

Figure 2.5. Caroline Bartlett Crane with Gilbert Worden, Everyman's House, Kalamazoo, Michigan, 1924: plans. *Source*: Western Michigan University Libraries, Archives and Regional History Collections, Caroline Bartlett Crane "Everyman's House" Collection.

States League of Local Building and Home Associations put it, "the safeguard of American liberties" in the face of such crises as the World War I, the postwar recession, and the Red Scare.[16]

One of the virtues of homeowning, for Crane as for its other proponents, was the incentive it provided for locational stability. The wage laborer aspiring to homeownership, she asserted, "must not be casual or peripatetic. He must be both willing and able to anchor in a home of some sort and become a part of the community."[17] By joining a building and loan association, Crane explained, a lot owner could expect to use the property as collateral in obtaining a loan for up to 80 percent of the construction cost of Everyman's House, with a twelve-year term at just under 7 percent interest. In some especially progressive cities, she noted, private lending associations specializing in short-term second mortgages could help provide financing to bridge any remaining gap between the borrower's savings and the costs in excess of the first mortgage amount. Everyman's House—like most new houses in an era of increasing mortgage indebtedness—was an anchor tying working families to place and polity through credit obligations. By cultivating a new set of bonds, dependencies, and disciplines in its purchaser, Everyman's House promoted a yeoman ideal of American citizenship even as it reflected the transformation of the house from a place of production to one of consumption within an industrial capitalist order.

The architecture profession participated in the real estate industry's "dreaming the American home." Studies of the building industry during the 1920s showed that only at the very high end did architects design a large proportion of projects. One architecture journal estimated the rate of "architectural control" as dropping from 95 percent among the top two-thirds of 1 percent of houses by cost, through 78 percent of the next 2 percent of houses, to a mere 15 percent of the remaining 97 percent—those costing less than twenty thousand dollars. Concerned about this low market share, architects sought to gain traction in the market for small, lower-cost houses, particularly those in the five-thousand- to ten-thousand-dollar range. Many entered competitions dedicated to recognizing good examples of affordable houses, including annual BHA competitions. The Architects' Small House Service Bureau, a nonprofit corporation founded in Minneapolis in 1920, promoted the use of architect-generated designs in the small house market. Endorsed by both the American Institute of Architects and Hoover's Department of Commerce, the bureau sold stock plans that owners, contractors, and architects could use in low-cost projects where an architect's design services posed a prohibitive cost, and it published these designs in its magazine, *The Small Home.*[18]

While the Small House Service Bureau embraced the principle that building more houses was the solution to the postwar housing shortage, some architects challenged the prevailing emphasis on building new single-family houses as the solution. Frederick L. Ackerman, an architect and policy analyst who emerged in the 1920s as a leading voice for socialization of the housing field, contended that the major problem in housing was not a shortage of units but shortcomings in financial accessibility to families of low and moderate incomes. Applying to housing the technocratic analysis that sociologist Thorstein Veblen had developed of industrial capitalist society more generally, Ackerman argued that the practices of market-based development, speculative investment, and difficult financing systematically withheld housing from potential occupants to maintain high-profit margins.

Before World War I had even ended, Ackerman and other progressives began promoting government-built multiunit social housing as a superior postwar alternative to market-based development and the single-family house. Charles H. Whitaker, Richard S. Childs, and Edith Elmer Wood, along with Ackerman, argued this case and analyzed suitable models in the article series "What Is a House?," published in the *American Institute of Architects Journal,* which Whitaker edited. Their solutions included not only new principles in planning and design, but also alternative mechanisms of ownership and financing to circumvent the complex and costly system of high down payment plus multiple mortgages. Among these were state development and ownership of housing, state financing of cooperative associations, the formation of nonprofit community land companies funded through bond issuance, and tax exemptions for housing developments that reflected progressive garden city ideals.[19]

The debates during and after World War I about the best means of designing, building, and financing American housing also stimulated innovations by other architects, such as the Dymaxion House concept that Buckminster Fuller developed in 1928. Fuller's designs for lightweight, mass-produced, portable aluminum dwellings on a hexagonal plan applied technocratic principles to rationalize the production of housing along the lines of Henry Ford's system of automobile production. While the production efficiencies Fuller sought to achieve through the Dymaxion House are well known, and the media systems within which he envisioned the house operating are increasingly recognized, less familiar are the distinctive methods of marketing and financing that he had in mind. Fuller devoted many pages of the *4D Time Lock,* the treatise in which he laid out his vision of industrialized dwelling, to outlining his plan for a "shelter service" business plan. In this plan a corporation—the 4D Control Syndicate—would not sell its housing products but would instead issue them to subscribers as part of a service contract to provide up-to-date housing. In other words, the house was to be an instrument of service rather than a product for direct sale.

Seeing shelter as a service subject to continual improvement, comparable to that achieved by telephone companies—which typically leased their equipment rather than selling it to assure interoperability across the network—Fuller envisioned a similar method for delivering housing. This service-contract business model was intended to circumvent the home finance business and to protect consumers from economic fluctuations by dissociating the provision of housing from the markets in land and credit, which historically have accounted for the bulk of housing costs. In Fuller's utopian imagination, mobile dwellings would stabilize the economy and eliminate neofeudal bonds by creating a self-regulating labor market in which workers followed jobs. The state would dissolve into a self-optimizing industrial economy in which consumers, disconnected not only from municipal infrastructures but also from less tangible forms of local association, dealt directly with transnational corporations.[20]

By addressing the house as a financial instrument drawing its consumers into new relations with one another, with markets, with corporations, and with the state through practices of ownership and finance, Fuller used design to rethink the political economy of housing. Whereas Crane sought through the house to settle workers whose mobility seemed to represent disengagement from community and social order, Fuller celebrated the increased autonomy and economic efficiency of a mobile workforce. Trusting the stock market more than the market in land to create value for investors and corporations alike, Fuller sought to accelerate the modernization and integration of a global capitalist economy that he believed afforded all parties increased opportunity for prosperity and happiness at lower risk.

The Interventionist State

The housing boom peaked in 1925, when construction of nonfarm dwellings accounted for nearly 40 percent of net capital formation in the national economy. Home loan foreclosures began to increase in 1925, and this trend accelerated rapidly following the stock market collapse in 1929. As the economy shrank, lenders began to demand repayment of short-term balloon loans when they came due, rather than granting the renewals that had been customary in better times, and this triggered foreclosures. Property values fell, in many cases below the value of the debt the properties had secured, and some properties became unmarketable given the weak economy and the tightened credit market. In Muncie, where some 63 percent of owner-occupied homes were mortgaged, homeownership peaked in July 1931, as bargain hunters sought to profit from the crisis. But foreclosures rose from an estimated ten or fewer in 1928 to more than a hundred in 1934, along with tax delinquencies. Mortgage lending at the city's leading building and loan peaked in 1928, then dropped by 1932 to a mere 4 percent of its peak volume in loan activity. "It was our fault for overselling them," said one of the city's real estate agents, "and the banks' fault for overlending. Everybody was buying a better home than he could afford." The expansion of homeownership through the liberalization of credit had afforded a large proportion of the population the opportunity of investment in homeownership but also exposed it to the risks of borrowing against so expensive a fluctuating asset as a house.[21]

The Depression spurred more direct federal intervention in the homeownership market than had been seen previously. As banks withdrew from mortgage lending, Congress and President Hoover established new programs and agencies dedicated to stabilizing the residential loan market. These included the Home Owners Loan Corporation and the Federal Home Loan Bank Board, a federally coordinated network of mortgage lenders following uniform lending standards and drawing on a common credit pool. Frankl Delano Roosevelt's New Deal greatly expanded the federal role, implementing through government authority policies that Hoover's administration had developed as proposals for voluntary industry adoption. The National Housing Act in June 1934 established the Federal Housing Administration (FHA) to provide mutual mortgage insurance on houses and low-cost housing projects. It also authorized FHA to charter national mortgage associations—the first of which would be the Federal National Mortgage Assocation (Fannie Mae) in 1938—to buy and sell FHA-insured mortgages, thereby establishing a secondary market to furnish greater liquidity for mortgage capital.[22]

FHA diminished the risk of mortgage finance for both lenders and borrowers, and it fostered closer adherence to convention in residential development and design. To qualify for FHA insurance, a mortgage loan and the property that secured it—as well as both borrower and lender—had to meet criteria laid out by the agency. Mortgages insured by FHA typically featured higher loan-to-value ratios that had loans in the 1920s, with longer terms (fifteen years at first, although terms rapidly lengthened until thirty years became the norm) and blended-payment amortization. The incentive of inexpensive federal insurance led lenders, borrowers, and builders to adopt FHA standards rapidly. The insurance protection, along with the homogenization it fostered, in turn allowed investors anywhere in the country to purchase a mortgage loan with greater confidence in its basic soundness, and Fannie Mae got the market going by purchasing insured mortgages from the primary lenders. These interventions rapidly created a national market in mortgage finance. In this way, housing entered the emerging mixed economy shaped by both government regulation and market action. Instead of socializing housing production, as Ackerman and others had advocated, the National Housing Act socialized risk.[23]

The impact of the National Housing Act was rapid and profound. Housing starts rose 40 percent in 1934, 70 percent in 1935, and 50 percent in 1936, and during the second half of the 1930s one in four occupied nonfarm dwellings added to national inventory was financed by an FHA mortgage. By 1940, FHA could claim that the monthly payment plan that went along with its insurance had become "the accepted mode of financing home repairs and home purchases in most communities" and that FHA-insured houses had become typical of new construction in the 140 largest housing markets in the nation. World War II brought new financial supports aimed at veterans that expanded on FHA insurance, further stimulating the markets in housing and home finance. State insurance of mortgage loans through FHA, guarantee of loans through the Veterans Administration (VA), and guaranty of the secondary market in mortgage debt through Fannie Mae allowed builders, brokers, and consumers to speculate more reliably in housing development.[24]

By assuming risk on mortgages that met its criteria, FHA used economic incentives to establish a powerful sumptuary regime shaping the consumption of land, housing, and credit. Its underwriting policies—the criteria whereby FHA assessed the soundness of a mortgage and the value and creditworthiness of the house that served as its collateral—soon became prescriptive for developers, purchasers, and lenders alike, and favored large tract developments consisting primarily of single-family houses on lower-cost land on the edges of developed metropolitan areas. The new regulatory regime of federal loan insurance and guarantees was geared toward institutional lenders and a new tier of large "merchant builders" or "community builders," companies that handled the entire development process from land acquisition and subdivision through construction to marketing. The FHA aesthetic agenda in its early years was "informed by the Better Homes ideal of the modest bungalow on a standard-sized tract of land, each house set back from the street by a standard distance," as Hornstein notes, leading to the proliferation of such developments.[25]

These new subdivisions were epitomized by the large-scale developments built in New York, New Jersey, and Pennsylvania by Levitt Brothers. Geared to FHA and VA financing—"5 percent down (nothing down for veterans) and 30 years to pay"—these Levittowns consisted of raised ranch and Cape Cod cottage designs with refrigerators, stoves, and even televisions built in so that they were included in the purchase price and the amortized mortgage. Modernist designs, as the agency cautioned in a technical bulletin advising underwriters, sometimes carried extra risk in resale and valuation due to potential "nonconformity" between the aesthetics of the house and its residential purpose, or between the house and neighboring properties in terms of siting and aesthetics. Large-scale financing, development, construction, and marketing of houses produced homogenous neighborhoods of nearly identical houses designed largely to meet FHA criteria and retain their resale value throughout the thirty-year loan term.[26]

In this way the sumptuary regime initiated by the New Deal channeled innovation into the elaboration of single-family house types, such as the saltbox, the colonial cottage, and the ranch house, as well as into the integration of house construction in the building of larger-scale community developments. Through incentive structures built into the federally underwritten, nationally integrated credit market, the federal government encouraged postwar purchasers to buy housing in standardized, preassembled packages adhering to widely shared conventions in development and design. This was a very different relation among individual, state, and market than had prevailed in cases like those of the Milwaukee Poles, who had helped one another build houses through incremental expansion, or even of the Everyman presumed by BHA literature. Anticipating that her reader would contract individually for construction of his house, and might need to defer the installation of some amenities until years after building the house, Crane outlined the relative values of different options in finishing and equipment, such as the specification of pine versus oak floors and the installation of one versus two bathrooms. Her book, like other documents of the 1920s, projects a consumer more actively engaged in producing his house than did later FHA policies and practices.

The federal regime of mortgage supports had broad social consequences. Combined with postwar prosperity, it gave the house a more central role in the accrual of equity for individuals and families, and it expanded the middle class. "The level-payment self-amortizing mortgage is one of the great social inventions," one scholar remarked as homeownership in the postwar period rose to nearly 70 percent. The parameters that FHA, Fannie Mae, and other institutions established for the planning, design, construction, and financing of houses stabilized the role of housing as a means of capital accumulation for institutional investors and house purchasers alike. At the same time, FHA underwriting guidelines institutionalized existing real estate industry practices based on the conviction that racial mixing, and indeed the presence of minority groups generally, lowered property values. The combination of market assumptions and federal policy led many lenders to "redline" neighborhoods with significant minority populations, refusing to lend in these areas, or encouraged them to change higher interest rates when lending in such neighborhoods. In this way, racial segregation was built into the formation of the middle class and its built environment through selective extension of credit and the risk-based pricing of mortgage loans.[27]

The Globalized Credit Market

From the early 1970s to 2006, the globalization of credit markets and a worldwide economic boom coincided with innovations that expanded the range, flexibility, and scale of mortgage financing. This combination yielded a

new sumptuary regime that diminished state regulation, increased both opportunity and risk, introduced new house designs, and shifted homeowner subjectivity toward a more entrepreneurial model than had prevailed during the
postwar period. Following the oil shock of 1973, inflation raised house prices,
making homeownership more challenging but also a potentially more reward-
ing investment. Many consumers began investing a greater proportion of their
money in housing, buying larger and more expensive houses as a way of turning their homes into speculative investments. The nation's mortgage lending
capacity was augmented in this period by the growth of the secondary market
in mortgage debt through federal intervention, loan securitization, and a proliferation of new loan types.

In the late 1960s the federal government restructured Fannie Mae and created the Government National Mortgage Association (Ginnie Mae) and the
Federal Home Loan Mortgage Corporation (Freddie Mac) to expand the supply
of mortgage credit by purchasing government-issued and market-issued mortgages, so that by 2008 the government owned or guaranteed nearly half of
the nation's total outstanding home mortgage debt. Computerization of mortgage origination and servicing allowed banks and other investors to securitize
mortgages by batching many loans into large debt pools generating monthly income streams, then selling securities backed by narrow slices of the aggregated
debt. With the nation's housing stock extensively conforming to FHA underwriting standards and federal or quasi-federal insurance protecting most loans,
mortgage-backed securities seemed like nearly risk-free investments. Institutional investors around the world, including central banks, pension funds, and
commercial banks, saw the federally regulated American mortgage market as a
low-risk, high-yield investment opportunity, especially once credit rating agencies began rating mortgage-backed securities issuances. In this way securitization in the secondary mortgage market created new links between individual
consumers and global capital markets.[28]

Capital, once scarce and only cautiously extended to house purchasers,
flooded the residential mortgage market as American home finance became
globalized. Lenders expanded their market by offering a range of new loan
types, including "jumbo loans" larger than the maximum amount insured by
FHA, forty-year loan terms, the reborn junior mortgage in the form of "piggy-
back loans," and adjustable-rate mortgages. Rising house values allowed many
homeowners to finance renovations, additions, or other expenditures unrelated
to housing by borrowing against the inflated house value through home equity
loans, which afforded lenders and borrowers alike another way of increasing
volume, profit opportunities, and risks. The combination of rising house prices
and the influx of global credit encouraged some finance companies in the 1990s
to extend credit for transactions that did not qualify for federal insurance.

Because taking on such "subprime" cases entailed assuming greater risk, these firms usually charged higher interest rates and higher loan origination fees. While such risk-based pricing expanded access to credit for borrowers, including for minority borrowers traditionally excluded from the market by redlining, it soon took a high toll as lenders introduced a raft of high-risk loan types that dispensed with key elements in FHA underwriting assessments. Among these were loans based on the applicant's statements of income and assets rather than on any verified data, and even a type known as the "no income, no assets" loan—which one mortgage broker called "a liar's loan." Because many loan originators and brokers realized a quick profit by reselling their loans for securitization in the secondary market, loan amounts frequently exceeded even optimistic property valuations as investment pressure in the credit market outpaced price inflation of the houses serving as collateral. Through these mechanisms, borrowers and creditors alike entered what one commentator termed an "imprudent partnership" of real estate speculation that yielded large profits but carried sizable risks.[29]

The rise in house prices had been accompanied by little change in income levels, so that the median house price, long two to three times median annual income, had risen to some four times median income. When house prices began to fall in many markets, in 2005 and 2006, subprime borrowers began to default at an accelerating rate. As had happened in the late 1920s and early 1930s, defaults triggered a sudden contraction in the credit market. Securitization had obscured the extent of subprime lending and had blended subprime loans into the larger pool of standard mortgages, so that nearly all investors in the credit markets had some risk exposure. By replacing traditionally bilateral mortgage lending with multilateral transactions, it had also intensified the likelihood of foreclosure by making it difficult for debtors and creditors to modify loan terms and craft the consensual workarounds that during the Great Depression had mitigated the negative consequences of default for borrower and lender alike. The interconnectedness created by securitization, meanwhile, spread the consequences of the real estate downturn into other economic sectors, triggering a worldwide economic recession. Once again, the federal government assumed a large volume in losses, socializing costs after years of private profit-taking, this time to protect investment banks as well as Fannie Mae and Freddie Mac. Many of the economic and social costs of the bust were thus absorbed not by the market participants but by the broader taxpayer base.

Before the credit crisis, however, homeownership had become an attractive way for middle-class consumers to speculate on credit. Even as average household size dwindled, the average size of a new single-family house increased from 1,660 square feet in 1973 to 2,521 in 2007. The value of new houses rose dramatically as well, from an average of $62,500 in 1978 to $313,600 in 2007.[30] The expanded range of loan products supported innovation by financing improvements to old inner-city houses that failed to meet FHA underwriting requirements, construction and resale of houses with inflated values that exceeded FHA insurance limits, and construction of new houses, townhouses, and condominium units tailored to niche markets, such as post–baby boom empty nesters.

Among the architectural dimensions of these changes was the rise of large tract houses pejoratively known as McMansions. These houses of three thousand to five thousand square feet typically occupy a high proportion of their suburban or exurban lot, their bulk articulated by complex rooflines. Though laden with signifiers of wealth, such as high-ceilinged foyers and "great rooms," these homes lack the construction quality and design detailing of the older or more expensive houses they evoke. Another result of the changed finance market was the "teardown," in which a house owner used savings and home equity credit to demolish an existing house and build a larger one with more luxurious finishes and updated services, typically on a valuable inner-suburb lot. Prompted as they were by financial rather than physical obsolescence, such teardowns highlighted the centrality of financing to the architecture of American houses (figure 2.6).

The mortgage-supported real estate speculation of the 1990s and early 2000s was captured in a spate of television shows built around the culture of "house-flipping": the practice of purchasing, improving, and then reselling a house at a higher price. As long as prices continued to rise, astute homeowners could use credit to finance a series of transactions that netted them good profit even once the transaction and renovation costs were deducted from the sale price. Television series titles included *Flip This House, Flip That House, Property Ladder, Designed to Sell, Flipping Out, Curb Appeal, The Stagers,* and *Extreme Makeover: Home Edition.* Within the genre of reality TV, these programs dramatized the possibilities of credit-fueled speculation, much as Better Homes demonstration houses (like Everyman's House) had explicated the economic and social potential of mortgage financing in the 1920s. They reflected and fueled a new culture of homeownership in which owner-investors saw themselves as commodity speculators using credit to make bets on anticipated inflation and on their ability to gauge evolving market preferences. Such purchases, renovations, and sales were not only investment strategies but also avocations for aspiring individuals and couples in a society where flexible labor relations and changed attitudes had increased geographical mobility and diminished the sense of rootedness in place and local community.

By liberalizing credit while reducing the regulatory influence of central banks

Figure 2.6. The teardown cycle as played out in Annandale, Virginia, in 2004, documented by resident Scott Evans. Above: postwar two-bedroom, one-bath slab-on-grade asbestos-shingled house before teardown; below: McMansion under construction on the same lot. Courtesy of Scott Evans.

Figure 2.7. Daniel Kariko, "#103, Lehigh Acres," 2009; view of an unmaintained tract house near Lakeland, Florida, from the series SpeculationWorld. Courtesy of Daniel Kariko.

and national governments, global processes have both facilitated homeowner-ship and made it riskier. A source of "stability, security, and investment" since the 1930s, as one study suggests, American homeownership has become "a site of uncertainty and risk in which some of the consequences of the chang-ing nature of work and welfare are played out."[31] The credit crisis that began in 2006 caused the restructuring of Fannie Mae and Freddie Mac, followed by broader changes in the legal and financial regime through which state and market structure the opportunities and risks of homeownership and the bal-ance between convention and innovation in house design. This re-regulation is likewise changing the subjective dimensions of homeownership and home finance—for subprime borrowers and house-flippers as for the millions of oth-ers in the mortgage market (figure 2.7).

Notes

1. Gilles Deleuze, "Postscript on the Societies of Control," October 59 (Winter 1992): 3–7. For additional analyses of liberal power, see Michel Foucault, Discipline and Punish: The Birth of the Prison, translated by Alan Sheridan (1975; New York: Pantheon, 1978); Michel Foucault, "The Subject and Power," in Hubert L. Dreyfus and Paul Rabinow, Michel Foucault: Beyond Structuralism and Hermeneutics, second edition (Chicago: University of Chicago

Press, 1983), 208–26; and David M. Halperin, *Saint Foucault: Towards a Gay Hagiography* (New York: Oxford University Press, 1995). On sumptuary regulation, see Alan Hunt, *Governance of the Consuming Passions: A History of Sumptuary Law* (New York: St. Martin's Press, 1996). For an analysis of the role of sumptuary regulation in the aesthetic of modernist architecture, see Jonathan Massey, "New Necessities: Modernist Aesthetic Discipline," *Perspecta: Yale Architectural Journal* 35 (2004): 112–33.

2. For accounts of the role played by mortgage lending in the credit crisis and broader financial crisis that began in 2007, see Alex Blumberg and Adam Davidson, "The Giant Pool of Money," *This American Life* (radio show), episode 355, first aired on May 9, 2008; Robert J. Shiller, *The Subprime Solution: How Today's Global Financial Crisis Happened, and What to Do about It* (Princeton: Princeton University Press, 2008); and Dan Immergluck, *Foreclosed: High-Risk Lending, Deregulation, and the Undermining of America's Mortgage Market* (Ithaca: Cornell University Press, 2009).

3. Andrew Berman, "'Once a Mortgage, Always a Mortgage': The Use (and Misuse) of Mezzanine Loans and Preferred Equity Investments," *Stanford Journal of Law, Business, and Finance* 11 (Autumn 2005): 76–125; and Michael Doucet and John Weaver, *Housing the North American City* (Montreal: McGill-Queens University Press, 1991), 252.

4. U.S. Department of Commerce, *How to Own Your Home: A Handbook for Prospective Home Owners*, prepared by John M. Gries and James S. Taylor, Division of Building and Housing, Bureau of Standards (Washington, D.C.: U.S. Government Printing Office, 1923), vii.

5. The characterization of the late-nineteenth-century development and financing system in this and the following paragraphs is based primarily on Doucet and Weaver, *Housing the North American City*; and Sam Bass Warner, *Streetcar Suburbs: The Process of Growth in Boston, 1870–1900* (Cambridge: Harvard University Press, 1962). For an overview of American single-family house development practices, see Dolores Hayden, *Building Suburbia: Green Fields and Urban Growth, 1820–2000* (New York: Vintage Books, 2003).

6. Thomas C. Hubka and Judith T. Kenny, "The Workers' Cottage in Milwaukee's Polish Community: Housing and the Process of Americanization, 1870–1920," in *Perspectives in Vernacular Architecture*, issue titled "People, Power, and Places" 8 (2000): 33–52. On the formation and role of savings banks, see R. Daniel Wadhwani, "Citizen Savers: Family Economy, Financial Institutions, and Public Policy in the Nineteenth-Century Northeast," *Enterprise and Society* 5, no. 4 (2004): 617–23.

7. Warner, *Streetcar Suburbs*, chapter 6, "Regulation without Laws," 117–52. On the national context of mortgage finance, see Kenneth A. Snowden, "Mortgage Lending and American Urbanization, 1880–1890," *Journal of Economic History* 48, no. 2 (June 1988): 273–85; and Lance Davis, "The Investment Market, 1870–1914: The Evolution of a National Market," *Journal of Economic History* 25, no. 3 (September 1965): 355–93.

8. Jeffrey M. Hornstein, *A Nation of Realtors: A Cultural History of the Twentieth-Century American Middle Class* (Chapel Hill: Duke University Press), 7.

9. My account of Hoover and homeownership campaigns is based primarily on Hornstein, *Nation of Realtors*, chapter 5, 118–55. Regarding BHA, see Jane Hutchison, "The Cure for Domestic Neglect: Better Homes in America, 1922–1935," *Perspectives in Vernacular Architecture* 2 (1986): 168–78; and Karen Altman, "Consuming Ideology: The Better Homes in America Campaign," *Critical Studies in Mass Communication* 7 (1990): 286–307.

10. Hoover to Harding, February 9, 1922, quoted in Hornstein, *Nation of Realtors*, 140; and Better Homes in America, *Guidebook for Better Homes Campaigns in Cities and Towns* (Washington, D.C.: Better Homes in America, 1929), 6, 48.

11. U.S. Department of Commerce, *How to Own Your Home*; see also Marc A. Weiss, "Richard T. Ely and the Contribution of Economic Research to National Housing Policy, 1920–1940," *Urban Studies* 26 (1989): 115–26.

12. Hornstein, *Nation of Realtors*, 122–23; and Robert S. Lynd and Helen Merrell Lynd, *Middletown: A Study in American Culture* (New York: Harcourt, Brace, and Company, 1929), 104.

13. Lynd and Lynd, *Middletown*, 98; and Doucet and Weaver, *Housing the North American City*, 169.

14. Better Homes in America, *Guidebook for Better Homes Campaigns*, 40; U.S. Department of Commerce, *How to Own Your Home*, vii; and Better Homes in America, *America's Little House* (New York: Better Homes in America, 1934).

15. Caroline Bartlett Crane, *Everyman's House* (Garden City, N.Y.: Doubleday Page, 1925), 3.

16. Ibid., 149; and Weiss, "Richard T. Ely and the Contribution of Economic Research," 117.

17. Crane, *Everyman's House*, 50.

18. Architects' Small House Service Bureau, Incorporated, *The Movement to Improve Small House Architecture* (Minneapolis: Architects' Small House Service Bureau, n.d. [ca. 1930]).

19. Charles Harris Whitaker, Frederick L. Ackerman, Richard S. Childs, and Edith Elmer Wood, "What Is a House?" *American Institute of Architects Journal* 5, no. 2 (1917): 481–85, 541–46, 591–639; and "What Is a House?" *American Institute of Architects Journal* 6 (1918): 14–18, 58–67. See also Gail Radford, *Modern Housing for America: Policy Struggles in the New Deal Era* (Chicago: University of Chicago Press, 1997).

20. Fuller's vision of a world reordered through "dymaxion" efficiencies is laid out in R. Buckminster Fuller, *4D Time Lock* (Albuquerque: Lamas Foundation, 1972); and Fuller, *Nine Chains to the Moon*, revised edition (Garden City, N.Y.: Anchor Books, 1971); see also Jonathan Massey, "The Sumptuary Ecology of Buckminster Fuller's Designs," in *A Keener Perception: Ecocriticism in American Art History*, edited by Alan Braddock and Christoph Irmscher (Tuscaloosa: University of Alabama Press, 2009).

21. Hornstein, *Nation of Realtors*, 119; and Robert S. Lynd and Helen Merrell Lynd, *Middletown in Transition: A Study in Cultural Conflicts* (New York: Harcourt, Brace, and Company, 1937), 554, 191.

22. Hornstein, *Nation of Realtors*, 148–50; and Radford, *Modern Housing for America*, 178.

23. U.S. Federal Housing Administration (FHA), *The FHA Story in Summary, 1934–1959* (Washington, D.C.: U.S. Government Printing Office, 1959).

24. Hornstein, *Nation of Realtors*, 42–45; Federal Housing Authority, *FHA Homes in Metropolitan Districts: Characteristics of Mortgages, Homes, Borrowers under the FHA Plan, 1934–1940* (Washington, D.C.: U.S. Government Printing Office, 1942), 5; and FHA, *FHA Story in Summary*, 15–18.

25. Hornstein, *Nation of Realtors*, 151. Regarding the emergence of large-scale subdivision developers, see Ned P. Eichler, *The Merchant Builders* (Cambridge: MIT Press, 1982); and Marc A. Weiss, *The Rise of the Community Builders: The American Real Estate Industry and Urban Land Planning* (New York: Columbia University Press, 1987).

26. Barbara M. Kelly, *Expanding the American Dream: Building and Rebuilding Levittown* (Albany: State University of New York Press, 1993), 77, 87; Federal Housing Administra-

tion, *Technical Bulletin #2: Modern Design* (Washington, D.C.: U.S. Government Printing Office, 1936); see also Keller Easterling, *Organization Space: Landscapes, Highways, and Houses in America* (Cambridge: MIT Press, 2001), 134, 175–89.

27. Martin Mayer, "Economics of Housing," in *Housing: Symbol, Structure, Site,* edited by Lisa Taylor (New York: Cooper-Hewitt Museum and Rizzoli, 1990), 100–101. On redlining and racial discrimination, see Kenneth Jackson, *Crabgrass Frontier: The Suburbanization of the United States* (Oxford: Oxford University Press, 1987), but also Amy Hillier, "Redlining and the Home Owners' Loan Corporation," *Journal of Urban History* 29 (May 2003): 394–420.

28. Berman, "'Once a Mortgage, Always a Mortgage,'" 91–93; and James R. Hagerty, Deborah Solomon, and Sudeep Reddy, "Treasury and Fed Pledge Aid for Ailing Mortgage Giants," *Wall Street Journal,* July 14, 2008, A1, A12.

29. Blumberg and Davidson, "Giant Pool of Money." See also U.S. Bureau of the Census, *American Housing Survey,* 2007, online at http://www.census.gov/hhes/www/housing/ahs/ahs.html, especially table 3-15; and Guy Stuart, *Discriminating Risk: The U.S. Mortgage Lending Industry in the Twentieth Century* (Ithaca: Cornell University Press, 2003).

30. U.S. Bureau of the Census, "Characteristics of New Housing Index, 2008," online at http://www.census.gov/const/www/charindex.html.

31. John Doling and Janet Ford, eds., *Globalisation and Home Ownership: Experiences in Eight Member States of the European Union* (Delft, Netherlands: DUP Science, 2003), 7. For a broader analysis of contemporary "risk society," see Ulrich Beck, *Risk Society: Towards a New Modernity* (London: Sage, 1992); and Beck, *What Is Globalization?* (Cambridge: Polity Press, 2000).

Selected Bibliography

Blumberg, Alex, and Adam Davidson. "The Giant Pool of Money." *This American Life,* radio show, episode 355. First aired on May 9, 2008. Online at http://www.thislife.org.

Doucet, Michael, and John Weaver. *Housing the North American City.* Montreal: McGill-Queens University Press, 1991.

Easterling, Keller. *Organization Space: Landscapes, Highways, and Houses in America.* Cambridge: MIT Press, 2001.

Hayden, Dolores. *Building Suburbia: Green Fields and Urban Growth, 1820–2000.* New York: Vintage Books, 2003.

Hornstein, Jeffrey M. *A Nation of Realtors: A Cultural History of the Twentieth-Century American Middle Class.* Chapel Hill: Duke University Press, 2005.

Immergluck, Dan. *Foreclosed: High-Risk Lending, Deregulation, and the Undermining of America's Mortgage Market.* Ithaca: Cornell University Press, 2009.

Weiss, Marc A. *The Rise of the Community Builders: The American Real Estate Industry and Urban Land Planning.* New York: Columbia University Press, 1987.

3

Boston's West End
Urban Obsolescence in
Mid-Twentieth-Century America

■

DANIEL M. ABRAMSON

N 1951, Boston's City Planning Board produced a comprehensive urban re-newal scheme detailing the city's woes and imagining a better future. Amid much dry data, one page spread stands out (figure 3.1).[1] On the left, a black-inked map of Boston's West End depicts a crooked maze of dense-packed blocks, back alleys, courtyards, and vacant lots. Atop reads the title "An Ob-solete Neighborhood" while across lies the pendant image titled "And a New Plan." Here is an imagined future cleared of congestion, modernist slab blocks arrayed in a park setting. A decade passed before the West End was infamously obliterated and the "New Plan" realized, but once singled out as "obsolete," the neighborhood's fate was largely sealed. How and why had the West End earned this dubious distinction?

Curious, too, is the choice of title. What did it mean to designate a neigh-borhood as "obsolete"? What and whose purposes did this assessment serve? Where, moreover, had the term "obsolete" come from in relation to urban form, and where was this rhetoric going? From the mid-1930s through the early 1970s the question of the obsolescence of neighborhoods and cities was posed regularly in discussions of American city planning and urbanism. Consequently, obsolescence became a key paradigm for conceptualizing and managing change in the American urban built environment, part of a national strategy for clearing urban land in the hope of improving citizens' lives and dwellings. This chapter offers a critical history of the idea of urban obsolescence using Boston's West End as a case study.

The "obsolete" West End of 1950 was an L-shaped, forty-eight-acre area in the northwest part of Boston close by the downtown business and civic district. Settled in the early nineteenth-century, the West End for a hundred years had

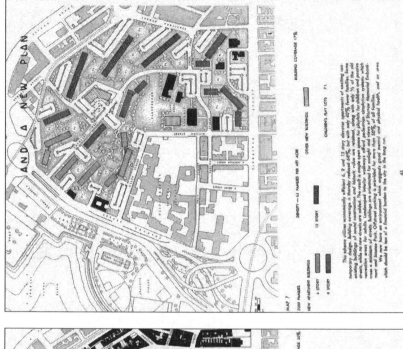

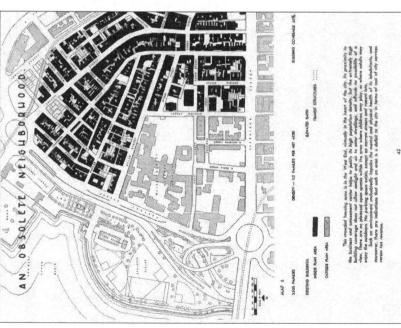

Figure 3.1. "An Obsolete Neighborhood . . . and a New Plan": the graphic that doomed the West End. *Source: A General Plan for Boston: A Preliminary Report* (Boston: Boston City Planning Board, 1951), 42–43.

been a district primarily of first- and second-generation immigrants. In 1950 working-class Italians represented a plurality of the West End's twelve thousand inhabitants, living alongside substantial Jewish and Polish communities, plus smaller numbers of Greeks, Albanians, Ukrainians, African Americans, students, artists, and hospital workers who had settled there for its low rents and central city location. Fragmented by ethnicity and income—the poorest concentrated in the dense center—the West End was never socially a "cohesive neighborhood," although it could look so because of its dominant working-class culture, architectural uniformity, and defined boundaries.[2]

Physically the West End was hemmed in on all sides: to the south by broad Cambridge Street, to the west by Massachusetts General Hospital and the Charles River, to the north and east by elevated rail lines and light industry. Within, the West End could feel claustrophobic. Only three of its two dozen streets ran all the way through; the rest extended a few blocks at most. Along cramped roadways and sidewalks a jumble of high, narrow, three- to five-story tenement buildings constructed in the late nineteenth and early twentieth centuries formed nearly continuous walls. Ground-floor stores and luncheonettes were ubiquitous. Trees appeared rarely in this brick and asphalt world. Density and disorder in the West End are the physical qualities of this "obsolete neighborhood" emphasized by the 1951 figure-ground plan.

Beneath the 1951 plan, statistics and a caption summarized the argument for the West End's obsolescence. Primary was the congestion of people and buildings: 112 families per net acre; building coverage of 55 percent that "does not allow sunlight and air to enter dwellings, and affords no possibility of a view."[3] These were densities, the *General Plan for Boston* noted, that "exceeded the standards set up by the American Public Health Association's Committee on the Hygiene of Housing."[4] The caption continues: "There are no pleasant open spaces within the area where children may play, or where adults may enjoy the outdoors. No parking space exists, except on narrow streets and vacant lots." Worse, the neighborhood's congestion "undoubtedly impairs the mental and physical health of its inhabitants." Most frequently cited was the neighborhood's high incidence of tuberculosis, which "ranked worse than 53 of 64 areas in Boston."[5] Ultimately, human distress and physical density exacted costs beyond the district's borders: "There are indications that such an area is a deficit to the city in terms of cost of city services versus tax revenue." From physical congestion to ill health to economic liability, this was the logic of the West End's obsolescence.

Subsequent planning studies of the West End from the mid-1950s filled in this outline. All featured a comprehensive housing survey whose conclusions were sobering. "Nearly 80% of all dwelling units in the West End rank as substandard or only marginally standard."[6] Of 631 West End buildings surveyed,

89 percent lacked rear stairs and 80 percent lacked fire escapes; 61 percent had trash strewn about; and 60 percent showed signs of rat infestation and 75 percent other vermin. Of the 3,671 dwelling units surveyed, 63 percent lacked washbasins and 64.8 percent had "larger" or "extreme defects" in their walls, windows, or floors.[7] This survey represented Boston planners' "main argument for describing the area as a slum," according to the sociologist Herbert Gans, then living among the West Enders.[8]

The survey that determined the West End's substandard obsolescence was conducted by "trained field inspectors using the American Public Health Association (APHA) technique."[9] Initially conceived in the early 1940s to help standardize wartime housing, the APHA's *Appraisal Method for Measuring the Quality of Housing* (four volumes in all, published in 1945 and 1946) was most widely used after enactment of the federal Housing Act of 1949, which required assessment of a city's existing housing stock before it could be replaced and improved. Upon publication the APHA manual was pronounced "without question the most scientific approach yet made to the measurement of housing quality on a large scale."[10] Twenty years later it was still "the best system yet devised for the appraisal of substandard housing."[11] Adopted by the United States Public Health Service, the APHA method was put to use at redevelopment agencies in a score of American cities, including Milwaukee, Philadelphia, Washington, Los Angeles, New Haven, and Saint Louis.

By APHA protocol, field inspectors with printed appraisal forms first canvassed a neighborhood to assess "penalty score points" on individual items from toilet facilities and sleeping arrangements to heating equipment and overall structural condition. One to three penalty points represented "slight threats" to public safety; maximum penalty points indicated "extreme and ever-present threats."[12] Separately, the whole neighborhood would be subjected to an "environmental survey," which assessed penalty points for items like land crowding, commercial nuisances, and inadequate community facilities. Field scores would be transcribed by office clerks onto punch cards for sorting, statistical analysis, and aggregation into block and neighborhood tables, charts, and maps. The sum of penalty points produced a neighborhood's total housing quality score, "the distinctive feature of the method" that expressed "complex relationships in a single figure."[13]

Fewer than 30 penalty points for a total housing quality score represented grade A "good to excellent housing." More than 120 penalty points indicated grade E "thoroughgoing slums." In the middle, a 60- to 89-point grade C score represented "mediocre housing districts in which extensive blight and obsolescence can be expected . . . housing which no official agency would condemn, but which may involve serious problems of blight and shrinking values during the next ten or twenty years."[14] For the category of the obsolescent vigilance was required: "The encroachment of grade C blocks into higher grade areas indicates a spreading blight which local agencies will wish to check both as protection to the remaining unspoiled neighborhoods and as a safeguard to the city's tax base."[15] Grade C obsolescent areas endangered the whole city and risked themselves collapsing into wholly obsolete slums. For that, intoned the APHA manual, "there is usually no practical remedy except rebuilding."[16]

Bureaucracy and abstraction characterized the APHA *Appraisal Method for Measuring the Quality of Housing*. The goal was to provide planners with a fine-grained, block-by-block, building-by-building analysis of urban housing conditions, indicating if an area needed "minor improvements," "radical rehabilitation," or "must be torn down."[17] Earlier classifications based on large-scale census tracts and just a handful of indicators had been imprecise and failed practically in guiding planners' decisions about which neighborhoods and blocks needed the most help first. Now the APHA had laid out a method employing dozens of criteria that could ideally target the citizenry most in need. One author forecast that an "official designation of substandardness by areas will serve as a beacon to guide the agencies of reconstruction."[18] The manual's grading rubric represented a "concise and quantitative picture . . . that will be understood by the busy public official or the layman."[19]

As a political tool, the APHA manual made the "determination of basic needs . . . a matter of quantitative measure" so that "it becomes possible to put all the housing cards on the table, where every group concerned may consider dispassionately its proper role in the reconstruction task."[20] The APHA method thus functioned as a kind of urban triage, officials and politicians using it to diagnose urban ills and prioritize areas for redevelopment surgery. The method's political effectiveness rested on its scientism and apparent objectivity, which could be used to transcend the usual class and ethnic divisions of American big-city politics seen as stymieing reform and social improvement.

The APHA *Appraisal Method for Measuring the Quality of Housing* reflected scientific methods traditionally applied by public health experts to sanitation engineering and infectious diseases. The manual also represented an expansion of public health into broader social concerns. "The public health of the future must be not only an engineering science and a medical science; it must also be a social science," proclaimed C.-E. A. Winslow, Yale University professor of public health and chair of the APHA's Committee on the Hygiene of Housing.[21] With financial support from the League of Nation's health organization, the U.S. Public Health Service, and philanthropies like the Milbank Memorial Fund and the Rockefeller Foundation, the APHA's Committee on the Hygiene of Housing began in the 1930s a decade-long study of housing matters from illumination and recreational facilities to housing survey procedures and standards of occupancy. Raising standards would decrease illness and accident rates and provide "esthetic satisfaction" and "refuge from the noise and tension of the street and market place," declared the APHA's *Basic Principles of Healthful Housing.* It would also protect against "the sense of inferiority developed in a home notably below the standard of friends and neighbors."[22]

The APHA's *Basic Principles* reflected long-standing views on the physical environment's determination of physical and social health, supplemented by a modern emphasis on the individual's mental health and happiness. Urban obsolescence now included a neighborhood fabric's failure to support individual self-esteem as well as moral and creative self-actualization, in terms developed at this time by the psychologist Abraham Maslow's "hierarchy of human needs." Modern, too, was the APHA housing study's organizational structure and institutional framework. Analysis of urban obsolescence exemplified the "big research" approach of the interwar years, bringing together government, academia, professional organizations, and foundations in a "totalist view of American life as an objectified, quantified mechanism."[23] For the APHA housing study some dozen separate interdisciplinary subcommittees were organized, each composed of experts from numerous fields.

The *Appraisal Method for Measuring the Quality of Housing* was authored specifically by the APHA's Subcommittee on Appraisal of Residential Areas, whose members included a statistician, sociologist, doctor, and housing specialist, plus the city planner Frederick J. Adams. Son of the famous planner Thomas Adams and himself founder in 1947 of Massachusetts Institute of Technology's Department of City and Regional Planning, Frederick J. Adams had since the 1930s been active in discussions on the obsolescence of American neighborhoods and cities. He was respondent to an important 1935 article on "Obsolescence in Cities" in the *Planners' Journal,* the leading professional publication that Adams edited from 1937 to 1940. He served on APHA subcommittees examining recreational facilities and home sanitation, and he chaired the subcommittee on environmental standards that authored *Standards for Healthful Housing: Planning the Neighborhood* (published in 1948).

Adams wrote widely on urban redevelopment, asserting that "the basic pattern and a large proportion of the structures in our cities are physically and economically obsolete" and that "the obsolete physical design of our cities is the major cause of the flight to the suburbs."[24] To replace obsolete neighborhoods, he proposed a comprehensive master planning process and universal metropolitan standards—the same in suburbs and cities—that legislated proper provision of direct sunlight, air circulation, noise abatement, usable outdoor space, municipal services, lot coverage, and population density to benefit all citizens regardless of class, race, and place of residence.

In 1949, Adams founded his own planning consultancy with two MIT colleagues, John T. Howard and Roland B. Greeley, "to study and advise on current and future problems of community development," according to the announcement of the partnership's formation.[25] Their first big job was none other than the *General Plan of Boston*, in which the West End was officially designated "obsolete." For Boston officials the choice of Adams's firm would not have been difficult. Adams was a leader in the planning profession, an expert in inner-city redevelopment. His consultancy offered "advice on layout and design . . . comprehensive land use and zoning" to supplement the City Planning Board's technical staff. And Adams's office was in downtown Boston on State Street, one street over from City Hall. The ideas and procedures Adams developed during the 1930s and 1940s the city of Boston was putting into practice in the 1950s. It is easy to imagine his leading role framing the *General Plan of Boston*'s vision and visuals, especially the page spread on the "obsolete" West End that conjoined public health rhetoric with city planning graphics. Adams represented a personal link between the APHA's housing standards methodology and the fate of Boston's West End. As a theorist and consultant, his fingerprints are all over the "obsolete neighborhood" designation and condemnatory housing survey. In effect, Frederick J. Adams had authored the West End's obsolescence.

Of course, Adams was not the sole inventor of the idea of urban obsolescence in midcentury America. A constellation of individuals and institutions from the 1930s through the 1960s produced the idea that America's cities were becoming obsolete. Significant among these included the planner Carol Aronovici, who edited an early 1932 collection of essays on "Obsolete Cities."[26] The planner George Herrold authored a seminal 1935 article on "Obsolescence in Cities" for the official journal of the American City Planning Institute.[27] Presidential housing adviser Miles Colean in 1953 wrote: "A city in which there were not at all times some worn-out or obsolete parts would not be a dynamic city."[28] Popular magazine articles from the early 1960s asked, "Are Cities Obsolete?" and "Are Cities Dead?"[29] Nearly forty years after debate began, there remained strong faith in "the basic message: the basic fact of life—which is that the city is functionally obsolete," as one urban policy expert put it in 1970.[30]

The term "obsolescence" was first applied by planners to urban neighborhoods and cities in the 1930s as a near-synonym for "blighted" and "decadent." In the dark "soul-searching" years of the Great Depression, "we are becoming blight-conscious as a people," observed the tax expert Mabel Walker in 1938, aware of the harm done to citizens and cities by substandard living conditions.[31] Boston's West End exemplified obsolescence's symptoms: overcrowding, narrow streets, heavy traffic, mixed commercial and residential uses; inadequate sunlight, fresh air, and open spaces; dwellings advanced in age and deficient in public health standards of sanitation and heating; and proximity to central business districts that obsolescent areas threatened to degrade economically.

Indeed, economic liabilities were the special mark of obsolescent areas measured by declining rents, property values, and tax receipts. These were factors distinct from and less tangible than the visible decay of a slum still profitable to its landlords.[32]

The planners' distinction between slums and obsolescent neighborhoods allowed policy makers to draw boundaries between urban areas more and less salvageable, or in transition from one state to another, as well as determine degrees of risk for effected districts and the surrounding city. The confluence of the terms "blight" and "obsolescence" from the 1930s through midcentury proved particularly effective in heightening and framing anxieties. Blight insinuated naturalistic contagion; obsolescence implied objective assessment of performance and value. Together the two played to emotion *and* reason. Blight's epidemiological connotations would help elicit a public health response; obsolescence framed urban ills as a matter of economic survival. The discourse on urban obsolescence triaged America's wounded cities, peering beneath surface impressions of social and physical decadence to deeper, equally if not more worrisome, currents of economic decline.

The fundamental economism of urban obsolescence derived logically from the first application of the term to the built environment in the 1910s and 1920s. Owners of downtown American office buildings puzzled over the unpredictable financial demise and early demolition of properties built only a few decades earlier, like the Gillender Building on Wall Street reduced to rubble in 1910 after just fourteen years of life. Economists and engineers began talking about buildings' "financial decay," adopting late-nineteenth-century industrial accountancy's terms for measuring the "service life" of capital assets like telephone poles, streetcar wheels, and railway stations.[33] Obsolescence, a factor distinct from physical wear-and-tear or depreciation, was understood as a loss of value and serviceability caused by competing new technology—for example, diesel engines obsolescing steam.

The federal corporate income tax, introduced in 1916, featured "a reasonable allowance for obsolescence," but without specifying a specific level of deduction. From this point on, the American corporate real estate industry took a vital interest in maximizing allowances for depreciation and obsolescence. Less building "life" in the eyes of the law would mean more profit for owners. Subsequently, the National Association of Building Owners and Managers embarked on a decade-long study of building obsolescence through analyses of downtown business districts and demolished structures, especially in its home base of Chicago, identifying contributing factors like changes in fashion and district character, competing buildings with better services, inadaptable interior layouts, and adjacent buildings blocking light and air.[34] Each and all could produce unpredictable, precipitous declines in an office building's financial worth and profitability to its capitalist owners, thus constituting a tax-deductible business expense under U.S. law.

In 1931 the building owners' efforts to establish the truth of short building lifespans bore fruit, when the Bureau of Internal Revenue produced depreciation tables that factored in obsolescence, defining commercial building lives at around a mere thirty years.[35] The political achievement had been to turn extreme cases of obsolescence in Chicago's Loop district into the standards of the U.S. tax code, producing windfall profits for building owners across the country. (By contrast, in Great Britain, where the tax code did not allow obsolescence deductions for buildings, no such similar discourse on architectural obsolescence appeared in the interwar years.)

The more general consequence was to establish in public consciousness the idea of building obsolescence as an inevitable truth of the modern built environment. By the 1930s the term "obsolescence" had become ubiquitous in the fields of real estate, finance, and city planning. A 1935 bibliography listed 125 articles related to the subject.[36] Newspaper articles propagated the concept of quick commercial building obsolescence.[37] When planning and public health professionals began defining urban obsolescence in the 1930s, they reflected this worldview and extended its particular economistic, not to say capitalist, outlook to residential neighborhoods and whole cities.

By the 1940s obsolescence had become a paradigm, a way of conceptualizing change in the built environment that presumed and quantified dramatic losses of value over shortened periods of time. What was in effect a proposition about how the built environment evolved—that the measurably better and new made expendable the insufficient old—came to be accepted as a reasoned if not natural fact. From an idea of single building obsolescence, the concept had been expanded by planners and other professionals into a related notion of urban obsolescence. And although there were differences between the commercial and urban applications of obsolescence—the former avowedly economic and focused on individual structures, the latter more generally social and encompassing whole environments—both commercial and urban obsolescence shared similar beliefs in quantifiable performance and the expendability of rapidly outmoded objects. Moreover, the discourse's collective basis, built up by researchers in a range of fields, helped persuade commentators, policy makers, and elite public opinion of the theory's truthfulness. What in effect had been in the 1920s an actuarial and political expedient for capitalist building owners became by midcentury a set of mythic beliefs, that short building lifespans characterized modernity and that the simple process of obsolescence underlay the dynamics of change in the modern built environment.

What then to do about America's urban obsolescence? Some commentators accepted obsolescence as a fact of modern urbanism, even a sign of vitality. Tax expert Mabel Walker explained: "If the city of the future is to have health and vitality it must be possible for these great human tides to flow in and out easily and readily. We must think in terms of a fluid city . . . these old cities of ours have got to be loosened up at their stiff old joints and elasticized in their hardened old arteries."[38] If marine metaphors reflected an essentially sanguine view of urban obsolescence, analogies to the human body usually reflected a darker naturalization. The planner George Herrold wrote of a "cure for obsolescence" and "preparing a patient for his operation."[39] Cancer, which had been a slum metaphor for decades, documented by the historian Robert Fogelson, became the "commonplace" metaphor for blight and obsolescence in the 1930s and 1940s.[40]

However one metaphorized obsolescence, always in its logic was the quandary, What to do with the obsolete object? On this point all concurred. "There's only one way you can cure a place like the West End, and that is to wipe it out," judged a Boston banker.[41] In midcentury America renewal by demolition was the consensus response to urban obsolescence. Politicians envisioned civic revival. Residents and unions envisioned housing and jobs. Capitalists envisioned profits. Boston mortgage bankers, advocating for the West End's complete demolition, argued "that it would be difficult to sell the cleared land were it surrounded by aging if well-kept tenements."[42] For their part, planners and architects envisioned cities remade by their guiding hands. Herrold asserted: "Obsolescence is a challenge, it is a test of human adequacy to master its environs."[43] The planner Carol Aronovici thundered, "Let the cities perish, so that we may have great and beautiful cities."[44]

The term "obsolescence," I would suggest, also contributed to this agreed, radical response. Obsolescence connotes a terminal process, an emptying of usefulness and value in competition with something new and better. But the suddenness and externality of obsolescence leaves the obsolete object intact, as opposed to slow, intrinsic, physical decay. The problem then becomes what to do with the superseded yet more or less whole artifact. The solution, by the logic of obsolescence, is to discard the old, to break with the past since by definition the old has lost its value in competition with the measurably superior new. The logic of obsolescence, applied to the built environment, represented in effect a clearance technique: a definitive devaluation of a building or neighborhood, a foreclosure of adaptability; a relegation to the past and emptying of relevance for the present and future; imminent replacement by the new and improved.

Obsolescence is thus of course also a politics. Implicitly it embodies an asymmetry of power, between those who make the designation of obsolete and those who must live under it. The politics of obsolescence allows those with power to deem dysfunctional, valueless, and out-of-time the habits and habitations of those without power.

Within American midcentury political economy, the paradigm of obsolescence played key roles. It facilitated the designation of neighborhoods for demolition, not least by helping to broker an elite consensus for redevelopment. Before the Housing Act of 1949, housing activists, business interests, and municipal politicians had failed to agree on solutions for America's urban problems, divided by different economic and social priorities. The paradigm of urban obsolescence helped break this deadlock by presenting a mutually agreeable framework for rebuilding and revaluing the urban landscape.

The obsolescence paradigm's fundamental economism resonated deeply with a conception of capitalism as creative destruction, in the economist Joseph Schumpeter's well-known phrase. In his famous 1942 book, *Capitalism, Socialism, and Democracy*—written while Schumpeter was teaching at Harvard and inspired by modern American industrial developments in steel, power, and transport—Schumpeter opposed static equilibrium theories of capitalism with the counternotion of a dynamic capitalism constantly roiled by entrepreneurial innovations deploying new technologies, products, organizations, and techniques. This process, thriving on obsolescence, Schumpeter called the "perennial gale of creative destruction . . . that incessantly revolutionizes the economic structure *from within*, incessantly destroying the old one, incessantly creating a new one. This process of Creative Destruction is the essential fact about capitalism. It is what capitalism consists in and what every capitalist concern has got to live in."[45] Analogous conceptualization of the urban built environment as governed by the process of obsolescence would have made inherent sense to entrepreneurial American capitalist interests. The paradigm framed America's urban ills as matter of economic development curable by a literal creative destruction.

In 1937 the first federal Housing Act had reflected the social concerns of housing activists, calling for the "eradication of slums" and "the provision of decent, safe, and sanitary dwellings for families of low income." Twelve years later, as the obsolescence paradigm took hold, the Housing Act of 1949, which would help fund ambitious inner-city redevelopment schemes nationwide, extended itself to "the clearance of slums *and blighted areas* . . . providing maximum opportunity for the redevelopment of project areas by private enterprise" and "the advancement of the growth, wealth, and security of the Nation."[46] The inclusion of these last phrases, plus the term "blighted areas," intertwined at the time with "obsolescent," elevated the importance of private market economic factors for residential area redevelopment schemes. Conceptualizing the problem of America's cities in terms of obsolescence's economism helped make federal urban renewal legislation palatable to American businessmen otherwise antipathetic to government social programs.

The government's role in urban reinvestment was key because capital interests on their own lacked the legal and financial resources to redevelop large urban areas. States provided eminent domain legislation to assemble sites without the obstacle of recalcitrant landowners. Federal funds covered two-thirds of the cost of acquisition and demolition before cleared sites were sold to private developers. In effect, government streamlined and subsidized the processes of capitalist reinvestment in obsolescent urban areas. From the perspective of local politics, the obsolescence paradigm also served useful purposes. Its bureaucratic logic disarmed opposition to redevelopment. As Boston authorities told critics: "To people who lived there for a long time the West End may not seem 'substandard.' But the preliminary studies made by the Housing Authority show that it is."[47] The APHA-sanctioned "official designation of substandardness" appeared objective, irrefutable, and apolitical. Resistance was futile against the technical judgment of obsolescence and expendability.

In fact, the West End's demise was as much political as scientific. The neighborhood was not statistically the city's worst. Other neighborhoods, like the North End, had even worse vacancy rates, land values, building conditions, and population densities than did the West End. The 1951 *General Plan for Boston* openly acknowledged the elite Back Bay's similar densities of people and aged buildings. Yet the Back Bay was officially deemed "old but not obsolete," its "preservation of permanent values"—that is, its immunity to obsolescence— depending on the Back Bay's apparently greater adaptability to change.[48] In truth, the West End lacked the Back Bay's cultural cachet and the North End's political clout as the center of Boston's Italian American community. Moreover, the West End's planned gentrification conformed to the agendas of downtown merchants anxious for nearby middle-class shoppers, of adjacent Massachusetts General Hospital desirous of higher-class neighbors, and of real estate developers covetous of the West End's Charles River views.[49] Against this array of factors, West Enders were powerless.

In Boston, as elsewhere, the administrations of postwar reformist mayors, like Boston's John B. Hynes, used the obsolescence paradigm to gain federal funding for urban renewal, marshaling planning expertise and public health techniques as alibis for political agendas and economic redevelopment. In many cities, including Boston, the political goals were replacing ethnic and black working-class neighborhoods with middle-class voters whose shopping dollars might reinvigorate nearby downtown retail districts and thus help struggling municipalities compete with their suburbs. "Boston must 'provide pleasant accommodations for the great American middle class, or perish,'" declared the chairman of the

Boston Finance Commission, reflecting the midcentury crisis mentality among urban businessmen and politicians around the country.[50]

From the point of view of city planners, the obsolescence paradigm served their profession's particular purposes, too. By the 1930s planners had abandoned City Beautiful–style fixed solutions for urban centers and came instead to favor techniques of quantitative analysis and notions of "dynamic equilibrium" at the metropolitan scale.[51] The obsolescence paradigm, in its economism and acknowledgment of suburban context and competition, answered to this shift in planning theory, which took the perpetual change of obsolescence to be the new normal urban condition under capitalism. For their part public health professionals varnished the paradigm's social component, with their commitment to human well-being, and provided a practicable scientific application with the APHA housing appraisal manual. City planners and public health experts alike used the idea of obsolescence to expand their disciplines into the social sciences, thus enhancing their professions' political relevance by offering policy makers a framework for managing the plight of America's cities. Moreover, the paradigm's long-term, collaborative, multidisciplinary research efforts—exemplified by the APHA's housing study—depended on financial and institutional support from universities, government, and charitable foundations, thus marshaling elite American civil society within the consensus for obsolescence.

The paradigm of obsolescence also possessed great cultural purchase in America's consumer economy, charmed by notions of "planned obsolescence" and expendable commodities. Since the late 1920s, marketers had enjoined Americans to accept "progressive obsolescence . . . a readiness to 'scrap' or lay aside an article before its natural life or usefulness is completed, in order to make way for the newer and better thing."[52] During the Depression government-sponsored "planned obsolescence" of the built environment was proposed as an economic catalyst: after twenty-five to thirty years a "building can be destroyed and a new one erected, with resultant stimulus to employment."[53]

In the affluent postwar period, obsolescence was even more compelling. Manufacturers accelerated the pace of product changes to quicken obsolescence and stimulate consumption. Marketers sold consumers on the desirability of the new and improved and the expendability of the obsolete. The goal was to keep refilling American homes and driveways with the newest gadgets and furnishings. Economically, business executives asserted, obsolescence stimulated growth: "Without installment buying and obsolescence, large sections of our billion dollar industries would rust."[54] Planned obsolescence and mass consumption appeared to embody essential American characteristics of change, abundance, and egalitarianism, as well as individual free will and pleasure. "You are not *forced* to buy new products," explained an industrial designer. "You *like* to do it."[55] Fears of economic stagnation destabilizing capitalism in contest with socialism underwrote ideological devotion to obsolescence from Depression-era through Cold War America. Like a marketer's vision, the "obsolete neighborhood's" aggressive disorder, as illustrated in the 1951 *General Plan for Boston*, would be replaced by the pendant "new plan's" genteel, modern openness —the city suburbanized, a new-and-improved neighborhood obsolescing the last century's model in performance and styling.

Finally, there were the obsolescence paradigm's racial and class dimensions, which underwrote its ideological effectiveness. Planners adopted real estate appraisers' bias that ethnic and racial heterogeneity signaled diminishing economic value, or obsolescence. "The area slipped down another notch and today is inhabited by some eighteen different nationalities," wrote George Herrold about a Saint Paul, Minnesota, neighborhood.[56] The Federal Housing Administration's 1938 *Underwriting Manual* listed "lower class occupancy, and inharmonious racial groups" as "adverse influences" in a neighborhood's Economic Background Rating, to be used in disqualifying "obsolete" neighborhoods for mortgage guarantees.[57] In terms of class, an obsolete neighborhood's congestion offended middle-class evaluators' beliefs about order, privacy, and safety, contrary to working-class residents' own experience. In the West End, children "preferred to play on the streets—where the excitement and action they valued was available," noted sociologist Herbert Gans who studied the neighborhood's social networks before their erasure.[58] "Even the sense of adjacent human beings carried by noise and smells," wrote other West End researchers, "provides a sense of comfort."[59] Precisely those elements of crowded public life and adaptation to physical density that best supported the localized social identity of a working-class neighborhood—the close congestion of streets and hallways, variety stores and taverns, children playing in the roads, women leaning out of windows, men on the street corners, families on their stoops—these were what middle-class evaluators, wedded to social ideals of individualism and mobility, found to be obsolete in public health surveys.

The 1951 designation of Boston's West End as obsolete thus represented a complex ideological construction, conjoining middle-class values and consumerism with state policy, capitalist methodologies, and multidisciplinary professional expertise. In midcentury America obsolescence's allure was overwhelming: simple in its dualism, a reflection of material abundance, progressive in its liberation from the past, promising a better future modeled on the spacious, car-centered suburban competitor that had apparently already bested the inner city economically and demographically. In Boston, as elsewhere, the consensus for obsolescence was seemingly unopposable. Even social service providers "approved of the redevelopment," as did Catholic churchmen, who "described the area as a slum [and] looked forward to the redevelopment of the West End, and hoped for a more middle-class group of parishioners."[60]

Ineffectively and too late, residents organized in 1956 a Save the West End Committee. Personalizing resistance by demonizing developer Jerome Rappaport and mayor John B. Hynes missed the point that impersonal bureaucratic techniques, not individual agency, undergirded the redevelopment process. Taking the fight to the city on its own terms, through a failed lawsuit that claimed housing survey statistics overstated the neighborhood's substandardness, did no good. Arguing about percentages of unsound buildings simply reinforced the underlying paradigm's validity. From the moment the West End was designated in 1951 as an "obsolete neighborhood," singled out and illustrated in the *General Plan* as the epitome of Boston's urban ills, the bureaucratic wheels were set in motion for its destruction. One report led inexorably to another and then another in the mid-1950s, largely out of public sight and with no apparent internal dissent, each new study substantiating the original designation of obsolescence until the whole bureaucratic sequence of approvals and funding for demolition and redevelopment had successfully run its course by the winter of 1957–58.

In the spring the City of Boston seized the whole of the West End by eminent domain. Rent was now due to the city that owned all buildings, residents began leaving, and those who remained received official notices to vacate their homes. By 1962 the demolition of nearly the entire West End was completed. Some two thousand families were displaced, scattered throughout the metropolitan area. Nine hundred buildings were demolished, leaving behind a flattened wasteland of dirt, brick, and ghostly streets. Out of this rose Charles River Park, a modernist complex of concrete and brick townhouses and towers in a park setting, loosely adapted from the 1951 "new plan" and renting mostly at market rates. Against this catastrophe the West Enders had been powerless, overwhelmed by the weight of professional expertise, institutional support, governmental policy, and bureaucratic technique. There was no counterlanguage or strategy to obsolescence.

The paradigm of urban obsolescence was something new for the twentieth century. In contrast with the divisive, personalized politics of Paris's Haussmannization in the nineteenth century, obsolescence's technocratic framework represented an evolution in tactics to clear and revalue urban land, working through a consensus of capital and the state, civil and consumer societies, conjoining economistic values of quantifiable performance and impersonal competition with a social theory of progressive change based on the identification of modernist planning with healthful social, physical, and psychological development.

In midcentury America obsolescence was the dominant paradigm for comprehending and managing urban change. (Elsewhere around the world, the term "obsolescence" appeared more sparingly in urban renewal discourse, never as emphatically as in capitalist, consumerist postwar America.)[61]

Yet obsolescence's efficacy survived hardly long enough to see through the West End's redevelopment. The terminology itself rarely appeared again in reference to Boston or other cities' redevelopment projects after the mid-1950s, when "blight" became the dominant term, having shared the stage equally with obsolescence for more than two decades. The planners offered no insights into the evolution of their vocabulary. Perhaps blight's naturalistic connotation of contagion was more useful in enlisting downtown business elites to support redevelopment of contiguous residential neighborhoods, which they might otherwise have cared little about. Perhaps, too, the term "obsolete" had become too risky in its own economistic implications. It threatened to reveal too much of the planners' cold-hearted thinking, at odds with the subjective realities of residential community life, unlike that of business districts' built environments not so easily reduced and governed by a capitalist logic of measurable performance and profit. "Obsolete" laid too bare the ideological alliance of capital and state. The economistic inflections, which had enhanced obsolescence's political effectiveness in the 1940s, ultimately helped discredit the paradigm.

Always there had been contradictions within the paradigm. How, for example, to square obsolescence's intangibility and unpredictability with the concreteness of its statistical determinations? Or how to overcome the contradiction between the paradigm's fundamental temporality and fixed solutions to obsolescence, exemplified in the West End's "new plan"? Or, again, how to reconcile the paradigm's economism with its social agenda? Which took priority? And what to do with the paradigm's conflation of the categories of the physical and social? In which realm was the West End an "obsolete neighborhood," physical or social, or was it both? The distinction never comes clear, nor the chain of causality from one to the other. A member of the APHA's own Committee on the Hygiene of Housing acknowledged, "there is little evidence that substandard housing per se causes sickness and death."[62] Indeed, slippage between the physical and the social allowed condemnation as obsolete in one category to justify reform in the other. The paradigm's effectiveness as a tool for redevelopment depended on obfuscation of its ambiguities and contradictions. Looking too closely might hamstring its operability.

Perhaps the most destabilizing contradiction involved the exceptions to obsolescence: those individual structures exempted from the overall neighborhood designation "obsolete." In Boston's West End five buildings stayed—two churches, a historical house, a school, and social service agency—officially because of their structural soundness and community usefulness, ideologically because they were the neighborhood's few elite-styled, historical constructions.[63] What remained served as reproach to the obsolescence paradigm's conse- quences, contradicted its totalizing logic. If these buildings were worth sav- ing, possessed of some intangible value, why could not others in the "obsolete neighborhood" also be immune to obsolescence?

By the mid-1960s elite consensus for the obsolescence paradigm was break- ing down. The West End's cataclysmic demolition and diaspora became a cause célèbre among social scientists and planners, who publicized the effects of relo- cation and the West Enders' satisfaction with their neighborhood and the grief of losing it.[64] Herbert Gans argued that the West End was "not really a slum" and that "obsolescence per se is not harmful; the judgment merely a reflection of middle-class standards."[65] In planning history, the lessons of the West End are credited with making "sure that Bostonians, and indeed the whole nation, would never forget the human impact of this sort of wholesale clearance and displacement of a still-viable neighborhood."[66]

At the same time, the consumer discourse of planned obsolescence lost its credibility, thanks to critiques like journalist Vance Packard's best-selling *The Waste Makers* (1960), which excoriated the consumer culture of planned ob- solescence as shallow, profligate, and manipulative.[67] Faith collapsed, too, in expert research's capacity for social good—think of Rachel Carson's 1962 en- vironmental call to arms, *Silent Spring*. Suburbia, which had seemingly rendered the inner city obsolete, now appeared itself superficial and inauthentic in com- parison with the ethnic, working-class, inner-city residential districts planners had once condemned. Now these neighborhoods (as long as they were white) appeared to embody civic health and economic vitality, according to commen- tators like Jane Jacobs, who wrote in her famous 1961 book *The Death and Life of Great American Cities*, "cities need old buildings. . . . Time makes certain structures obsolete for some enterprises, and they become available for oth- ers."[68] Subsequent historical events finished off the obsolescence paradigm. Ur- ban upheaval in America's black ghettoes was followed by economic austerity exacerbated by the 1973 oil crisis. All this put paid to the political and financial support for federal renewal programs, which had funded the designation and demolition of obsolete neighborhoods.

Once obsolescence had seemed the city's inevitable destiny: creative de- struction as axiomatic—shortened lifespans, expendable buildings, obsolescent cities as myths of modernity. But now, instead of representing a crisis, a prom- ise, a threat, a spur to new thought and action, obsolescence has been osten- sibly superseded by its opposite and today's ruling term: "sustainability." Most often identified with energy-efficient technology, the paradigm of sustainability properly encompasses a host of expert strategies to revalue rather than dis- card the old—from facilities management and life-cycle assessment, to historic preservation legislation and adaptive reuse techniques, as well as vernacularism, architectural postmodernism, and the heritage industry. These are all ways to reverse obsolescence, to revalue and retain the existing built environment.

In reaction to the excesses of obsolescence and then chastened by oil-crisis austerity, new environmental and historical sensibilities emerged in the 1960s and 1970s. These have led over the past thirty years to an emphasis on context and to the primacy of sustainability as architecture's dominant ideology of change, emblematized by the universal recycling symbol of three chasing arrows. If obsolescence embodied principles of discontinuity, supersession, and expendability, sustainability embodies opposite principles of continuity, conservation, and stewardship of architectural and natural resources. Yet the relation between architectural sustainability and obsolescence is as much filial as agonistic. Both depend on technology and measurable performance as markers of value. Adaptive reuse is a variation on the 1960s architectural megastructure: new components inserted into long-life frames. Architectural obsolescence and preservation both define the past as broken off from the present. In other words, we have not overcome the other side of the argument in the 1960s as much as the triumphalist narrative of sustainability might have us believe. Our time remains, as lived experience always is, polytemporal, in sociologist Bruno Latour's phrase—always new and old together, coeval, coexistent, sustainability *and* obsolescence.[69]

Some of this contemporary paradigm and its complexity can be seen in recent developments in Boston's West End. The owners of the Charles River Park complex recently rebranded it the West End to capture "the neighborhood spirit and electric energy of Boston's historic, wonderful and cherished West End."[70] Modernist townhouses are being replaced by foursquare, brick-faced buildings mimicking the shape and patina of the demolished tenements. The City of Boston along the area's streets has hung banners featuring large, grainy photographs of the old neighborhood. A new West End Museum founded by former residents commemorates the lost community.

The paradigm of obsolescence thus renders neighborhoods like the West End doubly mythic: first in the categorization of "obsolete," which abstracted and denied complex realities; now in the marketing and mourning of what was lost unnaturally under the rule of obsolescence. A national architecture critic pines for the West End's "memory, sensuality, intricacy, and location."[71] Among former residents, the sense of injustice a half century later remains palpable in the pages of *The West Ender*, the diaspora's quarterly newspaper. Steeped in memories and myths, the dislocated forget their complicated history—that when it existed, "the concept of the West End as a single neighborhood was foreign to the West Enders themselves."[72] The past, especially the recent past, is not sustained in the contemporary West End; it is whitewashed and effaced as effectively now as it was in the age of obsolescence.

What finally are obsolescence's ethics, the moral dimensions of the paradigm and its consequences? Here, alongside its mythologizing, must be denounced aspects of obsolescence's logic that leveled more or less functionally sound neighborhoods and exiled their inhabitants. The experts' diagnostic tools ended up as political weapons for wholesale clearance. Quantifications of performance paid little heed to the intangibles of lived experience and social satisfaction. Wasteful disregard for what exists counts heavily among obsolescence's sins. But alongside its authoritarian and destructive dimensions, obsolescence also possessed productive and progressive elements. Drawing attention to the crises of American inner cities, the paradigm laid out a decisive solution by striking at the status quo without remorse for the past, clearing the field not just for new physical approaches but also for more socially just redistributions of the city's resources, its housing, open spaces, and community facilities. Experts sought enhancement of human potential through physical alterations based on universal standards that did not discriminate by race, class, or geography. Those who subsequently perceived only the harm done by the obsolescence paradigm fail to credit its progressive instincts and successes and avoid accounting for the costs of the status quo: Who wins and loses if matters are left unchanged?

Left alone, districts like Boston's West End would not have remained the same. The gentrification that has scattered Boston's other inner-city communities, like the South End, to the winds would surely have done the same to the West End, just more slowly than urban renewal. What was irredeemably lost under obsolescence was physical, and what came out of obsolescence has its virtues. In architecture, belief in obsolescence, in short-life buildings and the need for flexibility, produced innovative design worldwide and on the urban level could replace tenement districts with landscaped spaciousness and admirable modern buildings, like the West End's Boston Synagogue (1971) and the Regina Cleri Home for Retired Priests (1973), which diversify Boston's traditionalist built environment.

Ultimately, it may be best to consider ethically the paradigm of obsolescence similarly to the way the critic Fredric Jameson once wrote about capitalism: "Positively *and* negatively all at once . . . as catastrophe and progress all together . . . at one and the same time the best thing . . . and the worst." This would mean acknowledging obsolescence's "demonstrably baleful features . . . along with its extraordinary and liberating dynamism simultaneously, within a single thought, and without attenuating any of the force of either judgment."[73] Such thinking would not foreclose moral assessments but would rather suspend judgment of good *or* bad for a more ethically difficult but historically more useful framework of good *and* bad. Obsolescence, like capitalism, would be understood as a historical force, which both responds to contemporary conditions and represents, to quote Jameson, "the framework, and the precondition for the achievement of some new and more comprehensive" mode, in our case, for conceptualizing and managing change in the built environment.[74] In this light, obsolescence was the phase that had to be passed through, for better and for worse, on the way to sustainability.

Notes

1. City Planning Board (Boston), *A General Plan for Boston: A Preliminary Report* (Boston: City Planning Board, 1951), 42–43.

2. Herbert J. Gans, *The Urban Villagers: Group and Class in the Life of Italian-Americans* (New York: Free Press, 1962), 11.

3. City Planning Board (Boston), *General Plan for Boston*, 42.

4. Ibid., 40.

5. Boston Housing Authority (Urban Redevelopment Division), *West End Project Report: A Preliminary Redevelopment Study of the West End of Boston* (Boston: Boston Housing Authority, 1953), 9.

6. Boston Housing Authority, *West End Project Report*, 14.

7. Boston Housing Authority (Urban Redevelopment Division), *Declaration of Findings Relative to West End Land Assembly and Redevelopment Project* (Boston: Boston Housing Authority, 1955), 14–16.

8. Gans, *Urban Villagers*, 313.

9. Boston Housing Authority (Urban Redevelopment Division), *West End Project Report*, 14.

10. *American Sociological Review* 11, no. 1 (1946): 124–25.

11. Carl Feiss, "Outer Skins and Contact Environments," *AIA Journal* 45 (June 1966): 61.

12. American Public Health Association (Committee on the Hygiene of Housing), *An Appraisal Method for Measuring the Quality of Housing: A Yardstick for Health Officers, Housing Officials, and Planners* (New York: American Public Health Association, 1945–46), vol. 1: 15.

13. American Public Health Association, *Appraisal Method for Measuring the Quality of Housing*, vol. 1: 14–15.

14. Ibid., vol. 1: 16, 45.

15. Allan A. Twichell, "A New Method for Measuring the Quality of Urban Housing," *American Journal of Public Health* 33 (June 1943): 738.

16. American Public Health Association, *Appraisal Method for Measuring the Quality of Housing*, vol. 1: 27.

17. Ibid., vol. 1: 2–3.

18. Allan A. Twichell and Anatole Solow, "A Technique for the Appraisal of Housing in Urban Problem Areas," *Planners' Journal* 8, no. 3 (July–September 1942): 28.

19. American Public Health Association, *Appraisal Method for Measuring the Quality of Housing*, vol. 1: 2, 1, 15.

20. Ibid., vol. 1: 50.

21. C.-E. A. Winslow, "Health and Housing," in American Public Health Association

(Committee on the Hygiene of Housing), *Housing for Health* (Lancaster, Pa.: Science Press, 1941), 14.

22. American Public Health Association (Committee on the Hygiene of Housing), *Basic Principles of Healthful Housing*, second edition (New York: American Public Health Association, 1939), 7, 23–24.

23. Joel Schwartz, "Robert Moses and City Planning," in *Robert Moses and the Modern City: The Transformation of New York*, edited by Hilary Ballon and Kenneth T. Jackson (New York: Norton, 2007), 131.

24. Frederick Johnstone Adams, "Rehousing vs. Rehabilitation," *Journal of the American Institute of Planners* 11, no. 3 (July–September 1945): 11.

25. Adams, Howard & Greeley, "Announcement of Partnership Formation," 1949, Loeb Library, Harvard University.

26. "Obsolete Cities: A Challenge to Community Builders," *Graphic Survey* (October 1, 1932).

27. George Herrold, "Obsolescence in Cities," *Planners' Journal* 1, no. 4 (November–December 1935): 73–75.

28. Miles L. Colean, *Renewing Our Cities* (New York: Twentieth Century Fund, 1953), 6.

29. Bernard Weissbourd, "Are Cities Obsolete?" *Saturday Review*, December 19, 1964; and Robert Moses, "Are Cities Dead?" *Atlantic Monthly* (January 1962): 55–58.

30. George Sternlieb, "Are Cities Obsolete?" *Trans-Action* 7, no. 6 (April 1970): 86.

31. Mabel L. Walker, *Urban Blight and Slums: Economic and Legal Factors in Their Origin, Reclamation, and Prevention* (Cambridge: Harvard University Press, 1938), vii.

32. Marc A. Weiss, "The Origins and Legacy of Urban Renewal," in *Urban and Regional Planning in an Age of Austerity*, edited by Pierre Clavel, John Forester, and William W. Goldsmith (New York: Pergamon), 55–56.

33. Richard Hurd, *Principles of City Land Values* (New York: Record and Guide, 1903); and Reginald Pelham Bolton, *Building for Profit: Principles Governing the Economic Improvement of Real Estate* (New York: De Vinne, 1911).

34. Earle Shultz, *The Effect of Obsolescence on the Useful and Profitable Life of Office Buildings* (Chicago: National Association of Building Owners and Managers, 1922). See also Daniel M. Abramson, "Obsolescence: Notes Towards a History," *Praxis: Journal of Writing + Building* 5 (2003): 106–12.

35. U.S. Treasury Department, Bureau of Internal Revenue, *Bulletin "F" (Revised January 1931). Income Tax. Depreciation and Obsolescence. Revenue Act of 1928* (Washington, D.C.: U.S. Government Printing Office, 1931).

36. Mary Ethel Jameson, "Obsolescence in Buildings: A Selected List of References," in *Selected Readings in Real Estate Appraisal*, edited by A. N. Lockwood and others (Chicago: American Institute of Real Estate Appraisers, 1953); originally published in *Journal of the American Institute of Real Estate Appraisers* (January 1935).

37. "Thirty Years Average Life Span of Modern Skyscraper," *New York Times*, January 18, 1931, 20.

38. Mabel L. Walker, "The American City Is Obsolescent," *Vital Speeches of the Day* 13, no. 22 (September 1, 1947): 697, 699.

39. Herrold, "Obsolescence in Cities: Concluding Discussion," 49.

40. Robert M. Fogelson, *Downtown: Its Rise and Fall, 1880–1950* (New Haven: Yale University Press, 2001), 349.

41. Quoted in Thomas O'Connor, *Building a New Boston: Politics and Urban Renewal, 1950 to 1970* (Boston: Northeastern University Press, 1993), 131.

42. Gans, *Urban Villagers*, 283.

43. Herrold, "Obsolescence in Cities," 75.

44. Carol Aronovici, "Let the Cities Perish," *Graphic Survey* 68, no. 13 (October 1, 1932): 439.

45. Joseph Schumpeter, *Capitalism, Socialism, and Democracy*, third edition (New York: Harper & Brothers, 1950), 83–84.

46. *United States Statutes at Large, 1937*, vol. 50, pt. 1 (Washington, D.C.: U.S. Government Printing Office, 1937, chapter 896, p. 888; and *United States Statutes at Large, 1949*, vol. 63, pt. 1 (Washington, D.C.: U.S. Government Printing Office, 1950), chapter 338, section 2, 102, pp. 413–14, emphasis added.

47. Quoted in Vale, *From the Puritans to the Projects* (Cambridge: Harvard University Press, 2000), 278.

48. City Planning Board (Boston), *General Plan for Boston*, 44.

49. Walker, *Urban Blight and Slums*, 64–66, figure 21; Walter Firey, *Land Use in Central Boston* (Cambridge: Harvard University Press, 1947), table 8, p. 173. Also, Boston City Planning Board, *The People of Boston*, vol. 1, *Population Distribution* (Boston: Boston City Planning Board, 1939); O'Connor, *Building a New Boston*, chapter 3; and Gans, *Urban Villagers*, 285–86.

50. Quoted in Vale, *From the Puritans to the Projects*, 276.

51. M. Christine Boyer, *Dreaming the Rational City: The Myth of American City Planning* (Cambridge: MIT Press, 1983), 205.

52. Christine Frederick, *Selling Mrs. Consumer* (1929), quoted in Glenn Adamson et al., *Industrial Strength Design: How Brooks Stevens Shaped Your World* (Cambridge: MIT Press, 2003), 4.

53. Bernard London, *Ending the Depression through Planned Obsolescence* (New York: Publisher, 1932), 14.

54. Paul Mazur, *The Standards We Raise* (1953), quoted in Ernest Black, "Planned Style Obsolescence," bachelor of arts thesis, Harvard University, 1962, 32.

55. Quoted in Jody Clowes, "Brooks Stevens: 'Ego-Inspiring Style' and the American Dream," in Adamson et al., *Industrial Strength Design*, 29.

56. Herrold, "Obsolescence in Cities," 73.

57. Federal Housing Administration, *Underwriting Manual* (Washington, D.C.: U.S. Government Printing Office, 1938), paragraphs 935, 918.

58. Gans, *Urban Villagers*, 312.

59. Marc Fried and Peggy Gleicher, "Some Sources of Residential Satisfaction in an Urban Slum," *Journal of the American Institute of Planners* 27, no. 4 (November 1961): 312.

60. Gans, *Urban Villagers*, 286, 113–14.

61. See, for example, Florian Urban, "From Periodical Obsolescence to Eternal Preservation," *Future Anterior* 3, no. 1 (Summer 2006): 25–35.

62. M. Allen Pond, *Public Health Report*, May 10, 1946, 667.

63. These five included two historic buildings on Cambridge Street by well-known architects, the Harrison Gray Otis house (c. 1795), by Charles Bulfinch, and West Church (c. 1806) attributed to Asher Benjamin; on Blossom Street the City of Boston Health Unit (originally West End House, 1930) and Blackstone Junior High School (originally the

Winchell School, 1915); and on Chambers Street St. Joseph's Roman Catholic Church and rectory (c. 1900). Two tenement buildings also survived the eminent domain process, at 25 North Anderson Street and 42 Lowell Street, still standing today as surreal fragments of a lost neighborhood. See Boston Housing Authority, Urban Redevelopment Division, *Supporting Documentation to the Redevelopment Plan: West End Land Assembly and Redevelopment Plan* (Boston: Boston Housing Authority, 1955), 1.

64. Fried and Gleicher, "Some Sources of Residential Satisfaction"; Chester Hartman, "The Housing of Relocated Families," *Journal of the American Institute of Planners* 30 (November 1964): 266–86; Marc Fried, "Grieving for a Lost Home," in *The Urban Condition*, edited by Leonard J. Duhl (New York: Basic Books, 1963); and Marc Fried et al., *The World of the Urban Working Class* (Cambridge: Harvard University Press, 1973).

65. Gans, *Urban Villagers*, x, 310.

66. Vale, *From the Puritans to the Projects*, 274.

67. Vance Packard, *The Waste Makers* (New York: David McKay, 1960).

68. Jane Jacobs, *The Death and Life of Great American Cities* (1961; reprinted, New York: Vintage, 1992), 187, 189.

69. Bruno Latour, *We Have Never Been Modern*, translated by Catherine Porter (Cambridge: Harvard University Press, 1993), 75.

70. Equity Residential, "The West End Apartments," promotional flyer, 2007; and Thomas C. Palmer Jr., "Once Supplanted by Charles River Park, the West End Returns," *Boston Globe*, May 17, 2007.

71. Robert Campbell, "Phantom Pain: A Neighborhood Lives On after Its Destruction," *Architectural Record* (April 2006): 63–64.

72. Gans, *Urban Villagers*, 11.

73. Fredric Jameson, "Postmodernism, or the Cultural Logic of Late Capitalism," *New Left Review* 1, no. 146 (July–August 1984): 86.

74. Jameson, "Postmodernism, or the Cultural Logic of Late Capitalism," 88.

Selected Bibliography

Adams, Frederick J., Edwin S. Burdell, Harry D. Freeman, and George H. Herrold. "Obsolescence in Cities: Discussion" *Planners' Journal* 2, nos. 1–2 (January–February and March–April 1936): 16–19, 46–50.

American Public Health Association (Committee on the Hygiene of Housing). *An Appraisal Method for Measuring the Quality of Housing: A Yardstick for Health Officers, Housing Officials, and Planners.* New York: American Public Health Association, 1945–46.

Bolton, Reginald Pelham. *Building for Profit: Principles Governing the Economic Improvement of Real Estate.* New York: De Vinne, 1911.

Herrold, George. "Obsolescence in Cities." *Planners' Journal* 1, no. 4 (November–December 1935): 73–75.

Shultz, Earle. *The Effect of Obsolescence on the Useful and Profitable Life of Office Buildings.* Chicago: National Association of Building Owners and Managers, 1922.

4

The Interface
Ergonomics and the Aesthetics of Survival

■

JOHN HARWOOD

*Some people think that the industrial designer is the equivalent
of a wonder drug like penicillin, to be used when sickness strikes.
Actually, we are preventative medicine.* —Henry Dreyfuss

THE term "ergonomics" and its adjectival derivative "ergonomic" have
become household words. Whether we have come to know them
through advertisements for office furniture, from pamphlets circulated
by OSHA or corporate HR departments, or from periodic trips to the physical therapist, "ergonomic" has come to connote a putatively correct quotidian
relationship between our bodies and our equipment. It is intuitive—rather, it
has become intuitive—that, say, the contours of a car steering wheel should
not be sharp enough to cut one's hands, that one's computer keyboard should
not engender carpal tunnel syndrome, and that the seat of a chair should be
wide, deep, and high enough to accommodate one's entire rump, regardless of
its size (figure 4.1)

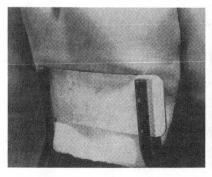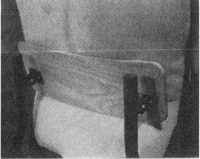

Figure 4.1. "A fixed back-rest cutting into the flesh." *Source:* K. F. H. Murrell, *Human Performance in Industry* (New York: Reinhold, 1965), 146.

Given the thoroughness of this naturalization, it is easy to forget that ergonomics is a theoretical concept and a discipline of very recent invention. Moreover, its origins and the contexts out of which it emerged remain poorly understood by even some of its most ardent apologists and practitioners. A close examination of the work of two of the most important designers involved in its articulation—the German architect Ernst Neufert and the American industrial designer Henry Dreyfuss—this chapter is intended to serve as a prolegomena to a critical history of ergonomics. So often taken to be a discipline that insists on the primacy of the body or the machine, ergonomics is neither. As the applied science of designing what is known as the "man-machine" system, ergonomics concerns itself with the hyphen between "man" and "machine," the means by which "man" and "machine" may be brought into dynamic and productive harmony.

This chapter seeks first to establish the definition of ergonomics and the fundamental differences between ergonomics and theories of work that preceded it, then moves to clarify the status of the human body as a normative model within ergonomics. Finally the chapter explores some of the consequences for our understanding of space that are the inevitable result of adopting ergonomics as a bedrock principle of design theory. At stake in such a history is the possibility of a critical view of numerous and rapidly proliferating metanarratives: that machines are becoming increasingly important agents within modern or postmodern culture; that "humanism" has been destroyed by the proliferation of mechanical and electronic systems; and that we reside in an age of perpetual crises, with the most important crisis being the constant, multivalent threat that our "environment" poses to our bodies.

From Taylorism to Ergonomics

At its most basic level, ergonomics is a technical discourse that emerged from a perceived problem of making the human being at home in an ever more mechanized environment. This is a familiar problem to any student of architectural and design modernism, the leitmotif of its most famous accounts—from Lewis Mumford's *Technics and Civilization* (1934), Siegfried Giedion's *Space, Time, and Architecture* (1941) and *Mechanization Takes Command* (1949) to Reyner Banham's *Theory and Design in the First Machine Age* (1960) and William Jordy's "The Symbolic Essence of Modern European Architecture of the Twenties and Its Continuing Influence" (1963).[1] These grand histories and critiques, all of which sought to understand the development of modern design from the nineteenth century to World War II as the creation of a so-called machine aesthetic, narrated designers' growing awareness of the threat posed by unbridled, disorganized mechanization. The machine—whether symbolized by the airplane, the automobile, the printing press, the steel beam, the jig, the gantry, the radio, or the machine gun—was to be both the archetype of a new architecture, and a threat to be ameliorated by the humanism of the architect.

Despite their many important differences, a common trope of these narratives—whether the histories themselves or the designs and manifestos upon which they were based—was one of integration. Written against the backdrop of mechanized warfare, frequent industrial accidents, and the crisis of cities, these authors argued that the human being simply could not survive an oppositional relationship with the machine. As Lewis Mumford put it in 1934: "Our capacity to go beyond the machine rests in our power to assimilate the machine. Until we have absorbed the lessons of objectivity, impersonality, neutrality, the lessons of the mechanical realm, we cannot go further in our development toward the more richly organic, the more profoundly human."[2] In other words, for the human being to be at home in this brave new world, the human being would have to become more machinelike, a "new man" possessed of objective qualities. Conversely, the machine would need to be humanized, given qualities of subjectivity that would allow it to interact meaningfully with people. At the site of the interaction between human being and machine—the interface—we would experience not pain but comfort.

Yet comfort is, like peace, a negative and tautological concept. Its standard definition is negative: "the absence of discomfort [or pain]." It is the erasure of an experience, pain, which itself has no positive qualities and is not linked to any particular sense organ.[3] Therefore, in the transition from a machine aesthetic to a fully articulated applied science of ergonomics, this erasure would need to be systematized, made into a baseline assumption in the design of any subject-object relationship. To put the question in the meanest possible terms, What could it mean that at some point in the mid-twentieth century, designers of all kinds, and especially architects, began to take it for granted that the basic assumption with which one begins designing an object—whether a book, a chair, or a building—is that we not experience the potential to cause pain that could be inherent in the object as such?

Already in 1934, Mumford was prepared to provide at least a provisional program for answering this question. If the problem was a rapidly diversifying and threatening propagation of machinic adjuncts, the solution must be a matter of "the simplification of the environment": "Precisely because there are so many physical organs, and because so many parts of our environment compete constantly for our attention, we need to guard ourselves against the fatigue of dealing with too many objects or being stimulated unnecessarily by their presence, as we perform the numerous offices they impose. *Hence a simplification of the externals of the mechanical world is almost a prerequisite for dealing with its internal complications. To reduce the constant succession of stimuli, the environment itself must be made as neutral as possible.*"[4]

At first glance Mumford seems to accept the terminology of Taylorism and even older sciences of work; the language of stimulus and fatigue harkens back to Victorian pathological theories of neurasthenia and psychic exhaustion.[5] Mumford, though, takes care to point out that neither the human being nor machine are the problem; the site of design intervention must rather be the surface between them mediating their relationship: "the externals of the mechanical world . . . the environment." This early euphemism would become the discipline of ergonomics: "human engineering."[6] The binary structure that seems to be at the basis of proto-ergonomic theory is in fact tripartite, as human and engine alike are reoriented around a third component: the interface.

It is a matter of great importance to the development of design theory that all of this theorizing precedes the invention of ergonomics. A neologism—coined at a British military research laboratory in 1949 from the Greek *ergon* ("organ" or "work") and *nomos* ("natural law")—ergonomics is a normative, synthetic discipline, seeking to apply the findings of psychiatry, psychology, physiology and anthropometrics, cybernetics and information theory, engineering, medicine, business management, and all branches of design to "the scientific study of the relationship between man and his working environment."[7] As such, ergonomics constituted a new configuration and instrumentalization of the human sciences. Earlier sciences of work, such as the system of "scientific management" championed by Frederick Winslow Taylor, had deployed anthropometric data and efficiency studies to "fit the worker to the job."[8] Taylorist principles had a profound impact on architectural and industrial design in the 1920s, as Mary McLeod has shown.[9]

However, in the face of the rigors of operating machinery that pushed the worker beyond his or her physiological and psychological limits during World War II, the Taylorist model was plainly insufficient. There was simply no such worker who could withstand the physical, sensory onslaught of operating high-altitude bomber aircraft. With such aircraft and other weapons being deemed absolutely necessary to the survival of civilization, scientists, engineers, and designers turned to what seemed to be the only possible solution. Instead of fitting the worker to the job, a new applied science would do just the opposite: "fit the job to the worker."[10] Having identified the "natural" limits of human ability or performance, the engineers and designers of these machines needed to learn how to design equipment that would compensate for these shortcomings and allow human beings to operate successfully in situations in which they otherwise would be overtaxed.

Put another way, it was necessary to increase the physical and psychological abilities of the human being through the addition of safe mechanical prostheses to the body. In short, the ostensible aim of ergonomics is to protect the body from a "hostile environment" to which it is exposed by the speed and power of modern technology, and to harmonize humans and machines in what is called a "man-machine system."[11] This was to be accomplished by using the same anthropometric data and psychological techniques as before but deploying them differently. This remarkable new brief for the designer entailed a wholesale redefinition of work. As the early ergonomist O. G. Edholm put it, "Work really includes all, or nearly all, human activity. Birth, marriage, death mean work for the midwife, priest and undertaker. One could even say that sex means work for the prostitute."[12] He concluded his textbook on the subject by paraphrasing Le Corbusier's most famous dictum: "a house is a machine for living in. And this vividly illustrates the ergonomic attitude."[13]

These sciences would now be applied as the basis for designing the medium—the *interface*—between the human being and the new environment into which it had been thrust by the power of the machine. This interface had dimension, even spatiality. As the man who coined the term "ergonomics," K. F. H. Murrell, put it in his first textbook on the discipline: "Ergonomics has been defined as the scientific study of the relationship between man and his working environment. In this sense, the term environment is taken to cover not only the ambient environment in which he may work but also his tools and materials, his methods of work and the organization of his work, either as an individual or within a working group. All these are related to the nature of the man himself; to his abilities, capacities and limitations."[14] The two-pronged program of ergonomics thus was (1) to redefine the human being through an analysis of "work" as encompassing all activity; and (2) to shape an ideal model of space (the "environment") around that working subject. By the very terms of the argument, these two objects of study and sites of reform—the body and the environment—could not remain stable.

Ergonomics, then, did not and could not emerge as Athena from the head of Zeus. Rather, it developed discursively, as a gradual—if rapid—integration of the increasingly shared assumptions in separate disciplines about the inadequacy of the human being alone as the determining criterion of the organization of work, space, production, and consumption. For these assumptions to coalesce into a freestanding synthetic discipline, however, a ground for synthesis was necessary. Perhaps surprisingly, it was architecture and the newly emerging discipline of industrial design that provided this ground: an image of the human body and its mechanical adjuncts that was capable of both inscribing limits around the body even as it denied the body's primacy to the definition of the "human environment."

From Taylorism to Ergonomics: Man as Measure and Target

Ernst Neufert's *Bauentwurfslehre* (Building design guide), of 1936, is arguably the founding text of what would become ergonomic design. Neufert's encyclopedic volume extended the purview of the architectural graphic standards manual to include a much broader range of designable objects and activities. It provided a compendium of ideal dimensions of everyday objects on every scale—from furniture and appliances to vehicles and buildings. These were meant to be used as guidelines or templates by designers, and since its initial publication, the guide has indeed proven its immense usefulness. Neufert's book is still in regular use by architects today and, having sold well over a half million copies in thirteen languages, is the most successful book on architecture in history.

Neufert was one of the first students at the Weimar Bauhaus and worked as an architect in Walter Gropius's office in the mid-1920s as the project architect for the Dessau Bauhaus building and the Meisterhäuser.[15] A committed modernist, Neufert was deprived of his professorial post in Thüringen when the Nazis entered the provincial government in 1930. Out of work for a time, like his countryman Konrad Wachsmann, and then employed as an architect to such industrial concerns as the Fagus works in Alfeld, Neufert turned his attention to learning about problems of mechanized building and mass production. Through this experience he accumulated the encyclopedic knowledge that formed his landmark work.

The core of what became the *Bauentwurfslehre* was a small pamphlet, published in 1935, that Neufert called *Mensch als Mass und Ziel* (Man as measure and target). This brief text and set of illustrations kept its title as it was integrated into the larger project as an introductory chapter outlining the central importance of anthropometry to the overall project. Despite all appearances to the contrary—after all, Neufert was hardly the first architect to consider basing architectural dimensions on the dimensions of the human body—Neufert attempted in his pamphlet to reformulate the core assumption of humanism, Protagoras's dictum "man is the measure of all things," to reflect the changing dynamic between man and technology.

In the first part of his definition of the human being (as "measure"), Neufert's text is straightforward enough, but with an interesting twist. He lamented the adoption of the overly abstract metric system, preferring instead measures that corresponded more closely to the dimensions of the human body. Neufert's preference for the "unity" of printmaker Albrecht Dürer's proportional systems as laid out in Dürer's work on geometry, *Underweysung der Messung* (Four books on measurement), led him eventually to invent a new synthesis between "organic" and metric measures: the *Oktameter* system, with the basic module of 1.25 meters. This newly measured "man" would become the starting point from which to determine the proper dimensions of every possible type of object.

Neufert's formulation of man as a "target," however, is much more complex. On the surface of the matter (and ergonomics is about surfaces), the target to which Neufert refers is a universally applicable average and ideal: a *norm*. As is well known, normativity is not limited to bell curves, nor to the simple settling of averages; as the medical philosopher George Canguilhem has shown in his pathbreaking work on *The Normal and the Pathological*, the norm is not static but rather expansive: "The normal . . . increases the rule at the same time that it points it out. It asks for everything outside, beside, and against it that still escapes it. A norm draws its meaning, function, and value from the fact of the existence, outside itself, of what does not meet the requirement it serves. The normal is not a static or peaceful, but a dynamic and polemical concept."[16] Yet the notion of man as target has another significance, no less powerful for being more literal. Neufert's man (figure 4.2) was, both in *Mensch als Mass und Ziel* and in the *Bauentwurfslehre*, literally under assault. The later book included

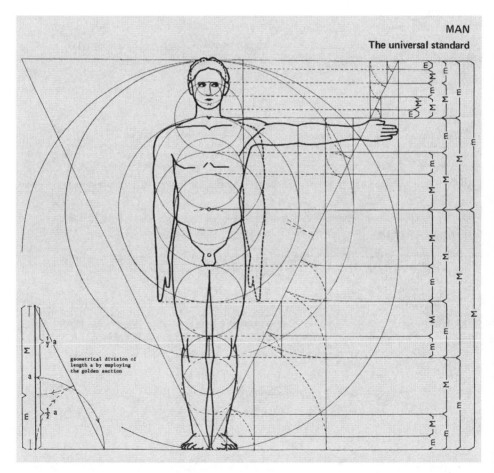

Figure 4.2. "Man: The Universal Standard." *Source*: Ernst Neufert, *Architects' Data*, edited and revised by Rudolf Herz, translated by G. H. Berger et al. (Hamden, Conn.: Archon Books, 1970), 1.

standards for vehicular and occupational safety, maximum population density, healthy posture, graves, and even air raid shelters (a topic to which Neufert devoted another small book).[17] The targeted man is treated as an object to be preserved from an increasingly threatening "environment" (*Umgebung*) through the articulation of a protective "habitat" (*Lebensraum*). Life is here transposed: it is no longer an inherent quality of man, instead a property of the objects and spaces in which man is inscribed.

Leading Nazi architect Albert Speer subsequently appointed Neufert to a series of high offices within his centralized office of the *Generalbauinspektor*. Neufert continued to pursue his research into standardized dimensions for every realm of human endeavor, with a particular focus on industrial and military architecture. The culmination of these efforts was another book, the *Bauordnungslehre* (*BOL*), of 1943, which sought to codify Neufert's research into a perfect system for architectural production. As Speer wrote in his foreword to the *BOL* when it appeared as a state publication under the auspices of the *Generalbauinspektor*: "Total war also forces the concentration of all powers in the science of building. . . . Through this organization . . . with a strong hand, in collaboration with industry, one must build a system of building organization [*Bauordnung*] in the widest sense of the word, coordinating the work of the planner, the manufacturer, and the building workers in the same direction, and ensuring the compatibility of the various parts."[18]

Neufert concluded the first chapter of the *BOL*, entitled "Ausblick," with a quotation from Nietzsche: "Morality creates a law book: the deep instinct for the fact that only automatism makes perfection possible in living and work."[19] This ambition toward "compatibility" (*Passfähigkeit*)—not simply of building parts such as prefabricated panels but also of the various building specialists themselves and of the user of the finished product—aimed at the establishment of an overall system, or set of rules, based on a firmly established norm. The norm in question was necessarily that of the human body, but that body was no longer that of the individual human being: it was only a module in a larger superstructure, itself impervious to bombing or disease. Neufert concluded the *BOL* by presenting a project of his own invention that neatly encapsulated this desire for total automatism: a moving factory for mass-producing housing in situ, a *Hausbaumaschine*. This limit-case fantasy of Fordism was a five-story-high trussed gantry system on rails, staffed by highly skilled workers working in perfect mechanical unison, each from his individual place, that could replace the buildings of Europe as quickly as they had been destroyed. Man might be a target, but if properly automated, it would hardly matter.

As noted, Neufert's work has remained a standard designers' reference in Europe to this day, translated rapidly into French and Italian and then into several other languages; however, the guide was not used in the English-speaking world until 1970, when it was translated for the first time, because of the difficulty in transposing the metric measures into the English system. The proliferation of metric measures has eased its passage into the English-speaking world in the ensuing decades, but the primary source in England, Canada, and America for graphic standards remains Henry Dreyfuss's *The Measure of Man*, originally published in 1959 and issued in updated editions ever since, with the addition of "and Woman" to the title in 1993.[20] Dreyfuss's work—issued in its first edition as a pamphlet accompanied by a collection of large format charts and figures, then later in increasingly massive tomes—is the first and most important comprehensive collection of "human engineering" or ergonomic data produced explicitly for architects and industrial designers.

The Measure of Man was long in the making. In his introduction to the first edition of the work, Dreyfuss described its genesis in an idiosyncratic collection of data from various sources: "Over the years, our pile of books, pamphlets, clippings and dog-eared index cards grew higher and more jumbled. When World War II came, the pile grew even faster." This was due to the fact that military engineers and scientists had begun to publish ever more anthropometric data; yet, Dreyfuss noted, "no one assembled these data into a single package that a designer could refer to and save spending days wading through his library and his files."[21] The spur to do so came while pursuing a typical project:

> Shortly after the war, our office was working on the interior of a heavy tank for the army. We had tacked a huge life-size drawing of the tank driver's compartment on the wall. The driver's figure had been indicated with a thick black pencil line and we had been jotting odds and ends of dimensional data on him as we dug the data out of our files. Surrounded by arcs and rectangles, he looked something like one of the famous dimensional studies of Leonardo. Suddenly it dawned on us that the drawing on the wall was more than a study of the tank driver's compartment: without being aware of it, we had been putting together a dimensional chart of the average adult American male.[22]

This epiphany—that the capacity to redefine the average human being was the function not of some inherent set of dimensions, or even of the gathering together and averaging of the dimensions of a statistical sample of bodies, but rather of inscribing those normative dimensions in "arcs and rectangles" within the compartment of the war machine—gave rise to Dreyfuss's invention of a new, wholly posthumanist model of the human being, entirely contemporaneous to the invention of ergonomics as a discipline of applied science. Dreyfuss dubbed this new male—drawn by his associate Al Tilley—"Joe" (figure 4.3) and his female counterpart "Josephine."

The major outcome of Dreyfuss's extensive involvement with industry and

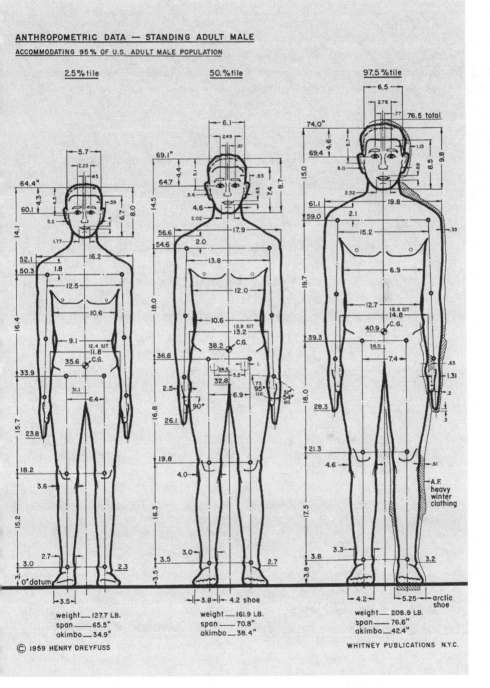

Figure 4.3. "Joe." *Source*: Henry Dreyfuss and Associates, *The Measure of Man: Human Factors in Design*, second edition (New York: Whitney, 1960), plate A.

the military before, during, and after World War II, Joe and Josephine became the spur for his first book on "human engineering," *Designing for People*, in 1955. A charming and disarming book, written in layman's terms and illustrated with lighthearted cartoons, *Designing for People* offered an explanation of the expanded purview of the designer in the postwar era. On the cover Dreyfuss printed his "creed," posted on the walls of his offices in New York and Pasadena:

> We bear in mind that the object being worked on is going to be ridden in, sat upon, looked at, talked into, activated, operated, or in some other way used by people.
>
> When the point of contact between the product and the people becomes a point of friction, then the industrial designer has failed.
>
> On the other hand, if people are made safer, more efficient, more comfortable—or just plain happier—by contact with the product, then the designer has succeeded.[23]

Like Neufert, then, Dreyfuss sought to "humanize" design. However, the terms of his creed are especially revealing of what this humanization of design entailed. The object is "worked on" and in so doing, "people are made"—that is, through the manipulation of the product's form and the use of that product ("contact"), the physical, economic, and psychological capacities of each person are increased ("safer, more efficient, more comfortable"). This is what Dreyfuss meant in using the term "human engineering." As he argued passionately at the outset of both *Designing for People* and the later *Measure of Man*, the "art" of design was entirely dependent on the success of reforming people themselves through the design of their equipment, their spaces, their experiences: "The industrial designer's task is twofold—to fit a client's wares to Joe's and Josephine's anatomies, and to explore their psychology and try to lesson the mental strains of this pressure age. It is not enough to seat them comfortably at their work. There is a responsibility also to remove the factors that impair digestions, cause headaches, backaches, fatigue, and give them a feeling of insecurity."[24]

The establishment of a set of norms for human dimensions was most explicitly *not* a simple matter of descriptive anatomy. Instead, the images of bodies that Dreyfuss and his associates produced were—in their very essence—images of biological and psychological processes. In particular, those processes were identified explicitly as pathologies. These processes were represented as *limits* to which the human body could be adjusted. Dreyfuss proposes to design bodies to be designed for: by selecting significant pathologies as the basis for the design of those bodies, creating images of those pathologies *as* bodies, and

then using those images to design products that would have an immediate effect on the actual bodies who made use of them. The key mechanism (in both
senses of the term) in this mode of design, not *for* but *of* people, was the "point
of contact between the product and the people." Central to Dreyfuss's creed,
everything hinged on this "point of contact." The touching of person and product was the site of an economic exchange of activity, the embodiment of uses
(riding in, sitting upon, etc.). Through this contact with the product, the qualities of the human being are literally produced; conversely, as Dreyfuss notes,
if the contact between body and product resulted in "friction," the person's
efficiency, comfort, happiness, and even safety were at risk.

Dreyfuss was explicit about this. "Joe and Josephine have numerous aller-
gies, inhibitions, and obsessions. They react strongly to touch that is uncomfort-
able or unnatural; they are disturbed by glaring or insufficient light and by of-
fensive coloring; they are sensitive to noise, and they shrink from a disagreeable
odor."[25] Joe and Josephine are barometers registering the degree of pressure
exerted upon them by the "environment." (It is also worth noting here that in
ergonomic discourse the designer constructs the normal human body in his
self-image, as a hypersensitive aesthete. Dreyfuss is hardly alone in this. One
might also think of Charles Eames's famous prosthetic projection of the mold
of his own leg onto every wounded leg in the U.S. Navy during World War II
with his leg splint, another product of wartime proto-ergonomic design.[26])

Through such reasoning, Dreyfuss and his associates came to view all use
objects as both potential threats to the body and extensions of the body. Early
in his book, Dreyfuss related an awestruck anecdote about the office's work
for the Veterans Administration on prosthetics for amputees: "We could see
how [the amputees] co-ordinated their muscles to operate the steel substitutes
for what they called their 'meat hands.' Some of them were so expert they
could select a dime or quarter from a collection of coins in their pockets. These
men had trained themselves to 'feel.' The hook had become part of them,
translating touch through cold metal."[27] Dramatically illustrated with a tightly
cropped photograph of an amputee outfitted with a hook signing his name (the
"Jo . . . " likely terminating in an "e"), Dreyfuss made the case for understanding Joe as just such a wounded body, healed by the application of a properly
designed mechanical prosthesis. It should come as no surprise, then, that in
the fully articulated charts of *The Measure of Man*, Joe and Josephine often appear clad in safety helmets, nearly always with their bodies (or at least "parts"
of their bodies) in contact with one or another mechanical surface. Without
this healthy contact with their prostheses, Joe or Josephine would be walking
wounded. This fundamental state of affairs is what separates Dreyfuss's approach from Neufert's: not only are the qualities of life transposed from figure
to ground, as it were, but the quality of the body is entirely dependent on the

interpenetration of product and body via the seemingly impenetrable surface of the interface.

Yet we would miss an essential point in Dreyfuss's reformulation of the human body as a wounded body in need of mechanical protection if we were to ignore the specific manner in which Joe and Josephine are delineated (figure 4.4). Neither Joe nor Josephine are anatomical studies: they are not sections, no skeletal structures or internal organs are shown. Their facial features are purely schematic, and sex organs are omitted (save for Josephine's breasts, rendered as featureless lumps). They are unbroken outlines, elevations, and plans of abstract bodies rendered purely as surface. Thus the most radical intervention in the articulation of the human body by ergonomic designers is not the mechanical prosthesis sutured onto or into the body itself, but rather the reimagined body as a surface that may then be laid in contact with the interface between body and machine.

It is now a commonplace of posthumanist media theorists—ranging from Marshall McLuhan to Donna Haraway to Friedrich Kittler—that the body has been penetrated by technology: we are "cyborgs" (cybernetic organisms) engaged in an economy of feedback with our "extensions" or equipment.[28] However, Dreyfuss's diagrams, and the countless similar diagrams that follow in the vast literature on ergonomics or "human engineering," make it clear that ergonomics considers neither machine nor body as a machine in its own right. Instead, they propose an alternative discourse. Looking to the diagrams, the situation is quite clear—all that matters is the articulation of the interaction of body and machine on the surface of the interface. This interface is located neither in nor on body nor machine. It is between these two centers. Therefore, it is a category error to label ergonomics as a "humanist" discipline (i.e., ergonomics is an ameliorative discipline designed to care for the body in a mechanical age). Likewise, it is also nonsense to assume that the body's former primary status in economies of work has been supplanted by the machine.

Rather, the ergonomic interface is the product of a third party—the designer or designers—who construct the interaction between the two as a full-fledged subject defined by the abstracted and coordinated limitations of machine and body alike. From the vantage point of ergonomic discourse, the act of sitting down is a matter of the surface on which the body is placed—or which places itself on the body—and the surface of the body placed on the machine, only ever rendered as surface. To take a more complex example, the ubiquitous diagrams of ergonomically correct attention coordinated by video screens and consoles show us a body surface and a machinic surface coordinated by a "cone of vision" corresponding to the rules of single-point perspective.[29] Here, the apparent depth of vision seems to hold out the possibility for considering the spatiality of ergonomics; however, closer inspection reveals that the size of video screens, distance of the seating apparatus, and the cone of vision are all coordinated to destroy any such perception of distance. This radical flatness of perception splayed out across the interface, it is probably hoped by the designers, will make the radar technician or programmer that much more able to extend his or her perception into far-flung territories surveilled by teletechnology.

In both cases the paired subjects of machine and body are inserted into a new model of space, one that is simultaneously flattened and extended. Both machine and body are quite literally *removed* from the "hostile environment" (i.e., the environment that would threaten both by exceeding their limitations) and placed into a new environment altogether. The qualities of this new environment, however, require careful analysis, for they do not obtain always and everywhere, nor do they wholly supplant the independent subjectivities of machine and body.

Habitability and the Aesthetics of Survival

The ergonomic subject is a compound surface. The complex "mechanical systems" and "biological processes" being brought into the systematic coordination of the "man-machine system" through ergonomics is accomplished through the production of a *compound surface*. This surface, the *interface*, is a radically mediated boundary through which the complexity of the coordinated systems is simplified and managed through the use of *limits*. Neufert and Dreyfuss alike understood that this exploration of limits would need to take on a spatial dimension, although they took different tacks in addressing the problem.

For the Taylorist Neufert the coordination of "man" and "machine" was a problem of *efficiency*, or doing the most with the least. This simple guiding imperative—"use less, get more"—conceals a complexity lurking just under the surface, however. Efficiency, of course, is a form of speed—that is, the amount of work accomplished in a given time—but significantly one that effaces any spatial element. In considering the spatial aspects of Taylorist or ergonomic efficiency, we see that *distance* is displaced, moving from the numerator to the denominator. That is, we move from the simple and familiar equation *speed* = *distance* / *time* to the compound function *efficiency (speed)* = *work* / *time* in which the denominator *time* is a function of *distance*. Therefore, within this logic of efficiency, the reduction of both time and distance results in increased speed or efficiency. Although this algebraic formulation may seem odd, this logic is instantly recognizable in the most famous of modernist architectural projects based on Taylorist principles, whether Greta Lihotsky's Frankfurt Kitchen or the multiple proposals in the Weimar era for the "minimum dwelling." In all of

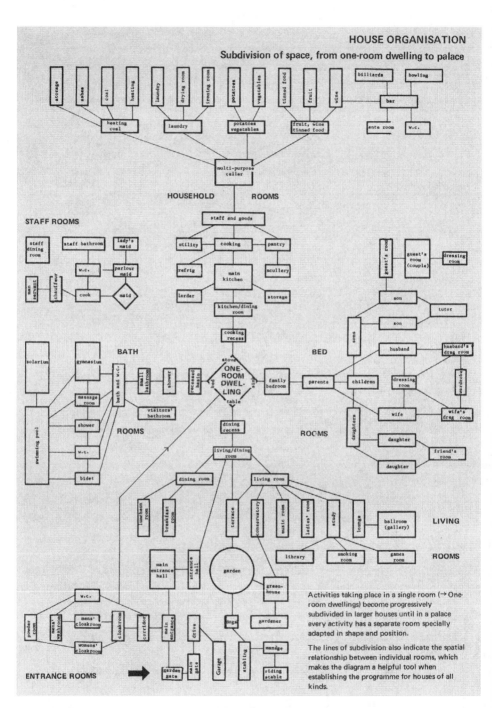

Figure 4.4. "House Organisation: Division of space, from one-room dwelling to palace." *Source*: Ernst Neufert, *Architects' Data*, edited and revised by Rudolf Herz, translated by G. H. Berger et al. (Hamden, Conn.: Archon Books, 1970), 39.

these, a Taylorist space is produced as a problem of *minimizing* space: of making it as small as possible, bringing related "functions" into as close a proximity as possible, reducing time and labor and increasing efficiency.

Knowing the crucial reversal between Taylorism and ergonomics—the reversal of emphasis between "man" and "machine"—we may ask, How is it possible to provide a space smaller and more efficient than that provided by Taylorist design logic? In Neufert's analysis, provided in his chapter on "Habitat" (*Lebensraum*), the solution is to be found in the organizational logic of the dwelling. Beginning with a bare-bones diagram of the minimal dwelling, Neufert shows the organization of a nearly infinite number of possible dwellings, ranging "from 1-room dwelling to palace" (figure 4.4) centered around a figure of a room outfitted with the essential technological fixtures (bed, table, sink, and stove). The boxes connected to this central box take their place according to a logic of need—as the family expands, either in numbers or economic means, each room in the flow chart can be added in the proper sequence. The innovative aspect of this strategem is that it is no longer necessary, as in earlier pattern books, to show specific model apartments, houses, or palaces; rather, only a series of relationships of generic spatial types (e.g., "living rooms," "entrance rooms," "household rooms," etc.) that can then be subdivided into subtypes according to function (e.g., "dining recess," "living," "ballroom," etc.).[30]

As indicated by the title of the diagram, the basic approach preserves a general sense of scale: as a building accommodates more functions, one may assume, the larger and more varied its overall plan will be. However, such a graphic approach to planning also dismantles a perspectival set of spatial relations—still preserved in the conventional logic of the projective orthogonal plan, section, and axonometric—to allow the designer to see many topologies of proximity at once. The overall effect is to reduce the question of space to one of equipment. The stove, sink, table, and bed are what organize the "house"—any structural enclosure is organized so as to house these functions. Any form of social function is reduced to an effect of technical function: a perfect case in point is the relegation of the "bar" space to a point further down the line of the flow chart from the core dwelling than "wine storage."

In modeling his own, properly ergonomic space, Dreyfuss takes the abstraction of Neufert yet one step further. In what is perhaps the most perplexing image in *The Measure of Man*, and one of only two in the book to address directly the character of ergonomic space, a one-page plan of a human being entitled "Environmental Tolerance Zones" (figure 4.5), Dreyfuss describes the human environment as a space defined not by any conventional measure of distance but rather of intensities of environmental stimuli. A set of sixteen lines radiating outward from the human body at the center pass through two concentric circles, giving a range of intensities of various phenomena—temperature, humid-

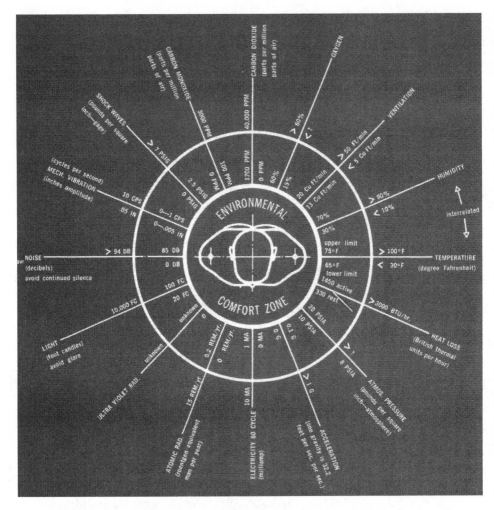

Figure 4.5. "Environmental Tolerance Zones." *Source:* Henry Dreyfuss and Associates, *The Measure of Man* (New York: Whitney, 1960).

ity, atmospheric pressure, speed and acceleration, radiation, light, noise, and vibration. The area between the body and the inner circle is identified as the "environmental comfort zone," a set of intensities of these stimuli below which the human body is putatively undisturbed (although other researchers soon noted, as did Dreyfuss in subsequent editions of the book, that understimulus could also produce deleterious effects). "The band between the [two] circles demarcates the bearable zone limit. Outside this limit great discomfort or possible damage is encountered." Outward, beyond the outer circle, one must assume (for Dreyfuss does not tell us), the environmental stimulus becomes fatal. "It is also necessary to consider," Dreyfuss added in this same note at the bottom of the page, "infra-red radiation, ultrasonic vibration, noxious gases, dust, pollen, and heat exchange with liquids and solids," although his office did not apparently have this information on hand.

What is surprising about Dreyfuss's diagram is the way in which it replaces a conventional model of space with a topological rather than a Euclidean model: the white space around the figure, and the concentric circles and radiating lines in that space, are in fact only extensions of the outer shell of the body. It is, as it were, an exploded diagram, spreading out the surface of the body to illustrate the range of the surface's durability and performance. Yet it is also inverted: the point at which some aspect of the "environment" would inflict "physiological harm"—that is, penetrate or damage the body—is rendered furthest from the outline of the body itself. It is difficult to imagine a more radical diagram of spatial enclosure. It would appear to offer a picture of the human being's range of "habitability," a broad space measured not dimensionally but in terms of temperature, light, and so on; yet this open field is only a surface pressed against the surface of the body.

The problem of habitability thus becomes one of enclosure. As Edholm put it in 1967, discussing the intensifying race to dominate outer space: "The Russians and the Americans have dramatically demonstrated that doors can literally be opened in this closed world [of outer space]."[31] However, he hastily notes, this is not possible without fully enclosing the astronaut within the masterpiece and idyll of ergonomic design—the space suit. Closed worlds are, for ergonomics, always already enclosed and any opening begets another enclosure. It is easy to capitulate to this relentless optimism that is at the heart of the rhetoric of ergonomic theory. Yet even the most influential theorists of this synthetic discipline frequently acknowledged the paradox at the heart of ergonomic thought and practice. Dreyfuss's contemporary and colleague, the industrial designer Walter Dorwin Teague, framed for the discipline very high stakes indeed, at the threshold of World War II. Speaking of the promise that ameliorative design practice had for "civilization," Teague too recognized an irony built into his own assumptions, that the very devices designed to protect human beings were also the very same machines designed to kill others.

> Now that a season of fruition has arrived, after all our labors, we are confronted with a conflict of destinies: unprecedented well-being within our power of achievement, immanent disaster threatening to lose for us all the advances we have made. It would be completely disheartening except for one thing—the strange unreality, the bizarre, nightmarish aspect of the impending danger. It is so obviously a reversal of all logical trends, so epileptic a seizure, so

stark a manifestation of frantic hysteria and manic psychosis; it has
an aspect of visionary impermanence, the kind of lapse from which
one wakes up suddenly to recovered sanity, and astonishment that
anything so utterly fantastic could be so violent.[32]

Teague was not alone in identifying a potential crisis in the theory and design
of "man-machine systems." Mumford himself made a seemingly shocking about-
face with regard to the discipline of human engineering in his two-volume epic
history *The Myth of the Machine*. Drenched in Cold War paranoia, the second
volume, *The Pentagon of Power*, offered a narrative of the increasing dominance
of "control systems" in civilizations ranging from ancient Egypt and Sumeria to
the space race. The book is typically read as a screed against the encroachment
of various technocratic regimes upon closely held tenets of humanism in the
1960s, and not without reason. However, it is essential to note that Mumford
relentlessly argues that it is the nature of control systems to expand through
a proliferation of surfaces. Moreover, he argues, these surfaces come into an
ever-more intimate relationship with the human body.

Positioning himself against the ergonomists (in attitude but not in theoretical assumptions), Mumford describes an irony of no small proportions (figure
4.6): the ideal equipment, a complete environmental system known as a "space
suit": "Behold the astronaut, fully equipped for duty: a scaly creature, more
like an oversized ant than a primate—certainly not a naked god . . . a kind of
faceless ambulatory mummy. . . . Here is the archetypal proto-model of Post-
Historic Man, whose existence from birth to death would be conditioned by
the megamachine, and made to conform, as in a space capsule, to the minimal
functional requirements by an equally minimal environment—all under remote
control."[33]

Mumford's grandiloquent anxieties about the "megamachine" make it easy
to miss that he is concerned here with the interface, the mediation between
body and environment that has taken on a fully spatial dimension and is radically
closed to the "hostile environment" beyond. He identifies, in the metaphor of
the ant (a worker par excellence), that within the systematicity of ergonomics, the true product is the interface, the product of a division of labor that no
longer deems labor an adequate or meaningful category. The interface is, as
Georges Canguilhem has noted in his discussion of the term *milieu*, "a between
two centers" that forms the paired subjects of human being and machine.[34] It
is expanded to cover all "human activity"; what is necessary to ergonomics is
to understand how to harness the a priori and continuous labor of the body
via the "externals of the mechanical world." Thus, if meaningful headway is to
be made in theorizing and historicizing ergonomics and its products, we must
take Mumford and the ergonomists quite seriously indeed. Rather than looking

Figure 4.6.
"Encapsulated Man."
Source: Lewis Mumford,
*The Myth of the Machine,
Volume Two: The Penta-
gon of Power* (Boston:
Mariner Books, 1970),
plate 14.

for the constituent qualities of ergonomically designed objects in the body, the
product, or the labor, we must interpellate it as a system. One is reminded of the
prescience of Marx in describing the diffuse nature of capital. Taking only small
liberties, we might restate his famous dictum: Ergonomics is not a thing; it is a
socio-technical relation between people and machines mediated by things.[35]

Notes

Epigraph: Henry Dreyfuss, *Designing for People* (New York: Simon & Schuster, 1955), 191.

1. See Mumford, *Technics and Civilization*; Sigfried Giedion, *Space, Time, and Architecture:
The Growth of a New Tradition* (Cambridge: Harvard University Press, 1941) and *Mechanization Takes Command*; Reyner Banham, *Theory and Design in the First Machine Age*, second
edition (New York: Praeger, 1972); and William Jordy, "The Symbolic Essence of Modern
European Architecture of the Twenties and Its Continuing Influence," *Journal of the Society
of Architectural Historians* 22, no. 3 (October 1963): 177–87.

2. Mumford, *Technics and Civilization*, 363.

3. On the difficulty of defining pain, see V. C. Medvei, *The Mental and Physical Effects of
Pain* (Edinburgh: E. & S. Livingstone Ltd., 1949); and Elaine Scarry, *The Body in Pain: The Making and Unmaking of the World* (New York: Oxford University Press, 1985).

4. Mumford, *Technics and Civilization*, 357, emphasis added.

5. For a good gloss on some of these terms and medical concepts, see Wolfgang Schivelbusch, *The Railway Journey: Trains and Travel in the Nineteenth Century*, translated by Anselm Hollo (New York: Urizen Books, 1977), especially chapters 7–10. A more in-depth study is Anson Rabinbach's *The Human Motor: Energy, Fatigue, and the Origins of Modernity* (New York: Basic Books, 1990).

6. This term endured as a synonym for ergonomics in the United States well into the 1980s; indeed, some British publications were given new titles when published in the United States. K. F. H. Murrell's *Ergonomics* was published in the United States as *Human Performance in Industry* (New York: Reinhold, 1965).

7. Murrell, *Human Performance in Industry*, xiii. It was Murrell himself who coined the term.

8. Taylor himself theorized this "fit" in no uncertain terms: "Now one of the very first requirements for a man who is fit to handle pig iron as a regular occupation is that he shall be so stupid and so phlegmatic that he more nearly resembles in his mental make-up the ox than any other type. The man who is mentally alert and intelligent is for this very reason entirely unsuited to what would, for him, be the grinding monotony of work of this character. Therefore the workman who is best suited to handling pig iron is unable to understand the real science of doing this class of work" (Taylor, *The Principles of Scientific Management* [New York and London: Harper, 1911], 59).

Rabinbach, in his otherwise excellent histories of the sciences of work and energy in the nineteenth and early twentieth centuries, has mistakenly identified this approach as "ergonomic." As I show here, and as the coinage of the term only in England in 1949 demonstrates, this usage is anachronistic and thus misleading. See Rabinbach, *The Human Motor: Energy, Fatigue, and the Origins of Modernity* (New York: Basic Books, 1990).

9. Mary McLeod, "'Architecture or Revolution': Taylorism, Technocracy, and Social Change," *Art Journal* (Summer 1983): 132–47.

10. O. G. Edholm, *The Biology of Work* (London: Wiedenfeld and Nicolson, 1967), 3.

11. On these notions, see, for example, Donna Haraway, "The High Cost of Information in Post–World War II Evolutionary Biology: Ergonomics, Semiotics, and the Sociobiology of Communication Systems," *Philosophical Forum* 13 (1981–82): 244–78; and Ernest J. McCormick, *Human Factors Engineering* [second edition of *Human Engineering* (1957)] (New York: McGraw-Hill, 1964). For an interesting discussion of the physiologically and psychologically "hostile environment" of the nineteenth and early twentieth centuries, discussed mainly in Freudian and Simmelian terms, see Wolfgang Schivelbusch's discussion of the "stimulus shield" in his *The Railway Journey: Trains and Travel in the Nineteenth Century*, translated by Anselm Hollo (New York: Urizen Books, 1979).

12. Edholm, *Biology of Work*, 7.

13. Ibid., 239.

14. Murrell, *Human Performance in Industry*, xiii.

15. The best source on Neufert, based on archival research and copiously illustrated, is Walter Prigge, ed., *Ernst Neufert: Normierte Baukultur im 20. Jahrhundert* (Frankfurt: Campus, 1999). The best source in English is Wolfgang Voigt, "Standardization, War, and Architecture: The Work of Ernst Neufert," *Archis* 10 (October 1995): 58–65.

16. Georges Canguilhem, *On the Normal and the Pathological*, third edition, translated by Carolyn Fawcett (Dordrecht: D. Reidel, 1978), 146. Compare with Ernst Neufert, *Baunormung als Ganzheit* (Berlin: Elsner, 1942).

17. Ernst Neufert, *Bombensicherer Luftschutz im Wohnungsbau* (Berlin: Volk u. Reich Verlag, 1942). See also Ernst Neufert, *Die Pläne zum Kriegseinheitstyp* (Berlin: Verlag der Deutsches Arbeitsfront, 1943).

18. Albert Speer, "Vorwort" (Foreword) in Ernst Neufert, *Bau-Entwurfslehre: Grundlagen, Normen, und Vorschriften über Anlage, Bau, Gestaltung, Raumbedarf, Raumbeziehungen. Masse für Gebäude, Räume, Einrichtungen und Geräte mit dem Menschen als Mass und Ziel: Handbuch für den Baufachmann, Bauherrn, Lehrenden und Lernenden* (Berlin: Bauwelt Verlag, 1936), n.p. The original German is: "Der totale Krieg zwingt zur Konzentration aller Kräfte auch im Bauwesen. . . . Bei dieser Ordnung . . . man musste mit fester Hand unter Mitarbeit der Industrie zuerst eine Bauordnung im weitestest Sinne des Wortes aufbauen, die dem Planer, dem Hersteller und den Männern am Bau in gleicher Weise das Arbeiten erleichtert und die Passfähigkeit der Teile untereinander gewährleistet."

19. Quoted in Ernst Neufert, *Bauordnungslehre* (Berlin: DIN, 1943), 13.

20. Henry Dreyfuss, *The Measure of Man: Human Factors in Design*, second edition (New York: Whitney, 1960), 4.

21. Dreyfuss, *The Measure of Man*, 4.

22. Ibid.

23. Dreyfuss, *Designing for People*, cover; reprinted in Dreyfuss, *Measure of Man*, 3.

24. Dreyfuss, *Designing for People*, 42–43.

25. Ibid., 27.

26. On the Eames splint, see John Neuhart, Marilyn Neuhart, and Ray Eames, *Eames Design: The Work of the Office of Charles and Ray Eames* (New York: Harry N. Abrams, 1989), 27–29.

27. Neuhart, Neuhart, and Ray Eames, *Eames Design*, 29. On the substitutional logic of prosthetics, see Vivian Sobchack, "A Leg to Stand On: Prosthetics, Metaphor, and Materiality," in *The Prosthetic Impulse: From a Posthuman Present to a Biocultural Future*, edited by Marquard Smith and Joanne Morra (Cambridge: MIT Press, 2006); and Vivian Sobchack, "Beating the Meat / Surviving the Text, or How to Get out of This Century Alive," *Body & Society* 1, no. 3 (November 1995): 205–14.

28. See Marshall McLuhan, *Understanding Media: The Extensions of Man* (New York: McGraw-Hill, 1964); Haraway, "High Cost of Information in Post-World War II Evolutionary Biology"; and Friedrich Kittler, *Gramophone, Film, Typewriter*, translated by Geoffrey Winthrop-Young and Michael Wutz (Stanford: Stanford University Press, 1999).

29. Ergonomic studies since the 1950s have gradually introduced more sophisticated models of attention that account for stereoscopic vision; however, the two-dimensional structure of perspectival perception remains wholly unchanged. See, for example, J. Long and A. Whitefield, eds., *Cognitive Ergonomics and Human-Computer Interaction* (Cambridge: Cambridge University Press, 1989).

30. The subtypes in Neufert's chart are preserved in contemporary editions of the book, despite the fact that they have become rather dated. Note, for instance, the presence of a relatively large "subdivision of space" devoted to refrigeration; on the curious and changing spatiality of refrigeration, see Michael Osman's chapter in this edited volume.

31. Edholm, *Biology of Work*, 240.

32. Walter Dorwin Teague, *Design This Day* (New York: Harcourt Brace and Company, 1940), 6–7.

33. Lewis Mumford, *The Myth of the Machine*, vol. 2, *The Pentagon of Power* (San Diego: Harcourt Brace Jovanovich, 1970), pl. 14–15.

34. Georges Canguilhem, "The Living and Its Milieu" (1946–47), translated by John Savage, *Grey Room* 3 (Spring 2001): 7–31, 8.

35. For the original formulation in English translation, see Karl Marx, *Capital*, vol. 1, translated by Ben Brewster (London: Penguin, 1972), 932: "Capital is not a 'thing' . . . [it is] a social relation between persons which is mediated by things."

Selected Bibliography

Canguilhem, Georges. *The Normal and the Pathological*. Translated by Carolyn R. Fawcett and Robert S. Cohen. New York: Zone Books, 1989.

Dreyfuss, Henry. *The Measure of Man: Human Factors in Design*. Second edition. New York: Whitney, 1960.

Giedion, Sigfried. *Mechanization Takes Command*. New York: Oxford University Press, 1948.

Mumford, Lewis. *Technics and Civilization*. New York: Harcourt, Brace & Co., 1934.

Neufert, Ernst. *Bau-Entwurfslehre: Grundlagen, Normen, und Vorschriften über Anlage, Bau, Gestaltung, Raumbedarf, Raumbeziehungen, Masse für Gebäude, Räume, Einrichtungen und Geräte mit dem Menschen als Mass und Ziel: Handbuch für den Baufachmann, Bauherrn, Lehrenden und Lernenden*. Berlin: Bauwelt Verlag, 1936.

PART II
Global States and Citizens

5

"Mejores Ciudades, Ciudadanos Mejores"
Law and Architecture in the Cuban Republic

■

TIMOTHY HYDE

THE Patronato Pro-Urbanismo (Pro-Urbanism Association), a civic group
organized in Cuba in 1942 to advocate for national planning legislation,
adopted a succinct slogan: "Mejores Ciudades, Ciudadanos Mejores"—
better cities, better citizens (figure 5.1). The phrase bound together formal order
and social order, cleverly employing grammatical symmetry to construe a reciprocal relationship between cities and citizens in which the latter are both the consequence and the prerequisite of the former. After winning independence from
Spanish colonial rule, Cuba had struggled to establish a stable political environment; corruption, partisan factionalism and violence, economic volatility, and the
hegemonic pressure of the United States all contributed to a persistent instability
in Cuban politics in the first decades of the twentieth century.

Professionals and intellectuals dismayed by the circumstances of civic life
in Cuba diagnosed Cuba's condition as a decline into decadence. In essays and
lectures on history and culture they attempted to discern the causes of this
decline, and through active associations they hoped to arrest and reverse its effects. One such association, the Junta Cubana de Renovación Nacional, was created by the sociologist Fernando Ortiz in 1924 to advance proposals for social
and political improvement, and its agenda for reform forged links between the
disciplinary perspectives of such members as the writer Jorge Mañach and the
architect Pedro Martínez Inclán. Three years later, another association similarly
composite in its membership, the Grupo Minorista, announced an explicit conflation of the aesthetic and the political in its declaration advocating modernism
in one passage and denouncing imperialism in the next. Out of these and similar activities, a narrative of social amelioration and political reform developed

ESTATUTOS

DEL

PATRONATO

PRO URBANISMO

DE CUBA

MEJORES CIUDADES,
CIUDADANOS MEJORES

HABANA

Figure 5.1. Cover of *Patronato Pro Urbanismo de Cuba* prospectus, 1942.

alongside a nascent modernism's aesthetic of progress. But as this movement for civic reform gathered pace, so too did political violence that culminated in the Revolution of 1933. President Gerardo Machado was forced to resign, his dictatorial regime besieged by an array of opponents and the threat of U.S. intervention, and the rival political groups that had fomented the opposition to his rule contested power through a succession of provisional governments. Now, in the late 1930s, the creation of a stable political sphere would require a difficult consensus of partisan groups divided into factions along numerous fissures, such as social class and generational difference.

By the time the Patronato Pro-Urbanismo coined its slogan, efforts toward political reform overlapped extensively enough with movements in other cultural domains for its proposed conjunction of urban form and social effect to possess considerable plausibility. In 1940 the drafting of a new Cuban constitution had catalyzed the participation of an array of cultural, professional, and intellectual fields in a common project: reconstructing the civic sphere of the nation. Disciplines such as architecture, law, or philosophy were already embedded within the contours of civic life but with the promulgation of a new national charter, a new discursive mode became manifest in their debates and accords. This chapter identifies that discursive mode as "constitutionalism," a conceptual form that enabled expressions of prerogative and assertions of legitimacy within any one discipline to be engaged with those of another and also to be positioned as constitutive aspects of the civic sphere.

Constitutionalism existed not independently but through its various invocations in the objects and practices that it sponsored: a civic group's advocacy for national planning, a Pilot Plan for Havana, an essay on legislation, or the 1940 constitution itself. Each of these depended for its expansive significance on the adoption of constitutionalism as a mode that enabled an instrumental conflation of politics and aesthetics, and thus constitutionalism opens a perspective on the potential agency of architecture. "Better cities, better citizens" could have served as the slogan of a number of other tendencies that married reformist intention to urban space—Hausmannization, the City Beautiful, and urban renewal, among others. The contextual surround of the Patronato Pro-Urbanismo—the confluence of nationalism, history, modernism, and, above all, politics—produced a specific situation in which a slogan conveyed not only its overt meaning but also the means of its discursive formation.

The Constitution of a Nation

While Cuba was still a Spanish colony, José Martí, the iconic figure of Cuban independence, posited the conjunction of a projected national sovereignty with the articulation of national identity. Writing in 1881, he insisted on the necessary correlation between a nation's government and its cultural and natural composition:

> One must see things as they are, to govern well; the good governor in America is not one who knows how government is conducted in France or Germany, but who knows the elements of which his country is composed and how they can be marshaled so that by methods and institutions native to the country the desirable state may be attained wherein every man realizes himself. . . . The government must be the child of the country. The spirit of the government must be the same as that of the country. The form of government must conform to the natural constitution of the country. Good government is nothing more than the true balance between the natural elements of the nation.[1]

With an echo of Montesquieu, Martí defined an organic relation between governmental forms and environmental, physical, and habitual conditions. Writing to incite a revolution, he avoided specific prescriptions for political structures in favor of a rhetorical appeal to republican virtue and civic conscience, but the link Martí fashioned had renewed relevance following the Revolution of 1933, when political and aesthetic pursuits in different disciplines converged with a reinvigorated and pervasive nationalism. Political consensus in such a factional moment required, alongside motivations such as economic gain, the general motive of a perceived national interest, which—though variously cast as national pride, community obligation, or simply progress—was also broadly construed as a civic conscience that was to be produced and cultivated in Cuban citizens.

Debates about the civic sphere and the public realm were therefore accompanied by arguments about Cuban history and culture that had in turn been explicated even before independence through the concept of *cubanidad*. *Cubanidad*, as an assertion of national identity and as a summation of the defining characteristics of Cuban life and experience, could be invoked to sanction revolt against Spain; to foster antipathy to North American influence; to lament political indifference; and to deplore political partisanship. In the wake of the revolution, *cubanidad* became in effect a medium for the expression of critical perspectives, and as *cubanidad* became a central preoccupation in art, literature, sociology, and other disciplines, its invocations remained inseparable from their surrounding political context.

Essays in the avant-garde journal *Revista de Avance* and paintings by the Vanguardia artists sought to reveal *cubanidad,* as did the novels of Alejo Carpentier and the Bonet House, designed by Eugenio Batista in 1939 as a modern architecture derived from what he regarded as the fundamental elements of Cuban architecture. The descriptions of *cubanidad* in these various manifestations varied by discipline but most made reference as Martí had done to the natural environment as a determinate factor. In 1940, Fernando Ortiz published *Contrapunteo cubano del tabaco y el azúcar* (Cuban counterpoint: Tobacco and sugar), a historical and sociological study of the development of the Cuban character from the encompassing cultural and economic effects of the island's twin crops, tobacco and sugar. The book's opening essay proposed an allegorical rendition of their counterpoint that defined *cubanidad* as the synthesis of their contrasting traits and influences. Ortiz advanced a theoretical concept, "transculturation," to identify the process by which such cultural syntheses emerged from an initial "deculturation," an uprooting from an existing culture, through a subsequent "neoculturation," the establishment of a new cultural condition.

Cuba's history, Ortiz argued, was a constant process of transculturation that had produced "the extremely complex transmutations of culture that have taken place here, and without a knowledge of which it is impossible to understand the evolution of the Cuban folk, either in the economic or the institutional, legal, ethical, religious, artistic, linguistic, psychological, sexual, or other aspects of its life."[2] Presenting transculturation in the model of an organic process produced an echo of Martí but, more important, enabled Ortiz to suggest that *cubanidad* was not an immutable characteristic; quite the opposite, Ortiz's conceptual coinage, particularly in the conclusive term "neoculturation," defined *cubanidad* as the evolving cultural manifestations of a continuing transformation.

This part of Ortiz's argument paralleled in key respects the ideas of other prominent intellectuals. Jorge Mañach and, more emphatically, the members of the Orígenes group that formed in the mid-1940s, suggested that Cuba was defined by its *lack* of origins, by the absence of surviving indigenous populations or their aesthetic practices or social structures.[3] To the Orígenes writers, Cuba was a nation without a past. Similarly, Mañach in his essays outlined Cuba's past as a punctuated historical narrative, depicting signal persons and events as incomplete episodes with their potential to establish a stable republic left unfulfilled. He argued that the war for independence had not initiated but actually halted the achievement of national sovereignty because the decades that followed had only reinforced the tendencies of the colonial period. The task for his generation was not to restore a lost golden age from Cuba's past, Mañach proposed; it was to assume responsibility for fulfilling the deferred promises of that past.

In tandem, the arguments put forward by Mañach and Ortiz displaced the understanding of *cubanidad* as an essence to be discovered at its historical origin. They depicted *cubanidad* as an outward expression at a given moment that defined an orientation toward prior events, influences, and trajectories; not a cause, then, but a consequence to be discerned differently along the procession of historical contexts. This conception further suggested that earlier manifestations of *cubanidad* could be recast as responses to the exigencies of the present moment, enabling a critical shift from an attitude of discovery to an attitude of invention; critical because the aesthetic projects of cultural production were bound up with the political crisis of the civic sphere. The proximity to the colonial period—the recent past in Cuba's case—and the diagnosis of a declining cultural arc since that period forestalled any resurrection of prior models for the present.

Even as they competed, often violently, for power, rival political groups agreed that Cuba needed new civic and governmental structures, a consensus that led to the drafting and promulgation of a new Cuban constitution in 1940. In February of that year, delegates elected to represent the political parties assembled in Havana as the Constitutional Convention. In drafting the new constitution, the delegates confronted the paradoxical task of summoning into being a nation that already existed. Cuba had been a republic for four decades, a coherent cultural entity for four centuries, and yet the constitution of 1940 was to be as much the formulation as the affirmation of its existence. This paradox came clearly into view as the delegates considered the degree to which the charter should accommodate the existing reality of Cuba and the extent to which it would legitimate new orders and intentions superimposed upon that reality.

The prevailing legal structure was an amalgam of statutory codes inherited from the colonial period and laws passed under the elected and dictatorial governments of the early republican period, all authorized by the 1901 Cuban constitution drafted during the U.S. occupation of the island. These legal remains could not be wholly discarded—some were closely bound to institutional practices or to customary rights—but they had to be drawn into a coherent order by a new charter that supported the social and political aims of the new republic. In addition to such legal structures, delegates also had to consider the relevance of existing social and physical factors. A commission charged with preparing for the constitutional convention had already invoked Martí's proposition regarding the relation between government and natural elements. The commission concluded that "if the constitution principally organizes the government of a people, it is indisputable, then, that to draft it natural elements should be taken into account."[4]

At the same time, delegates desired the new constitution to promote changing aims and to induce novel potentials. While the foundational constitutions of the Enlightenment had declared universal principles and rights, a more recent wave of new constitutions in the Soviet Union, Weimar Germany, and

Republican Spain mandated the more deliberate management of social development within national contexts. Active constitutions such as these, with their declaration of specific social ideals, supplied the more relevant model. The provisional governments of the 1930s in Cuba had promoted a series of new social policies that were to be incorporated into constitutional terms. The charter would eventually come to nearly three hundred articles, providing a thorough and detailed formulation of the organic structure of government and its corresponding social responsibilities. Most individual rights, such as habeas corpus and freedoms of association and religion, had already been guaranteed in 1901, but the new charter went much further, defining social rights classified under the four "cornerstones" of family, culture, work, and property.[5] Finally, and crucially for both the delegates and the citizens, the new constitution was to fulfill the still unrealized promise of an independent and sovereign Cuba conceived at the start of the independence wars in the nineteenth century.

The 1940 constitution derived much of its juridical pedigree from the theory of the Viennese jurist Hans Kelsen, who had several adherents and even a former student among the prominent jurists in Cuba. Kelsen advanced what he called the "pure theory of law" against two prevailing legal philosophies, the metaphysics of natural law and the empiricism of legal sociology. A legal order should be fixed neither by transcendental principles nor by social reality, Kelsen argued, for law is properly normative, a hierarchical order in which any given norm is a presupposition, understood to be validated only by a superior norm. A legal order might consist of any set of presuppositions with a basic norm (conventionally expressed as a constitution) at the apex of their pyramidal structure, where it provided the primary or root presupposition. Kelsen argued that norms, being presuppositions, could be neither consequences nor causes of actual events; they are of the "ought" as opposed to the "is." Here he discerned a fundamental distinction: "Whereas an 'is' statement is true because it agrees with the reality of sensuous experience, an 'ought' statement is a valid norm only if it belongs to such a valid system of norms, if it can be derived from a basic norm presupposed as valid. The ground of truth of an 'is' statement is its conformity to the reality of our experience."[6]

Jurists in Cuba adopted Kelsen's normativism as the basic precept of constitutionalism but alloyed it with somewhat greater concern for the phenomenological interpretation of social reality. One jurist, while acknowledging that Kelsen's theory offered an escape from the essentialism of natural law, argued that the difficult problem of *apriorismo* remained. The presupposition of the norm, he argued, had to be elucidated from a "material a priori"—that is, from the realities of Cuba.[7] Calibrating the relation between the real and the normative was a decisive issue in drafting the new constitution precisely to fulfill the historical claims of Cuban independence. Mañach, who was one of the convention delegates, had already proposed the discontinuous nature of Cuban history, a view that suggested the present possibility to now bring the first revolutionary declaration signed in 1861 to fruition as a foundational moment. But the constitutional framework would have to extend beyond abstract principles to incorporate the specificities of this interrupted history. The realities of the Cuban nation—its climate, its people, its customs and habits—all these coalesced into el hecho cubano (the Cuban fact) that was to be reflected in the articles of the new constitution.

The constitution was to provide the underpinning for a stable civic sphere through the authorization of statutes but, in a further difference from earlier constitutions that had defined only the rights of citizens, it also stipulated the obligations of citizens. These required each citizen "to comply with the Constitution and the Laws of the Republic and to observe civic conduct, instilling it in one's children . . . promoting in them the most pure national conscience."[8] Other articles supported this condition, including several relating to education that mandated that courses be taught on civics and on the constitution and that all teaching tend to inspire "in a spirit of cubanidad . . . the love of country [and] its democratic institutions."[9] The obligatory cultivation of civic conduct and conscience revealed the desire to produce a reflexive citizenship, an awareness of the condition of being a citizen. As Mañach had argued several years before, "the sense of civic responsibility [civismo] is not a natural attribute in an individual or in a people, but a result of more civilized coexistence."[10] In requiring the citizen to maintain and foster civic conscience, articles such as these installed a principle of reciprocity as the operative mode of the civic sphere, which would consist in the reciprocal relation between individual citizens and the legal order that encompassed them. This reciprocal structure would itself be one of the primary registers of constitutionalism as it emerged in other disciplinary practices.

Although the 1940 constitution never fully coincided with the actualities of the political sphere over the next two decades, it nevertheless did produce effectual political and cultural consequences. The Constitutional Convention had assembled with the sanction of Fulgencio Batista, the military leader who had consolidated power following the Revolution of 1933 and subsequently wielded his influence from behind the provisional governments. In lawful democratic elections held after the promulgation of the constitution in 1940, Batista became president and began some of the transformations required to effect its provisions. Four years later in the next election his chosen successor lost, but Batista acceded to a peaceful transition that seemed to evidence the maturing of the political process. A third election in 1948 extended this period of democratic governance, although increasing corruption and decreasing governmental competence accompanied a recurrence of political gangsterismo. Then, in 1952,

Batista seized power illegally and commenced the seven-year dictatorship that is his familiar infamous legacy by suspending the constitution.

Although the charter now no longer authorized political events, it was neither unimportant nor ineffective because it still functioned as a representation of a civic sphere to which the nation aspired and as a measure of its distance. Batista's opponents eulogized the constitution to assert its construct of civic conscience. The writer Francisco Ichaso, for example, argued that it had already produced in the Cuban people sufficient "reserves of *civismo*" to compel the return to legal transfers of government, while the rebel leader Fidel Castro declared the restoration of the 1940 constitution as one of the principles of his revolutionary guerrilla movement.[11]

Both invocations distinguished in the constitution an instrumental potential to produce cultural actualities in advance of social and political realities. It performed a cultural role independent of its legal status, preserving the category of citizenship in unadulterated form at a remove from the corruptions of present political life and maintaining an ideal civic sphere at a remove from the damages of the prevailing events. Furthermore, the constitution sustained the guarantee of constitutionalism, which had by then developed as a conceptual mode propagated through other discourses. As the constitution, even in extremis, possessed a reserve of instrumental capacity, so too did constitutionalism before and after the moment of political crisis carry the potential to foster the civic sphere through discourses such as planning or architecture. Could constitutionalism, through a normalization that bracketed disparate and prior elements into a coherent and prospective whole, resolve the challenge of *particularismo*, the diffuseness of Cuban identity that impeded the consolidation of a civic conscience? Could its forecasting of a historical past fulfilled by contemporary actions resolve through these other discourses the challenge of *apriorismo*, the integration of Cuba's history and its existing structures into unprecedented but accommodating configurations?

The Civic Image

In 1942 the Patronato Pro-Urbanismo started its campaign for a coordinated program of planning to be authorized under a National Planning Law. The Patronato resembled the reformist groups founded during the Machado regime, linking the aims of the planning profession to broader concerns for civic betterment. One of the founders, the architect Pedro Martínez Inclán, had been a member of the Junta Cubana de Renovación Nacional. Another, Eduardo Montoulieu, was a younger architect who had recently studied city planning at the Harvard University Graduate School of Design. Other members included a journalist and a sculptor who had been in the Grupo Minorista. They,

along with the historian of the City of Havana, and the president of the Lyceum y Lawn Tennis Club, a leading cultural institution in Havana, expanded the
array of disciplinary interests now associated with the advocates of planning.
Through this influential and professionally diverse membership, the Patronato
commenced a systematic publicity campaign that explicitly linked national planning to the new constitutional project, casting a national plan as both a historical
and a pragmatic necessity.

The group's prospectus (which itself imitated the form of a constitution)
stipulated seven objectives; in addition to supporting "Laws, Regulations, Ordinances and all measures that are favorable for the urban improvement of the
nation," the Patronato also sought to "encourage patriotism and civic pride by
means of the enlargement of our cities."[12] These aims presumed the coordination of urbanism, law, and civic conscience, a presumption legitimated, according to the group, by the 1940 constitution. As only one example of how the
new constitution either required or presupposed regulatory activities encompassed by the concept of planning, Montoulieu pointed to Article 277, which
obliged the state "to foresee, guide and design scientifically the safe, beautiful,
economical and utilitarian growth of its towns, cities and regions."[13]

In September 1942 the group presented *La Exposición sobre Urbanismo* (Exhibition on urbanism) at the Lyceum y Lawn Tennis Club, advertised as the first
exhibition of urban planning in Cuba. The exhibition panels, whose didactic
tone was established in preliminary sketches by Montoulieu, readily revealed
the concept of planning they elaborated. In his first sketch a pointed finger confronted the viewer to ask: "You plan your clothes, your house, your hobbies,
your work, studies, travels, food budgets, in short, your life . . . but . . . who
plans the surroundings? The streets, parks, schools, hospitals, shops, industries,
houses, theatres, museums, etc. . . . in the cities, in the country?"[14]

Why, the question implied, tolerate improvisation in the public sphere if you
would refuse it in the private? Both private and public contexts are improved,
indeed are made functional, by the conscious activity of planning. The pointed
finger confronted the viewer again in Montoulieu's second sketch to exhort:
"You as an important part of the citizenry can and should participate in the planning process by means of an active civic conscience!" A third sketch included
the citizen as one of three constituent elements of the planning process: citizens
educated about the intentions of planning and able to define their future needs
and ambitions; technicians able to assess the demands of citizens and devise the
means for their satisfaction; and governments interpreting and resolving the demands of citizens without recourse to political exigencies. Montoulieu's sketch
presumed the reciprocity between the state and the citizen as defined by the
constitution but added the provision that that reciprocity was to be contrived
through the mediating mechanism of planning. The citizen, equipped with the

reflexive awareness of "an active civic conscience," would elaborate demands addressed to the state, while the state, armed with the instrumental capacities of the plan, would regulate the environment of the citizen. The third constituency, the technicians, was responsible for the agencies and methods of planning.

The concept of planning during this period in Cuba necessitated both a neologism in Spanish—*planificacíon* competed with two rival terms, *planeamiento* and *planeación*—and extensive definitions. Montoulieu was one of the first to supply the latter, enumerating the benefits of planning in the propaganda of the Patronato Pro-Urbanismo and continuing to develop and disseminate the concept of planning through the 1950s. The words and images of the exhibition panels described planning as a deliberate coordination of interests and resources toward a determined result. This coordination was produced by an assessment of past and present conditions to ensure the appropriate translation of those conditions into a future form. But the term *planificacíon*, which combined root meanings of planning *and* constructing, was understood to place an emphasis on present action. To plan, Montoulieu's sketches concluded, is "to know what is, to define what should be, to define what is to be done." This active process, he and the other members of the Patronato concluded, required the formation of a central planning board responsible for the framework of a coherent national plan, a recommendation that did not meet with unanimous approbation.

Although the articles of the constitution did indeed presume planning, they included no explicit provision for such a planning authority; and although the new charter promoted a republican ideal of civic participation, it also confirmed the liberal presumption of the inviolability of property. Planning carried political associations that unfavorably colored its reception. Some critics connected it with authoritarianism; others with the economic controls of state-managed economies. Supporters therefore had to argue the merits of planning as a remedy to the existing faults of improvisation and corruption without encouraging even the perception of state regimentation. Mañach, for one, addressed planning in relation to processes of political and social change. Cuba needed, he stated, "not so much a severely planned society as a society capable of planning or of planning intelligently, which is not the same."[15] He regarded planning as a practice of self-regulation that could manage the relation between citizen and state just as it managed the transformation of past and present into future conditions. The capacity to plan would correspond to an acceptance of extensive transformations in the civic sphere without the necessary accompaniment of either political repression or political revolution.

Mañach maintained this view of planning in conjunction with the observation that the consciousness of Cuban citizens was typified by a behavior he called *quijotismo*. This trait, by his account, had emerged in Latin America following the

independence wars of the early nineteenth century as the new nations began
to define their political and social structures. Their intellectual inheritance from
Spain met with the demanding American environment, combining a contemplative idealism and a determined sense of action into a tendency Mañach named
quijotismo to acknowledge the paradigmatic illustration of a relentless determination to summon up the ideal as reality itself. *Quijotismo*, he wrote, was "an affirmation of the ideal against the grain of experience, and often behind its back;
an essentially contemplative attitude, that the cervantesque paradigm wanted
to bring to action."[16]

Mañach did not disapprove the idealism of *quijotismo*, which was already
embedded within his valorization of the civic sphere, but he was concerned that
its disconnection from reality inevitably rendered it ineffectual. How might such
idealism actually be brought to action? As construed in Cuba, planning was in
fact a specific mode of idealism, but one that, in Montoulieu's definition, guided "that which is" toward "that which ought to be done."[17] Planning, in other
words, guided reality *toward* the ideal. Planning might begin to do so through
the enabling institutions of government, but to create a venue for the reciprocal
obligation of the *mejor ciudad* and the *ciudadano mejor* that Montoulieu and his
colleagues promoted, it would have not only to devise the terms of the better
city but also to foster the orientation of the better citizen.

In 1925, Inclán had contributed to the reformist debates what might be
called an image of the civic, a representation of forms and arrangements that
would correspond to desired conditions of civil society. He published this as a
prospective plan for Havana, with the existing city transformed by a network
of radiating boulevards connecting public plazas and monuments (figure 5.2).[18]
In 1949, Inclán contributed a renewed image of the city, this time in the text of
a pamphlet titled *Codigo de urbanismo* (Code of urbanism). Below this title on
the cover, Inclán added, "A contribution to the promulgation of the Charter
of America, taking as a base the Athens Charter"—carefully chosen words
that conveyed its constitutional pretension. The pamphlet reproduced verbatim
the articles of the Athens Charter, the modernist creed drafted in 1933 at the
Fourth International Congress of Modern Architecture (CIAM) that had broadcast the modernist narrative of amelioration through a theory of urbanism.

In the former colonies of Spanish America the origin of a deeply embedded relationship between the law and the city lay in the sixteenth-century ordinances drafted by Spanish kings to regulate the colonization of the New World.
These Laws of the Indies defined how towns were to be founded, specifying
both their structure of government and their physical arrangement in a grid
of *cuadras*, or blocks, that surrounded an open central plaza. The Laws of the
Indies were a historical relic until their relevance was precociously identified
in the mid-1940s by Cuban scholars, who revisited them as regulatory instru-

ments devised to bind together civic order and urban form.[19] Inclán's *Codigo de urbanismo* traced its own provenance directly to the Athens Charter but would have been received through the concurrent attention for the Laws of the Indies (which Inclán mentioned in the text) and the constitution of 1940. Participating in the circulation between these three antecedents—the Laws of the Indies, the Athens Charter, and the 1940 constitution—it took on their presumption of a discursive binding between constitutions and architecture but absorbed as well the compound of modernism, history, and nationalism that they together represented.

The Athens Charter outlined precepts by which to plan the Functional City, and its polemical text was supplemented over time by various urban propositions advanced by CIAM members. Inclán began by appropriating the text itself; in the *Codigo de urbanismo* he added, modified, and excised articles to tailor the original charter to the Cuban situation. The new and modified articles were distinguished with italics, so that the elaboration of what he understood as a model constitution for the modern city was visibly evident. Inclán placed his first insertion to the Athens Charter immediately after the original first article, which declared the city to be part of the region; he added that the region's urbanistic problems were connected to those of the nation, thereby asserting the role

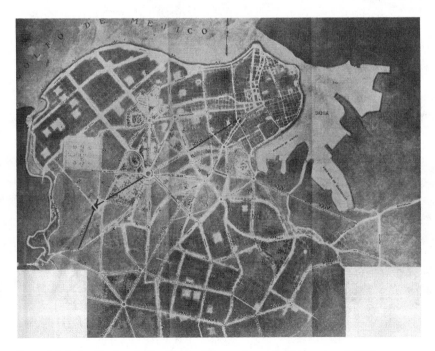

Figure 5.2. Pedro Martínez Inclán, Plan for Havana. *Source: La Habuna Actual,* 1925.

of urbanism in the larger project of the nation. As well as modifying individual articles, Inclán also included entirely new sections. One of these, entitled "Urban Aesthetics," categorized beauty as a necessary urban quality, an appeal to the nonscientific that the drafters of the Athens Charter would not likely have tolerated. He elevated the quality of beauty to a function of the city, affirming its value in a crucial appendage to one of the concluding articles of the Athens Charter:

> 156: The cycle of daily functions: dwelling, work, recreation, will be regulated by Urbanism with the strictest economy, with dwelling considered to be the very center of urbanistic concerns and the focal point of all measures.
> 157: This does not mean, however, that of the three graces of Contemporary Urbanism, hygiene, circulation, and beauty, the last should be sacrificed in any considerable manner for economic reasons. Spiritual values ought to balance material ones in social life and therefore in the Planning of Cities.[20]

The seeming anachronism of Inclán's emphasis, at a time when he acted as one of the strong proponents of modernism in Cuba, resulted from several factors; the most important was his concern for the expressive value, or in other words the civic character, of urban elements. This prompted him to make detailed comments on the social role of monuments and boulevards.

In 1925 the Cuban government had commissioned the French urbanist J. C. N. Forestier to design a Plan for Havana to regulate the expanding form of the rapidly modernizing city. Forestier worked with a large team of Cuban professionals and absorbed into his proposal several ideas then circulating in Cuba, including the outline of the plan published by Inclán that same year. Forestier's Plan for Havana consisted of a radial network of boulevards linking existing locations of civic importance, such as the National Capitol or the University of Havana, and future ones, such as a projected civic center. So in 1949 what might have seemed a reactionary regard for the City Beautiful movement likely resulted from the fact that even though only a few components of Forestier's Plan for Havana were realized, they served as actual examples for the potential civic effect that Inclán sought to cultivate in the new constitutional framework. Certainly Inclán remained committed to a projection of civic order that corresponded to the influence of the constitutional project, and he now selected the Athens Charter as the explicit template to advance that aim.

But sharp distinctions differentiated the implications of constitutionalism from the theoretical and practical presumptions of earlier planning modes, not only Forestier's but also the influential polemics of the Athens Charter. The earlier civic image, the City Beautiful, required a stable framework of consensus, such as that provided by a ruling political class or a fixed national ideology; the later civic image, the Functional City, distanced itself entirely from the contingencies of nationalism, asserting its scientific and nonrepresentational character. The Cuban situation required a more elastic conceptual frame to accommodate the still fragile political consensus of constitutionalism and to enable representations of national identity sufficient to address both the citizen and the city. Inclán's *Codigo de urbanismo* mitigated the generality of the Athens Charter by supplemental specificities and its abstraction by the addition of a new section on "Legislation." There, announcing the law as a cultural code through which architecture could be enacted, Inclán's text implied that architecture, through the framework of planning, would contribute to the shaping of citizens by functionally and aesthetically shaping the city.

The *Codigo de urbanismo* lacked, at the moment of its publication, an accompanying plan, a representation through architecture of the civic image it proposed. First were needed the enabling structures of national planning, for which Inclán and his colleagues continued to advocate. In 1955, three years after having seized power, Batista established the Junta Nacional de Planificación (JNP), a national planning board authorized to formulate master plans for several Cuban cities. The JNP retained, along with other expert consultants, Charles Haar, a professor at Harvard Law School to collaborate with the architects on the enabling legislation for these plans. Haar had recently published an article entitled "The Master Plan: An Impermanent Constitution," in which he argued that a master plan aspired to contain both a set of objective principles and a set of tangible effects. He held that the contradictory requirements for stability and flexibility could undermine the necessary cohesion of the master plan. Haar proposed the conceptual compromise of an "impermanent constitution" in which the master plan would be impermanent, susceptible to change to preserve the advantages of flexibility yet able to claim the foundational privileges of normalization.[21] Haar's idea, in conjunction with the tenets of the *Codigo de urbanismo*, provided an opportunity for an elaboration of the concept of constitutionalism through architecture. The existing city could be regarded as a representational form *and* as a regulatory structure, with its civic code already contained in its aesthetic dimensions and therefore accessible to the prerogatives of design.

A Constitutional Modernism

To develop master plans for Havana and other Cuban cities, the National Planning Board retained the firm Town Planning Associates, led by architects José Luis Sert and Paul Lester Wiener, internationally prominent protagonists of modernism.[22] Over the next three years Sert and Wiener worked with the Cuban architect Mario Romañach to develop the Pilot Plan for Havana. Like the Forestier Plan for Havana, this master plan aimed to regulate the physical order of the entire city from its historic core to the new districts expanding toward the west and the south. Its morphology was very different, however, with older colonial quarters and new speculative developments integrated into a system of sectors and a network of roads classified according to a hierarchy of speeds and use; residential densities, commercial activities, public spaces, civic functions were all subject to a normalizing intention that could be seen most vividly in the proposed reconfiguration of Habana Vieja, the old colonial core (figure 5.3).

Here the city's dense historical fabric confronted the projective ambitions of urban renewal. In accordance with articles of the constitution that pertained to the state's obligation to sustain national culture, several buildings in Habana Vieja had already been legally designated historical monuments. A 1944 decree signed by Batista not only protected monuments like the Cathedral but also included unexceptional buildings facing onto the Cathedral Plaza and the adjacent streets entering into it, indicating that such groupings were judged to possess historical civic value as complete entities. But in 1955, now as a dictator distanced from the progressive consensus of the early 1940s, Batista signed another decree giving broad legal sanction for the "Rehabilitation of Ancient Havana." This new decree did not obviate the perquisites of the older law, although it reflected a change in emphasis from preservation to development.[23] Given the recognized presence of such significant historical elements in the district, the development of Habana Vieja was quite distinctly a problem of *apriorismo*.

In a preliminary sketch, as the architects began work on the Pilot Plan, Wiener outlined the new development program over the existing blocks of Habana Vieja, designating a six-block area to become a financial sector to accommodate the banks that had long been the principal commerce in the area. He marked three historical sites: the Cathedral Plaza, the Plaza de Armas, and the Plaza Vieja. Subsequent sketches showed several more blocks reconfigured as high-rise buildings set back in superblocks, with the area of new blocks extended much further toward the historical monuments in the northeastern corner of Habana Vieja. In these sketches the significance of the colonial fabric was addressed directly for the first time. Wiener proposed a "historic zone" that would enclose the Plaza de Armas and the Cathedral Plaza and buffer the historical buildings from the redeveloped area. In a composite drawing compiled from these studies, the area of redevelopment extended to the edges of the plazas, directly contravening the terms of the 1944 decree. It showed also that the dense existing fabric of Habana Vieja was largely to be demolished and replaced with superblocks, towers and high-rise slabs. No privilege was accorded

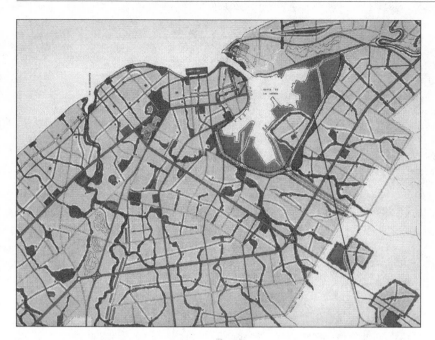

Figure 5.3. Pilot Plan for Havana, Town Planning Associates, 1955–58. Courtesy of the Frances Loeb Library, Harvard Graduate School of Design.

to the existing district as a concretion of a civic order, nor to its monuments as the residue of that order. But some further sketches hint that consideration was later given to these two aspects. Wiener traced several studies that tested different arrangements and scales of street and block, some of which began to recuperate existing dimensions. Another sketch rendered the historical zone in sufficient detail to imply an intention to integrate the historical buildings into an encompassing civic landscape.

These intentions coalesced in the final plan devised by Sert and Romañach. The array of superblocks was reduced to a linear band, and low-rise blocks with open courts were proposed for the remaining area (figure 5.4). This configuration maintained the courses of almost all of the streets, and therefore the block perimeters as well, so that the existing configuration would persist in the relation of figure and ground. Alternate streets would be widened to ease traffic while the others, reserved for pedestrians, would "preserve the scale and charm of the old streets."[24] Typical diagrams indicated that existing property lines might be maintained after rehabilitation, with the irregular plots laid out in the colonial period coexisting with the more regular geometry of the new courtyards. The architects also acknowledged the need to preserve certain historical clusters. Their detailed drawing suggested how the Cathedral

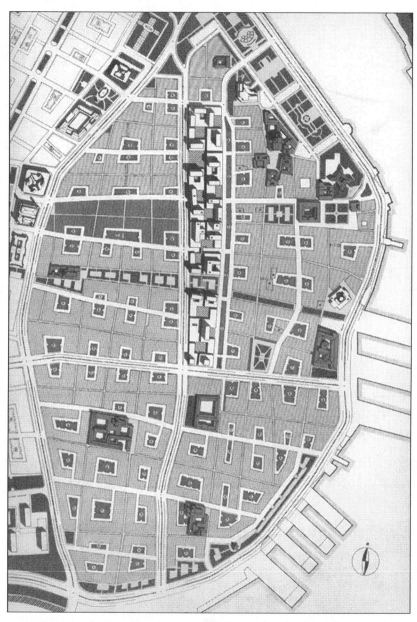

Figure 5.4. Havana Vieja, Pilot Plan for Havana, Town Planning Associates, 1955–58.
Courtesy of the Frances Loeb Library, Harvard Graduate School of Design.

Plaza might have coexisted with the new organization by being integrated within blocks, while other remaining lots might accommodate new constructions, rehabilitated buildings, or some combination of the two.

This proposal contained an important conceptual premise. Describing the configuration as a "new approach to the '*cuadra*' or grid pattern," the architects averred its genealogical link to the Laws of the Indies, which had marked out a legal configuration of social hierarchy and property ownership in the physical configuration of a grid of *cuadras*, or blocks.[25] In the context of constitutionalism, this reference to the Laws of the Indies would have been received with a plenary meaning not limited to only a correspondence in form. Indeed, Inclán's specific reference to the Laws of the Indies in his *Codigo de urbanismo* fashioned a link between that text and the new Pilot Plan for Havana such that architecture manifested the larger structure of constitutionalism. Compared with the foundational cities of the Laws of the Indies, the rigidity of the grid was eased in the new proposal for Habana Vieja by the incorporation of the irregularities of the existing streets, but this did not compel an abandonment of what was manifestly a normative order.

To the contrary, it revealed the characteristic advantage of a normative system: the capacity to absorb such contingencies and transform their significance within a superimposed order. Recall that a normative system, in the conceptual mode of constitutionalism, consists of a set of presuppositions asserted with a plain regard for their consequence and not for their origin. The presuppositions of the normative system—in planning, the *cuadra* as a conceptual and a literal instrument of urban order—project a condition that "ought" to be, enframing within that projection the objects and events of the condition that "is." In Habana Vieja, as in the Cuban situation generally, the pure presupposition of normalization was tempered by the problem of *apriorismo*, not only the awareness of historical realities but of the need for those realities to authorize the projected futures. By effecting a calibration of the real and the normative and introducing a systemic potential for flexibility and variation, the Pilot Plan for Havana achieved the requisite balance of Haar's impermanent constitution. Its framing of the historical moments within the normative *cuadra* was no longer a gesture of preservation but a conferral of legitimacy; quite simply, an act of constitution.

The typical neighborhood sector proposed in the Pilot Plan for the future expansion in other districts of the city was also organized into *cuadras*, each filled with single-story attached dwellings to create an even fabric of patio houses (figure 5.5). Architects like Romañach had identified the *patio*, or courtyard, as one of the architectural manifestations of *cubanidad*. Sert also had emphasized the recurring figure of the patio, defining it more abstractly as a physically bounded space of social interaction, whether a courtyard in a house or the plaza of the public square. In the typical neighborhood sector, designed by Sert and Wiener in association with the firm Arroyo & Menendez, the patio figure was proposed as a module, so that the patio in a house was affiliated to the patio that provided a neighborhood plaza, which was in turn affiliated to the patio that served the district.

Through this modular scale, the social relations of the home and those of the neighborhood were to mirror the social interdependence made visible by the civic center. The juxtaposition of the domestic and the urban evoked Montoulieu's earlier exhortation for planning: "You plan your clothes, your house, your hobbies, your work, studies, travels, food budgets, in short, your life . . . who plans the surroundings? The streets, parks, schools, hospitals, shops, industries, houses, theatres, museums, etc.?"[26] Equally, it recapitulated the succinct motto of the Patronato Pro-Urbanism: "Better Cities, Better Citizens." The architectural figure of the patio, when understood as a scalar component, elided the boundaries that otherwise seemed to segregate different spheres of social

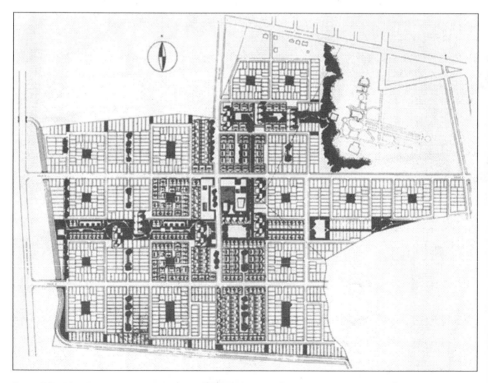

Figure 5.5. Typical Neighborhood Sector, Pilot Plan for Havana, Town Planning Associates, 1955–58. Courtesy of the Frances Loeb Library, Harvard Graduate School of Design.

activity, and through this elision made possible a more immediate correlation of the individual and the nation.

At the Eighth CIAM Congress in 1951, Sert had described a constitutive act to indicate the significance of the public square. He quoted the philosopher José Ortega y Gasset, who claimed that man's secession from the undifferentiated space of nature was the foundational act of civilization. "The square," wrote Ortega, "thanks to the walls which enclose it, is a portion of the countryside which turns its back on the rest, eliminates the rest and sets up in opposition to it."[27] From this constitutive act—which was the designation *and* the performance of foundation—Sert traced out the lineage of the public square from the agora to the plazas of colonial Latin American cities. Cuban architects, historians, even Cuban law similarly affirmed the plazas of Habana Vieja as representatives of this civic lineage. Sert proposed that the public square would be "a frame where a *new civic life* . . . could develop [through] direct contacts and exchange of ideas," suggesting a sequential production, new conditions from the repetition of earlier ones.[28]

In other words, if the *cuadra*, a normative instrument for the regulation of city fabric, were further supplemented by the patio at its center to become a figure for the projection of social effects, then the *cuadra* defined by the master plan would be capable of constituting the civic. The habits of social interaction would be transposed onto the conceptual plane of *cubanidad*, as the outward expression of historical circumstances revealed as national identity and as political agency. The civic sphere, the legible reciprocity between citizens and political circumstances, would in turn be conjured by the now equally legible relation of citizen to the city.

In January 1959 the Cuban Revolution led by Fidel Castro brought an end to this constitutional modernism. Fulgencio Batista was overthrown, the projects he patronized were left unrealized, and the 1940 constitution was superseded by the ideology and laws of the revolutionary government. Seen through the historical sensibility of Mañach and his colleagues, the constitutionalism discursively defined in the *Codigo de urbanismo* and the Pilot Plan and projected in formal devices such as the *cuadra* and the patio joined prior deferrals of democratic civic order in Cuba. Insofar as an enduring civic order was not established through the affiliation of law, planning, and architecture, the potentials that inhered in their conflation remain unfulfilled. The conclusion to be drawn, though, is not the crude diagnosis of a failure of the forms of modernism, for the Cuban situation in fact revealed their greater potential once they were loosened from the narrow disciplinary constraint of architectural formalism.

Reconstructing the motives and processes of the cultural context in Cuba, particularly in the significance of the law as a cultural mode during the period, reveals how the ambitions of formalism to construe a social order were actually to have been pursued. Different from the expressive emphasis of the City Beautiful, or the analytic scientism of the Athens Charter, or even the doctrinaire pragmatism of urban renewal, this constitutional modernism proposed a supple means for cultural and political engagement by which architecture would assist the formulation of the new civic sphere. The formula "better cities, better citizens" did not merely claim the resonance of architectural form but asserted the disciplinary capacity of architecture to participate fully in the cultural mode of constitutionalism.

Notes

1. José Martí, *The America of José Martí*, translated by Juan de Onís (New York: Noonday Press, 1953), 141. Recent publications that elucidate the invocations of Martí as a figure in Cuban nationalism include Lillian Guerra, *The Myth of José Martí* (Chapel Hill: University of North Carolina Press, 2005); and Mauricio A. Font and Alfonso W. Quiroz, *The Cuban Republic and José Martí* (Lanham, Md.: Lexington Books, 2006).

2. Fernando Ortiz, *Cuban Counterpoint: Tobacco and Sugar* (Durham: Duke University Press, 1995), 98. Ortiz's particular focus was on the significance of *mestizaje* as a defining condition of race in Cuba. He elaborated this fact of *mestizo* racial identities into a larger conception of the essentially hybrid nature of *cubanidad*.

3. See Duanel Díaz Infante, *Mañach o la República* (Havana: Letras Cubanas, 2003); and Rafael Rojas, "*Orígenes* and the Poetics of History" in *Essays in Cuban Intellectual History* (New York: Palgrave Macmillan, 2008), 65–92.

4. Gustavo Gutiérrez y Sánchez, "La convención constituyente y la Constitución de 1940," in *Historia de la nación Cubana*, edited by Ramiro Guerra y Sanchez (Havana: Editorial Historia de la Nación Cubana, S.A., 1952), 118.

5. For the full text of the 1940 constitution, see Andrés María Lazcano y Mazón, *Las constituciones de Cuba* (Madrid: Ediciones Cultura Hispánica, 1952).

6. Hans Kelsen, *General Theory of Law and State* (Cambridge: Harvard University Press, 1945), 111.

7. Miguel Jorrín, "La fenomenología y el derecho [II]," *Universidad de la Habana Publicación Bimestral*, no. 24–25 (May–August 1939): 215.

8. Lazcano y Mazón, *Las constituciones de Cuba*, 849.

9. Ibid., 864.

10. Jorge Mañach, *Pasado vigente* (Havana: Editorial Trópico, 1939), 112.

11. Francisco Ichaso, "La nueva conciencia cubana y la constituyente de 1940," *Cuadernos de la Universidad del Aire*, no. 40 (1952): 286; and Fidel Castro, "History Will Absolve Me," in *The Declarations of Havana* (London: Verso, 2008), 28.

12. Patronato Pro-Urbanismo, "Estatutos del Patronato Pro-Urbanismo de Cuba," Havana, 1942.

13. Eduardo Montoulieu, "Architect Explains Need of City Planning Body in Cuba," *Havana Post*, September 6, 1942.

14. Permission to examine and quote from the original sketches, which are in the personal archives of Eduardo Montoulieu, was generously granted by Eduardo Montoulieu.

15. Jorge Mañach, *El pensamiento de Dewey y su sentido americano* (Havana: Comisión Nacional Cubana de la UNESCO, 1953), 23.

16. Mañach, *El pensamiento de Dewey y su sentido americano*, 29. Mañach first presented his idea of *quijotismo* in lectures that were published in Cuba as Jorge Mañach, *Filosofia del quijotismo* (Havana: Universidad de la Habana, 1947). Although Mañach himself did not draw an explicit connection between his ideas on history, planning, and *quijotismo*, their theoretical and temporal proximity is evident when considered through the lens of constitutionalism.

17. Eduardo Montoulieu, "Enfoque sobre el urbanismo contemporáneo," *El cusol*, June 17, 1942.

18. This drawing was published as an illustration appended to Pedro Martínez Inclán, *La Habana actual: Estudio de la capital de Cuba desde el punto de vista de la arquitectura de ciudades* (Havana: P. Fernández y Cía., 1925).

19. The historical study of the Laws of the Indies was initiated by Zelia Nutall, an American archeologist who published a partial translation of the Ordinances in 1921. Historians in Mexico introduced further research in the 1930s, but the first theorization of the Laws of the Indies, one that took regard of their contemporary relevance, was published in Cuba in 1945 by Francisco Domínguez Compañy, *El urbanismo en las leyes de Indias (estudio histórico y jurídico-social)* (Havana: González y compañía, 1945).

20. Pedro Martínez Inclán, *Codigo de urbanismo: Carta de Atenas, Carta de la Habana* (Havana: P. Fernandez y Cía, 1949), 26. The italics in the original were used to signify Inclán's additions to the Athens Charter text.

21. Charles M. Haar, "The Master Plan: An Impermanent Constitution," *Law and Contemporary Problems* 20, no. 3 (Summer 1955): 353–418.

22. José Luis Sert was the president of CIAM and also dean of the Graduate School of Design at Harvard University. He and Wiener founded Town Planning Associates in 1942 and worked subsequently on a number of projects in Latin America, where Wiener had traveled extensively on lecture tours. Sert had resided in Cuba for a few months in 1939, and when the firm received independent commissions in Cuba in 1953, he was able to renew contact with several Cuban colleagues, including Nicolás Arroyo. When Batista named Arroyo his minister of public works and head of the Junta Nacional de Planificación in 1955, Arroyo retained Town Planning Associates as consultants.

23. Contemporary preservation practices, as well as contemporary cultural practices give a consistent valuation of the historical significance of Habana Vieja that has led to its designation as a UNESCO site. But it is necessary to consider the Pilot Plan for Havana within the prevailing attitudes and values of its own historical period. At that time the concept of the "historical district" was only just developing, and historical districting and urban renewal were in some cases viewed as parallel endeavors. The city of San Juan in Puerto Rico offers one such example.

24. Town Planning Associates, *Plan piloto de la Habana* (New York: Wittenborn Art Books, 1959), 32.

25. Town Planning Associates, *Plan piloto de la Habana*, 32.

26. Permission to quote from the original sketches was generously granted by Montoulieu.

27. José Ortega y Gasset as quoted in the José Luis Sert Collection, Folder D14, Frances Loeb Library, Harvard University.

28. Sert as quoted in the José Luis Sert Collection, Folder D14, Frances Loeb Library, Harvard University.

Selected Bibliography

Lejeune, Jean-François, ed. *Cruelty and Utopia: Cities and Landscapes of Latin America.* New York: Princeton Architectural Press, 2005.

Mumford, Eric. *The CIAM Discourse on Urbanism, 1928–1960.* Cambridge: MIT Press, 2000.

Rama, Angel. *The Lettered City.* Durham: Duke University Press, 1996.

Sert, José Luis. *Can Our Cities Survive? An ABC of Urban Problems, Their Analysis, Their Solutions.* Cambridge: Harvard University Press, 1942.

Tugwell, Rexford G. *The Place of Planning in Society.* San Juan: Puerto Rico Planning Board, 1954.

6

Dwelling, Dispute, and the Space of Modern Iran

■

PAMELA KARIMI

A T the end of the nineteenth century, a group of Iranian reformist intellectuals began to criticize the effectiveness of the rule of the Qajar dynasty (1794–1925).[1] After Nasir al-Din Shah's assassination in 1896, Iran saw a vital new period due to the expansion of modern schools and the growth of publications with themes ranging from geographical discoveries and political conflicts to scientific developments and adventure novels. These educational venues afforded the Iranian public insights into the world beyond their own country.[2] The 1906 constitutional revolution led the parliament to draft laws enacting more centralized state control, but the political turmoil of World War I put the intended reforms on hold. It was not until the founding of the new Pahlavi dynasty by Reza Shah that the country underwent major infrastructural reforms affecting the look of its cities and residential neighborhoods.

During Reza Shah's reign (1925–1941) the norms for urban public spaces were dramatically altered, not only through the construction of wide streets, new shops, and modern administrative buildings but also by the introduction of public areas for social interaction and entertainment. The development of transportation infrastructure and the revamping of such services as schooling and health care, together with the new cinemas and parks, brought about an expansion of the public sphere. By the 1920s educational reforms had helped produce a homogeneous modern middle class, much of which was employed by governmental institutions.[3] Mindful of the destructive side effects of industrialized urban modernity, the government tried its best to prevent disorder and to create a society made up of educated, disciplined, and productive individuals.[4] This required the expansion of new state-run projects regarding the population's well-being even beyond the traditional areas of taxation, levying soldiers, and preventing anarchy.[5] The improvement of home life as a major factor in making Iranian society healthier and more productive received further attention during the early Pahlavi period. More than ever before, women's magazines and the press proclaimed the importance of the actual residence itself and its impact on the health of the family and society as a whole.

The discourse of domesticity gradually crept into the field of state policy, which sought to build better homes.[6] During the reign of Reza Shah, housing development plans were implemented mostly through foreign contractors. From the 1920s until 1951, when Iran nationalized the oil industry and evicted the Anglo-Iranian Oil Company, such oil cities as Abadan and Masjid Suleiman saw massive expansion to house laborers and oil-industry specialists who had arrived from the United States, Europe, India, and the Persian Gulf states.[7] Many other foreign architectural firms and consultants were involved in the building of residential neighborhoods in Iran's industrialized cities, among which were the Scandinavian consortium SENTAB (Svenska Entreprenad Aktiebolaget) and the Austro-Hungarian industrial enterprise Škoda. In addition, there was the housing for trans-Iranian railroad-company employees constructed mostly by Italian consultants.[8] These projects were accomplished according to foreigners' specifications, and it was not until the beginning of Muhammad Reza Shah Pahlavi's reign (1941–1979) that the Iranian government itself began to formulate standards for housing. These codes were implemented through a number of development plans.

As Iranians struggled to come to terms with the country's identity on the brink of widespread Westernization, the house and its contents became one focus in the clash of traditional ways with the pressure to modernize and achieve a better standard of living. This topic gave rise to much fervent political debate and also to many discussions about moral and ethical problems within Iranian society. Contemporary writers in Iran watched the process of domestic modernization with doubt and called instead for reform of the cultural and moral character of the families who would occupy the newly constructed houses. Although Western ideas were certainly catalysts and influences in the movement to bring Iran into step with up-to-date and possibly beneficial technology in the home, Iranians themselves were actively engaged on a local level in figuring out which aspects of contemporary Western home life actually worked for them and which did not. The outcome depended on the question of adjusting a national and personal identity to rapidly changing times—something that only the people of Iran themselves would ultimately be able to do.

Not at Home: The Home Economics of the Left

Between 1941, when Reza Shah was forced to abdicate, and 1953, with its coup against democratically elected Prime Minister Mohammed Mosaddeq (in office 1951–1953) sponsored by the American CIA and the British MI-6, political activists in Iran experienced a freedom of expression and free elections not previously permitted. At that time the most prominent Marxist group was the Tudeh party, whose activities were not only political but also cultural. *Bidari-e Ma* (Our awakening), the women's bimonthly publication of the pro-Communist Tudeh party, presents a vivid picture of the latter enterprises.[9] Its writers considered coveting new fashions and the latest household commodities to be irrational, and encouraged women to "go local" rather than to rely on imported medicines and cosmetics. The healing properties of water, for example, were stressed: drinking plenty of water was seen as the key to beauty, and water was said to be able to heal most bodily ailments, including nervousness and anxiety. Creative methods for recycling disposable materials were also presented. Above all, working outside the home was encouraged. In an October 1944 article titled "Home and Its Limits in the Modern Age," contributor Farah Laqa Alavi emphasized the statement that most of women's traditional responsibilities (such as training children, preparing food, and so on) should now be taken care of by the society at large beyond the confines of the home.[10] In step with early Soviet ideology, the main concern of *Bidari-e Ma* was to get women out of the house.

This rejection of domesticity was more vividly addressed through the symbolic way in which the magazine represented the nation as a house inimical not only to women but to all Iranian citizens. The cover of every issue featured the headline, "We [Iranian women] also have Rights in this House." Writing in the first issue of *Bidari-e Ma* (in June 1944), in an article titled "Bidar shavid!" [Wake up!], contributor Maryam Firouz (founder of the women's branch of the Tudeh party) regarded Iranian society as a dark house filled with cigarette and opium fumes. Under the influence of these drugs, the people trapped in this house had become listless and lazy. They did not even bother with opening the windows to let in fresh air. The home's residents sometimes saw the beautiful outside through this curtain, but because of their fatigue, they found it almost impossible to reach the outside. The author mentioned that although men sometimes had a chance to get close to this window and possibly get some fresh air, women were always forced away from it and had no opportunity to access the world outside.[11] The house and its tasks were seen as the reason for the limitation of female life.

Domesticity was thus rejected altogether, and the magazine deemed Soviet society to be the most advanced when it came to the affairs of women and families. Quoting the Iranian Marxist and Tehran University professor Said Nafisi, who periodically paid visits to Russia to attend cultural events, the magazine portrayed Soviet women as open-minded and active in the public sphere. The magazine also reported that despite their simple look and modest outfits, Soviet women possessed a unique natural beauty that surpassed women of other nations.[12] "Hard work has allowed these women to stay fresh and in shape," he wrote. "There is hardly any fat or out-of-shape woman and most of the time you see young women around you. It seems as if the Soviet woman never gets old."[13] Nafisi seems to have been captivated by the views of Bolshevik activist Aleksandra Kollontai, who depicted the ideal Communist woman as a very simple and slim type.[14]

The more popular Iranian newspapers did not describe Soviet life in such positive terms. In a 1952 article titled "Love in the Soviet Union," the popular biweekly *Taraqqi* (Progress) reported on the difficulties of married life in Russia. A caption to a picture portraying a family jammed into a small bedroom reads, "Family life in Russia: Most families have no more than one or two bedrooms."[15] While acknowledging that love and family life were different before Stalinist times, the newspaper still found these domestic issues in the early days of the Soviet Union to be problematic. Featuring passages from Kollontai, the article refers to the time of Lenin, when free love, antimarriage, and antimonogamist thoughts were advocated by some.[16] As a result of these ideas, the Soviets were not only endangering needed population increase but also causing high rates of abortion and single-motherhood.[17] Such criticisms of the USSR had increasingly occupied the pages of the popular press since the late 1940s and were not unfounded.

The Azerbaijan Crisis of 1946, when the Soviets threatened to overstay their wartime occupation of parts of Iran, became one of the major means that shifted the United States to a Cold War mind-set.[18] The American struggle to keep Iran from communism led to the 1953 CIA and MI-6 sponsorship of the coup against Prime Minister Mosaddeq. This marked the beginning of heavy U.S. support for the Pahlavi monarchy.[19] In its effort to prevent Iran from falling into Soviet hands, the American government did not restrict itself to "political" means alone. In fact, the United States hoped that a "quiet diplomacy," instead of war and violence, would produce the desired results. "You should not start to fight if you cannot win; sometimes just to be right is enough."[20] This statement came from a short American film made soon after the Azerbaijan Crisis. The documentary opens with a speech by U.S. president Harry Truman about Iran and goes on to celebrate America's success in the Azerbaijan conflict, saving "a small nation" from becoming Communist. Interestingly, Iran was personified in this film as a bride at a village wedding. The ceremony is upset by the approach of Russian soldiers but as soon as help from the United States arrives and the Soviets are driven away, the ceremony takes place and the whole village comes to life. Spring replaces the dark winter, and nature's beauty blossoms.

However, by 1951 economic and political relations between Iran and the Soviet Union were already reestablished, and a demarcation agreement was signed in Tehran by a Soviet-Iranian joint commission. This Soviet-Iranian rapport prompted Associate Justice William O. Douglas of the U.S. Supreme Court to assert that "we [the United States] will write their history instead of letting Soviet Russia do it."[21] American foreign-policy makers became determined to furnish Iran with ideas, commodities, and technologies in an effort to integrate the underdeveloped country into the global capitalist economy. In this sense, the agenda of Truman's Point IV Program of economic aid to Iran shared much in common with the broader post–World War II discourse of international development, which sought improvement in such sectors as health care, education, agriculture, housing, and urban planning.

Model Homes: Reforming Domestic Skills

In addition to building dams and roads, improving rural life, and eradicating numerous contagious diseases, the Point IV Program for Iran established a home economics department supervised by the U.S. Department of Education.[22] The affairs of women, along with their families and homes, were a focus of American intervention in Iran. Part of the program looked to improve the Iranian woman's domestic situation.[23] Helping young women to create a less labor-intensive way of life and to develop "good taste" in decorating and furnishing their homes was seen as a pathway leading eventually to an improved economy.[24] Inevitably this approach indirectly stimulated a desire for Western commodities.

Despite earlier efforts, systematic and nationwide transformation of Iranian home life had to wait until after World War II, when the financial and technical assistance provided by the Point IV Program reached Iran. Changes brought about by the program were not in and of themselves unique, as hygiene and domestic improvements had been a focus of Iranian reformers and missionaries to the country since the second half of the nineteenth century. The novelty lay in that these changes indirectly reoriented the Iranian economy toward mass-market consumption even though the project's emphasis was placed on supplying women with new skills and know-how in the domestic sphere. Bernice W. King, the attaché to the U.S. Department of Education and head of its Home Economics Department in Iran, conducted extensive research in Iran.[25] According to her, the introduction of Western domestic furnishings and Western models of living "gave a real opportunity . . . to raise the level of living for the country as a whole."[26] For home economics specialists, developing an appreciation for discipline and order in bodily habits and effecting changes in Iranian home life were crucial. The 1959 Moscow "Kitchen Debate" between the USSR premier Nikita Khrushchev and the U.S. president Richard Nixon demonstrated that Cold War animosities functioned on wildly diverse levels and featured not just missiles and spheres of interest but also automobiles, washing machines, and toaster ovens.

The Point IV Program's Division of Education and Training began its work by setting up a unit for home economics in the capital.[27] Later similar units were established in other cities.[28] The programs were designed for girls of high-school age and took place in model houses built for the purpose, wherein the students were to spend the hours allotted to homemaking and then return to their high schools for the remainder of their classes. Point IV specialists planned to help these young Iranian women refine their domestic skills; improve the quality of their food and cooking methods; consider their family's health and hygiene; and develop "good taste" in decorating and furnishing their homes, through which process they would be able to create more labor-saving kitchens and living rooms on their own. The desired result was illustrated in the actual arrangements of the model houses and were intended to serve as preliminary blueprints for future Iranian homes. The models' design ran from landscaping at street front to color combinations for each room—including furnishings, walls, floors, and ceilings—as well as the china, wood, silver, and glassware to be used. Each of the model houses was furnished with upholstered sofas, coffee tables, armchairs, and such. Rooms with specific uses, such as the dining room, were configured according to American ideas based on a small nuclear family. However, modes of familial interaction and privacy in the model homes differed from those prevalent in the usual Iranian courtyard house lived in by an extended family (figure 6.1).

In most Iranian cities the traditional plan was an open rectangular courtyard with rooms on two or four sides. These rooms often housed members of an extended family in single-family units. During the day each single-family unit ate in the same room where at nighttime the family would spread its cushions and blankets for sleeping. Such quintessential Western spaces as the dining room and living room were not immediately identifiable in the traditional Iranian house, which was more of an amorphous communal unit wherein multiple functions often took place in a single room. The courtyard house evolved from the geographic, topographic, and climatic conditions of various regions in Iran, and the overall arrangement of the interior of such a house was based on kin relations; although it was not just the structure of the family that determined the specific architectural layout. In the traditional house some herbs and vegetables were grown in the courtyard, and much of the comestible meat and dairy products came from animals raised on the premises. Many of these homes included the addition of an isolated courtyard (narinjistan). Its small scale and four thick walls retained the warmer daytime air and thus made possible the growing of citrus fruits that would otherwise be impossible given the cold desert winters of arid areas. The traditional house was a self-contained entity. The introduction of different recipes and new rituals in meal preparation and in dining required revised spatial arrangements. The availability of new products to fill these dif-

Figure 6.1. An example of suggested interior designs for the living room at Shiraz Division. *Source*: The Album of the Home Economics Department, Division of Education and Training, U.S. Department of Education, 1954, n.p. By permission from the Library of Congress. Photo courtesy of the U.S. Department of Education.

ferent spaces transformed the holding's previous economic sufficiency into a fledgling unit of consumer spending.

In the Point IV curriculum, besides food preparation, spatial arrangement, and the choice of furniture, there was also the subject of body position to be achieved through the "table service and etiquette" portion of the program. The disciplined female figures stand out in the photographs taken by staff members of the Point IV Division of Education and Training.[29] The schooling was meant to change both the thinking of the Iranian housewife and her actual positioning and movements within the home through the formation of "rational habits" in place of the "mindless routines," in the American educational reformer John Dewey's sense of the expression.[30] To avoid the inefficient pitfalls of traditional housework in Iran, such as sweeping the floor with a short broom or cooking while squatting on the floor (figure 6.2), it was deemed necessary to follow Dewey's principle of developing critical self-awareness so "that habits be formed which are more intelligent, more sensitively percipient, more informed with foresight, more aware of what they are about, more direct and sincere."[31] Although it is hard to trace the actual ways in which Point IV specialists adapted educational principles advocated by Dewey, drawing a connection between U.S. educational policies abroad and contemporaneous pedagogical themes espoused by important American didacts does not seem farfetched. In fact, the desire to inculcate "rational habits" in a traditional society represents a microcosm of the Point IV Program's larger agenda: "Nations, like men, must learn to crawl before they can walk."[32]

Training included efforts to make Iranian women rethink their "place" within the home, in a quite literal sense (figure 6.3). Every step of women's activities within the kitchen was recorded. Mopping the floor or cleaning the

Figure 6.2. An Iranian woman cooking at a traditional stove while in a seated position. *Source*: The Album of the Home Economics Department, Division of Education and Training, U.S. Department of Education, 1954, n.p. By permission from the Library of Congress. Photo courtesy of the U.S. Department of Education.

Figure 6.3. Students in the kitchen in a Tehran school. *Source*: The Album of the Home Economics Department, Division of Education and Training, U.S. Department of Education, 1954, n.p. By permission from the Library of Congress. Photo courtesy of the U.S. Department of Education.

windows (activities that undoubtedly existed before) took on new meanings as performed by women dressed in Western attire (figures 6.4 and 6.5). In fact, what in many cases may have been "mindless routine" suddenly became a "rational habit" when performed within the confines of the model house. The whole program was bound to new environments, garments, furniture, and appliances.[33] Without encountering this new economy, Iranian women could hardly become modernized. The model and its contents became a new "habitus" (in French anthropologist Pierre Bourdieu's sense of the term). Although at first glance the program seems geared toward women, the rhetoric of masculinity and femininity worked powerfully to reconstruct the identity of both sexes. Certainly, changes in cooking, hygiene, and other domestic activities that were taught at school meant that a new female desire was being created for Western products to use in advanced kitchens and houses. These innovations also tended to bring about a new male desire concerning both the house and the housewife. Not long after the program began, some Iranian men remarked that they "would not marry any girl who had not received some of the new training in the Home Economics."[34]

Morphing Homes: Household Consumption Patterns in Transition

For obvious reasons the Point IV Program kept its rhetoric far from questions of market transformation and preferred instead to emphasize the more innocuous terms of "official home life" and "healthier life-styles." Nonetheless, these boilerplates occasionally revealed their hand most transparently. Something as simple as readymade ice cubes helped to create a market for ice storage devices and other related facilities for the mass production of ice for household consumption. Ice cubes were first introduced to a large majority of Iranians by the Point IV specialists in the early 1950s, ostensibly for health purposes. Until that time people in rural areas and smaller cities used to collect the supposedly unhealthy natural ice at the bases of mountains. When Point IV specialists had a hard time convincing people not to use this naturally occurring and hence free ice, as in Isfahan, they resorted to making the easily accessible free sources undesirable by contaminating them with colored liquids.[35]

Not long after this occasion, the American York Corporation introduced facilities for manufacturing readymade ice cubes and ice storage devices.[36] Imported home appliances found a growing number of consumers as American companies (more than any other Western companies)—such as General Electric, Carrier Corporation, Hoover Company, McGraw Edison, Electric Bond and Share Company (EBASCO), Coleman, International Harvester, Emerson Electric, and CertainTeed—introduced their building materials, cooler chests, washing machines, vacuum cleaners, ovens, dishwashers, and shiny utensils into

Figures 6.4 and 6.5.
Students learn how
to clean the house
at a school in Shiraz.
Source: The Album
of the Home Eco-
nomics Department,
Division of Educa-
tion and Training,
U.S. Department
of Education, 1954,
n.p. By permission
from the Library of
Congress. Photo
courtesy of the
U.S. Department of
Education.

Iranian kitchens. By the final months of the Pahlavi regime (in late 1978), the Public Service Company of Iran (Shirkat-i sirvis-i hamigani Iran), which distributed appliances from companies ranging from American Philco, Hoover, and General Electric to the British Indesit, had established itself in twenty-two cities.[37]

The distributor encouraged its regular customers to buy even more appliances by launching a lottery competition whose winner would receive a round-trip ticket to England, along with ten days' accommodation at a quality London hotel.[38] Over the next couple of decades, American exports to Iran expanded so that by the second half of the 1970s, the Iranian market was saturated with them—from the fast food of Kentucky Fried Chicken to Westinghouse refrigerators. In 1970 the value of U.S. exports to Iran amounted to $326 million, while from 1970 to 1973 this figure increased significantly and then more than doubled over the next five years.[39] The demand for these commodities, as the anthropologist Arjun Appadurai has put it in another context, eventually became a "socially regulated and generated impulse, not an artifact of individual whims or needs."[40]

In 1966 this consumerist approach expanded to envisioning the form of future residential neighborhoods in the capital. Victor Gruen, an Austrian-born commercial architect known for introducing gigantic malls into American cities (thus earning him the moniker "the architect of the American dream"), proposed a new design for Tehran, a certain indication that consumerism in the Iranian capital had gained a firm foothold.[41] A utopian project, Gruen's comprehensive or master plan for Tehran surely enough included residential complexes that were developed around shopping malls (figure 6.6).[42] These neighborhoods were also suitable for "an automobile society" in a capital that, in Gruen's mind, was a rapidly growing business and holiday center in the region.[43] The diagrams and illustrations of his master plan presented an ideal life realized through the city's revamped form. Unlike earlier initiatives, Gruen's design for Tehran was neither geometricized nor smothered in strategies for order and control. The plan was programmed to accommodate commercial markets and to facilitate the movement of automobiles.[44]

By the end of Muhammad Reza Shah Pahlavi's regime in 1979, Gruen's plan was only partially realized; but as early as 1950, many Iranians (including those in smaller cities) had already begun to remodel their homes based on recently available commodities and technologies. The introduction of new appliances, furniture, and building materials resulted not only in the construction of modern neighborhoods and houses but also in the refurbishment of already existing traditional domestic structures. It is important to grasp the manner in which Iranian notions regarding domesticity were evolving, rather than understanding home modernization as merely a top-down imposition dictated by Cold War politics. The discourse targeting a more hygienic environment successfully persuaded Iranians to change their homes. Large glass windows allowed natural light into rooms, replacing dark-colored windows. Cement tiles or mosaics (*muzaik*) paved the muddy courtyards. The introduction of Western appliances altered the physical appearance of the house even further.

The Iranian contemporary architect Ali Saremi has traced this transformation in a single courtyard family house built in 1921 in the northwestern city of Zanjan.[45] Saremi described what he considered to be five distinct stages that occurred over the course of the decade from 1950 to 1960. During this time new building materials and appliances either transformed the rooms serving traditional functions into new spaces with novel purposes, or eliminated par-

Figure 6.6. A sketch of an upper-class neighborhood (with the shopping mall at the center) from the proposed master plan for Tehran. *Source*: Consultancy report produced by Victor Gruen and Abdol Aziz Farman Farmaian of Tehran, 1966, n.p. Courtesy of the archives of Iran's Organization of Finances and Planning (Sazman-i barnameh va budjeh).

ticular spaces altogether. First, iron beams replaced the old wooden beams that had earlier been topped with a gabled metal roof (the addition of the gabled roof itself was a Western phenomenon and had become popular at the beginning of the twentieth century). Second, the use of gas for cooking as well as heating made possible the removal of the old masonry charcoal-burning oven in the kitchen and allowed more space for the new electric refrigerator. Third, the addition of a washing machine, vacuum cleaner, and other time-saving appliances eliminated the need for a maid; thus the vacated maid's room became another bedroom.

The fourth step involved the plumbing. Formerly the toilet was in a corner of the home's courtyard, and the neighborhood's public baths obviated any need for a shower in the home. New plumbing helped bring both the toilet and a shower inside the precincts of the house. *Huzkhanih*, the traditional summer room with its small pool, was turned into a simple shower area.[46] In eastern cities this room was also a ventilation wind tower or wind catcher.[47] Plumbing also left no use for the pool in the middle of the courtyard. The pool was therefore filled and covered with mosaic, allowing more clear space within the yard for parking an automobile. Finally, bringing the car into the yard also required the removal of little flower boxes, the widening of the traditional vestibule, and the replacement of the small wooden double entry doorway (with its two different-sounding door knockers to indicate the visitor's gender) by a large metal gate.

The process of transforming a house through the introduction of Western ideas and products shows the extent to which post–World War II changes in home life were impacted by Iranians' desires regarding the modernization of their homes (not counting these changes as a mere consequence of direct U.S. initiatives and other Western interventions). One also finds a surfeit of modern-izing—even Westernizing—tropes throughout the popular media of the period. For instance, an article titled "How Do You Sit?" from a 1946 issue of *Taraqqi* (Progress) emphasized that one demonstrates a certain level of sophistication by using a chair, a piece of furniture that did not exist in traditional homes. The author claims that the people featured in the article are genuine Americans and encourages his readers to model their sitting habits after the gentlemen and ladies of New York City.[48] One picture shows an Iranian man with his legs crossed on the desk in front of him, with a caption indicating that the "newly Americanized Iranian youth" who follows this manner of sitting does not re-alize that well-cultivated New Yorkers would never position themselves like this.[49] Such visually assisted advice gave rise to specific habits in using imported furniture. The modernizing vision did not pertain to the mere acquisition of Western furniture and appliances but also to their use, replete with social fears about potential faux pas in the encounter with a new material environment. After World War II, Iranians sought to keep up both with Western consumers and with compatriots who had earlier acquired foreign products.

Consider an ad from a 1950 issue of the popular magazine *Tehran musavvar* (Illustrated Tehran) (figure 6.7). A woman stands by a wide-open Electrolux refrigerator filled with food, as she says in Farsi: "My Electrolux refrigerator, which works with both electricity and gas, has made my friends envious."[50] This ad becomes more interesting when seen against some of the postwar American literature on the subject of economic development. In his 1953 book *Problems of Capital Formation in Underdeveloped Countries*, the Estonian Ameri-can economist Ragnar Nurkse wrote that "in developing countries, the growing awareness of advanced living standards does not depend on the idea of 'keep-ing up with the Joneses.'"[51] He added: "The propensity to spend . . . depends on . . . demonstration leading to imitation. Knowledge of or contact with new consumption patterns opens one's eyes to previously unrecognized possibili-ties. It widens the horizon of imagination and desires. It is not just the matter of social snobbishness."[52] However, Nurkse's pronouncement falls somewhat short in the Iranian case.

Traditional Iran was certainly not devoid of "Joneses"-type expressions. The well-known saying "chishm u ham chishmi" (being concerned about one's appearance and status after seeing those of others) could well be an equivalent of "keeping up with the Joneses." Nonetheless, Nurkse's account helps us understand how, at least in part, the desire for consumption of foreign goods in

Figure 6.7. The caption reads: "My Electrolux refrigerator which works with both electricity and gas has made my friends envious." *Source: Tehran musavvar* 385 (Day 1329/December 1950), n.p. Image courtesy of Princeton University Libraries.

Iran explicitly resorted to such socializing devices. The Electrolux refrigerator ad exemplifies this production of desire; it shows how both the idea of "keeping up with the Joneses" and the imitation of foreign modes of living epitomized the Iranians' desire to be modern. The push for change within the domestic milieu was thus driven by two coterminous "envies": by Iranians' standing in relation to their neighbors and by Iran's position relative to the more technologically advanced Western countries.[53] This petit-bourgeois tendency has been well described by the French anthropologist Pierre Bourdieu. "In order to survive in the world of their aspirations," he wrote, "they are condemned to 'live beyond their means' and to be constantly attentive and sensitive, hypersensitive, to the slightest signs of the reception given to their self representation."[54] Iranian advertising in the mid-twentieth century seems to suggest that Iranians were meant to follow the path of the West and, like the European petit bourgeois, to "live beyond their means."

Records from this period certainly show us that Iranian homelife had conformed to what Nurkse had already written in the early 1950s: that even though there may have been "people of ascetic bent who have no use for American gadgets, most people seem to like them. . . . The goods that form part of American consumption patterns are 'superior.'"[55] The Point IV Program and other American- and Western-initiated efforts thus deeply impacted indigenous notions regarding the Iranian home and the practices within it in both conceptual and real senses. The results may be found in the most unlikely places, including among the pages of Ayatollah Khomeini's illustrated *Risaleh-i Novin*. The *Risaleh* or *Tawzih al-Masai'l* is a handbook of behavior governing homelife, among other issues. It was first written down in the seventeenth century by the *mujtahids,* or highest-ranking authorities of Shiite Islam.[56] It has been revised several times during the twentieth century to correspond to Iranians' changing life styles.[57] Khomeini's illustrated *Risaleh-i Novin* is the most modernized version of these handbooks, both in its content and form.

Ayatollah Abdol Karim Biazar Shirazi (hereafter Shirazi) had always intended to bridge the gap between Western knowledge and traditional Shiite Islam. Illustrations helped Shirazi to fill this gap in a way that was not too removed from his intended audience's experience. In the late 1970s Shirazi—a graduate of Montreal's McGill University in the religious studies department who had also spent some time in the United Kingdom—translated, edited, and designed Khomeini's *The New Risaleh*, previously available only in Arabic, titled *Tahrir al-Valisilah*, and first published in 1947.[58] The newer version, in progress for some years, was eventually released at the dawn of the revolution (1980) in four volumes, including two on personal and family matters. The Americans who attempted to reform the Iranian home in the 1950s had come from a generation that used charts and graphs, and these now rather dated materials seem to have inspired Shirazi's editorial work. He claims that the *New Risaleh* became a best-seller and influenced the youth in exactly the same way that colorful magazines of the Shah's period had captivated them. It was able to compete with "dozens of attractive alternatives such as Marxism, and Western pop culture."[59]

The commentaries in the *New Risaleh* define the modern home and practices within it from a religious perspective that sought to recalibrate the determination of the sacred and the profane, setting it within the context of modern products, situations, and activities. Khomeini's tract displays a continuous conflation of ritual purity, as required in the performance of religious obligations, with the concept of cultural purity. An important theme in the book is the dichotomy of *taharat* and *nijasat* (purity versus filth), which is seen to regulate bodily functions and habits. Shiite regulations governing water (*ahkam-i ab*) come to determine the ways in which a believer should use foreign appliances. According to *The New Risaleh*, the purity of clothes washed in the washing machine should be determined by the amount and source of water used in the appliance. Detergents have no place in this process of cleansing.[60] Likewise, the use of foreign toilets is legitimate only if one brings a bottle of water to use for washing after visiting the toilets (figure 6.8).

In attempting to bring back Iranians' everyday life to be more in line with orthodox tenets, the diagrams and charts of the *New Risaleh* were also an effort toward standardization and rationalization of religious information (figure 6.9). In this sense they embodied the Western orderliness and discipline that had long been encouraged by the Pahlavi state. The *New Risaleh* also helped translate the abstruse language of the Shiite religious texts into a popular form. In doing so, Khomeini's *New Risaleh* (albeit perhaps largely through the editorial and graphic contributions of Shirazi) sought to modify Shiite domestic practices within the context of the modernized home. Just as religious ideas in the *New Risaleh* were adapted to a modern context, the reality of everyday life in Iran from the early 1950s to the late 1970s shows that there was neither total conformity to Western life styles and commodities nor a steadfast embrace of "traditional values."

This strategy of combining foreign and traditional forms and practices may be found in both middle-class and upper-class homes. The Khodadad residence in northern Tehran is a case in point. Hossein Khodadad was an affluent merchant. In the mid-1970s, with the help of a modern Iranian architect and a local craftsman, he designed a house that used a hybrid mixture of traditional Iranian and Western architecture. The exterior seems to have been mainly inspired by older European styles. Triglyphs and metopes derived from ancient Greek temples appear on an architrave band that adorns the edge of the roof. Corinthian capitals decorate the columns, and rococo stucco reliefs replete with convoluted scrolls, tendrils, and other pliant forms shape the window frames. The windows them-

قلیل به روی آن در صورتیکه در مرتبه اول آب از آن خارج گردد پاک می‌شود و باید بعد از هر دفعه با فشار آب آن خارج شود.

در مورد پیشاب کودک شیرخوار یک بار کافی است.

توالتهای خارجی

کسانی که در کشورهای خارجی اقامت دارند و یا به خارج سفر می‌کنند و مجبورند در راه، در هواپیما و در شهرهای اروپایی از توالتهای فرنگی استفاده کنند. تکلیفشان چیست ؟

در چنین توالتها می‌توان از بیده، یا شلنگ یا ظرف لوله‌داری مانند ظرفی که برای آب دادن گلدان مصرف می‌شود، استفاده کرد و خود را با آب شست و یا با کاغذ توالت خود را پاک کرد همچنانکه می‌توان حتی با سنگ، کلوخ، پارچه پاک خود را تمیز کرد. و میزان برطرف شدن آلودگی و پاک شدن است و همانطورکه در رساله تحریر الوسیله آمده:

Figure 6.8. A page from Khomeini's *Tawzih al-Masai'l*, showing how to use washing machines and foreign toilets. *Source: The New Risaleh,* volume 1, *Worship and the Development of Self,* edited by Abdol Karim Biazar Shirazi (Tehran: Moassisey-i Anjām Kitāb, c. 1980), 54. Courtesy of Abdol Karim Biazar Shirazi.

selves are screened by star-patterned openwork wood frames holding panels of dark-colored glass, as used in traditional Iranian courtyard homes to minimize both the intense natural light and direct visual access from outside.

The same mixed approach may be seen in the first-floor interior, where a

traditional music room, used for the reception of occasional visitors, is embel-
lished with rococo stucco reliefs and furnished with Western-style furniture.
This music chamber is a replica of that in the early seventeenth-century Ali-
Qapu palace in Safavid dynasty Isfahan (1502–1736). Khodadad's music room
exemplifies a plan used in many Iranian middle- and upper-class interiors:
therein, a single traditional room strongly contrasts with the rest of the more
modern house. Thus, although the overall plan and form of the interiors of
many homes were borrowed from the West (including the furniture in them),
an "Iranian room" helped preserve the grand heritage of both pre-Islamic and
"Islamicate" Iran. This room was typically furnished with traditional cushions
and carpets and was frequently occupied by male guests, who were often en-
tertained with *hookah* (water pipe) and traditional music. By restricting their
heritage to a single room, Iranian householders simultaneously celebrated and
marginalized their traditional customs. Khodadad's house limits the custom of
floor-sitting to its so-called Iranian room.

The Khodadad residence contains another room that was popular among
the upper class and perhaps unintentionally mixed modern and traditional thinking. The study-office of the man of the house is itself a Western concept, but
it also helped to perpetuate the importance of the male within the domestic
setting. While modern homes, unlike the traditional courtyard house, certainly
allowed for more flexible intermingling between men and women, they also
reinforced the male's dominant family role by dedicating certain spaces to him
(and his male companions), although this arrangement was often contested and
then negotiated depending on the family's dynamic (figures 6.9 and 6.10).

Domesticity: The Discourse of the Deprived

By the 1970s the class status of an individual was not so much defined by
the ways in which he or she used a chair, as in the 1946 issue of *Taraqqi* (Progress), but was determined primarily by whether one actually owned a chair. In
the capital, owning better homes, Western-style furniture, and advanced commodities identified residents of *shomal-i shahr* (north of the city), while living
in traditional homes or in shanties defined those of *jonub-i shahr* (south of the
city). Within a short time period a large number of poor Iranians encountered,
but were at a remove from, the abundance of Western-style material goods.
They had no access to what the cultural historian Jordan Sand has described
within the context of domesticity in modern Japan as a "culture of abundant
knowledge."[61] According to Sand, the highly literate population of late-twentieth-
century Japan could connect with Western appliances and furnishings (without
necessarily possessing them) through such publications as women's magazines
and architectural journals. Most illiterate lower-class Iranians and the really

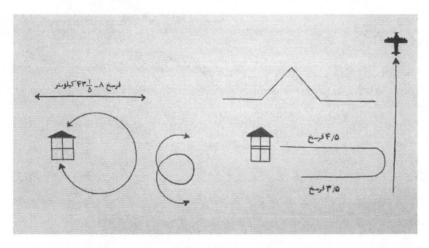

Figure 6.9. Diagrams showing rules of prayer while away from one's home. *Source: The New Risaleh,* volume 2, *Economic Issues,* edited by Abdol Karim Biazar Shirazi (Tehran: Moassisey-i Anjam Kitab, 1980), 101. Courtesy of Abdol Karim Biazar Shirazi.

Figure 6.10. Image of the interior of the Khodadad's house. The interior of the music room is a replica of the music chamber of the seventeenth-century Ali-Qapu Palace. Photograph by Pamela Karimi.

poor, however, merely witnessed the passing flow of Western commodities without being able to discern anything about the culture associated with them. Even those who found some connection confronted great difficulties in actually acquiring and possessing these Western goods.

Under the Skin of the Night (1974), a movie by Iranian filmmaker Freydoon Golé, vividly demonstrates this phenomenon. An underprivileged young Iranian man who sells tickets at a Tehran movie theater meets a young American tourist who is to leave Iran that evening. The man offers to accompany her throughout her final day in the city, and by the late afternoon the two wish to make love. As a fresh migrant to the city, however, he spends his nights in public shelters and so has no place to take her. In their wanderings, they eventually stop by a furniture shop, where they stare at a king-size bed behind the display window. The camera captures the imagination of the man as he envisions the American girl lying naked on the bed with himself at her side shortly thereafter. A group of street men watch them through the window.

By the time of the film's release, the new master bedroom for married couples—as opposed to the common sleeping room of the traditional extended family—had altered the most intimate exchanges between men and women. Sexual relations among Iranian couples had become more private and romantic. The film turned the notion of the sheltering bedroom into a stage set for public voyeurism. The scene encapsulates what the German sociologist Georg Simmel once alluded to in his 1907 work *Philosophy of Money*. It is the remoteness of the object of desire that gives it greater attraction.[62] By the end of the movie the two main characters have left each other without having had a chance for fulfillment. For the underprivileged Iranian, the attractive American female (and also, perhaps, other foreign objects of fantasy, such as the fancy furniture in the shop) becomes iconic of what is present and within reach but ultimately inaccessible.[63] *Under the Skin of the Night* perfectly expresses the frustration of a disadvantaged class that has been torn from the security of traditional life but also denied the riches of a modernized society.

Indeed, this crisis of cultural identity with its feelings of anomie was not confined to the urban poor. Iranian intellectuals had many reasons to oppose the society that represented the Shah's regime. They not only thought that Iranian families were ill at ease with the imported modern life but insisted that these families were completely alienated from it. Iranian writer and social critic Jalal Al-i Ahmad addressed these concerns in his seminal book of 1962, *Occidentosis: A Plague from the West.*[64] "We are all like strangers to ourselves," he wrote, "in our food and dress, our homes, our manners . . . and, most dangerous, our culture."[65] Al-i Ahmad developed a stinging critique of Western technology. He argued that the decline of traditional Iranian industries was the beginning of Western "economic and existential victories over the East." A decade after his death, Al-i Ahmad's message became part of the ideology of the 1979 Iranian Revolution, which emphasized nationalization of industry and economic self-sufficiency.

The revolutionary elite criticized Western imports in their evaluation of the moral character of household items and commercial goods, drawing a sharp distinction between local and foreign-made goods. Antinomies such as *halal-haram* and *taharat-nijasat*—terms once applied mainly to the human body and its environment—now were more strongly applied to imported commodities. Joint Iranian-Western enterprise (so-called montage) was considered *haram*, as described in early postrevolutionary books such as Hasan Tavaniyanfard's *Karkhanejat-i montage: Iqtisad-i shirk* (Montage factories: The sinful economy). Thus it is no surprise that later editions of Khomeini's *New Risaleh* actually excluded any and all images of Western household furniture. Architectural journals, such as *Maskan va inqilab* (Housing and the revolution), likewise rejected Western norms and encouraged pious homelife. The media showcased the "humble" household of Ayatollah Khomeini. *Kukh-neshini* (residing in shanties) stood in stark contrast to *kakh-neshini* (residing in palaces).[66] In accord with this, the revolutionary elite saw the so-called montage culture of the Shah's era as *mobtazal,* a term implying that which is corrupted, in poor taste, and slapped together.

The ideas concerning domesticity and daily life explored in this chapter show the interplay between Western initiatives and the active contributions of Iranians in refashioning or rebuffing these influences to fit their needs. Whether attempting the modification of Shiite domestic practices to be in step with modernization or criticizing Western ideas wholesale, the different voices analyzed have something in common. Rather than regarding modernization as the necessary adoption of Western institutions and norms, the protagonists introduced in this chapter were searching for alternative means by which to transform their traditional society. Most studies of Islamic domesticity give the impression that it was predominantly Westerners who shaped modern trends within the Iranian home. This chapter emphasizes the role of indigenous figures whose ideas and work should not be seen merely as a reactionary rejection of Western influence or a slavish acceptance of it but rather as a key factor in the creation of a non-Western modernity.

Notes

1. Shaul Bakhash, *Iran: Monarchy, Bureaucracy, and Reform under the Qajars: 1858–1896* (London: I. B. Tauris, 1991), 305–73.

2. Abbas Amanat, "Qajar Iran: A Historical Overview," in *Royal Persian Paintings: The Qajar Epoch 1785–1925,* edited by Layla Diba and Maryam Ekhtiar (London: I. B. Tauris, 1999), 28.

3. Schayegh, "Sport, Health, and the Iranian Middle Class in the 1920s and the 1930s," *Iranian Studies* 35, no. 4 (Fall 2002): 341–69; the information appears on page 342.

4. Darius M. Rejali, *Torture and Modernity: Self, State, and Society in Modern Iran* (Boul-

der: University of Colorado Press, 1994), 52; cited in Schayegh, "Sport, Health, and the Iranian Middle Class in the 1920s and the 1930s," 341–69.

5. Schayegh, "Sport, Health, and the Iranian Middle Class in the 1920s and the 1930s," 343.

6. This strategy entailed improvements, even more rigorously, in medical treatment, bodily hygiene, and public health.

7. The company that in 1909 built most of Abadan was the Anglo-Persian Oil Company (APOC), which changed its name to the Anglo-Iranian Oil Company (AIOC) in 1935. For more information about architectural undertakings in Abadan, see Mark Crinson, *Modern Architecture and the End of Empire* (London: Ashgate 2003), 53.

8. Mina Marefat, "The Protagonists Who Shaped Modern Tehran," in *Téhéran, Capitale Bicentenaire,* edited by Ch. Adle and B. Hourcade (Paris: Institut français de recherche en Iran, 1992), 102–3. Marefat refers to several sources regarding such contributions, among which are *Gozareshat* (Reports) 1 (1936): 21; "Italia Illustrata, numero speciale della Rivista Illustrata del Popolo d'Italia," special issue of *Italia illustrata* (1937); *Journal de Teheran* (Journal of Tehran) (March 1946), as well as multiple articles from the 1930s and 1940s in Iranian newspapers, such as *Ettela'at* (Information) and *Iran-i Emruz* (Iran today).

9. The publication was that of the Association of Women of the Tudeh Party. The magazine was edited by Zahra Eskandari-Bayat. Apart from the West and capitalism, *Bidari-e Ma* criticized the Pahlavi regime. The Tudeh Association of Women became a member of the International Democratic Foundation of Women in 1947 and was represented in international conferences in Budapest (1948) and Beijing (1949). The association was banned in 1949, and two years later it was replaced with the Democratic Association of Women. See Parvin Paidar, *Women and the Political Process in Twentieth Century Iran* (Cambridge: Cambridge University Press, 1995), 124–25.

10. Farah Laqa Alavi, "Home and Family and Its Limits in Modern Age," *Bidari-e Ma* 3, no. 1 (Mihr 1323/October 1944): 13. In addition, the magazine criticized the harem in traditional Iranian dwellings and categorized any socioreligious ideas connected to this all-female space as superstitious; see Azam Sorush, "Societal Superstitions," in "Fundamental Reforms in Womens' Lives)," *Bidari-e Ma* 2, no. 1 (Murdad 1323/August 1944): 8–10; note appears on page 10.

11. Maryam Firouz, "Wake Up!" *Bidari-e Ma* 1, no. 1 (Tir 1323/June 1944): 9–13.

12. "Interview with Said Nafisi," *Bidari-e Ma* 3, no. 2 (Shahrivar 1324/September 1945): 17–21.

13. "Interview with Said Nafisi," 21.

14. For further information about Aleksandra Kollontai's depiction of the ideal Soviet female body, see, for example, Eric Naiman, *Sex in Public: The Incarnation of Early Soviet Ideology* (Princeton: Princeton University Press, 1997), 208–49. It is noteworthy that in the 1920s, fashion designer Liubov Popova created outfits that intentionally obliterated the female body's curves; see Christina Kiaer, *Imagine No Possessions: The Socialist Objects of Russian Constructivism* (Cambridge: MIT Press, 2005), 132.

15. Under the Soviets the vast majority of the urban population lived under cramped conditions. In 1926 per capita living space in Moscow was 5.7 square meters. In 1956 the figure had been reduced to 4.8 square meters. This decrease was generally duplicated throughout the country and was sometimes even more dramatic. See James Bater, *The Soviet City: Ideal and Reality* (London: Arnold, 1980), 100; cited on 477 of Robert Porter,

"The City in Russian Literature: Images Past and Present," *Modern Language Review* 94, no. 2 (April 1999): 476–85.

16. Two other major advocates were philosophers Vladimir Solov'ev (1853–1900) and Nikolai Berdiaev (1874–1948), for whom birth represented the "bad infinity of physical reproduction." It was a reminder of the change of generations and of the seeming inevitability of human decay. See Naiman, *Sex in Public*, 28–31.

17. "In Russia Marriage Is Very Easy but Divorce Is Extremely Difficult," *Taraqqi* 9, no. 37/473 (Bahman 1331/February 1952): 6, 22.

18. This mention of Azerbaijan refers to a Turkish province in northwestern Iran and not what was then a Soviet province or what is now the independent country of Azerbaijan. The crisis in 1946 stemmed from a Soviet refusal to relinquish Iranian territories that had been occupied by the Red Army since 1942.

19. Following World War II, oil and military deals as well as America's technical assistance strengthened the contacts between Iranians and Americans. By 1979 some thirty thousand Americans were living in Iran.

20. Motion Picture Archives, MP 72-65, reel 1, Harry S. Truman Library and Museum, Independence, Missouri.

21. In his 1950 speech at the University of Tehran, Douglas said that Iran needed a reform program of "perhaps 10% communism, 15% capitalism, and 75% something else." See John Donovan, *U.S. and Soviet Policy in the Middle East 1945–1956* (New York: Facts on File, 1972), 97–98.

22. The Point IV Program was established to promote U.S. foreign policy and to assist with the development of certain economically underdeveloped countries. The program's section in Iran was meant to improve Iranian industry, communication, transportation, general services, housing, and labor efficiency. The process was carried out through joint operations involving American officials and various Iranian ministries, agencies, and institutions. See *Act of July 1, 1951–June 30, 1952 on The Point Four Program in Iran Report* (Tehran: Agriculture College of the University of Tehran, 1952).

23. It is noteworthy that of the total budget of $85,620,000 for the Point IV Program for the Near East and Africa, Asia and the Far East, as well as the so-called American Republics (Latin America), $17,306,400 was dedicated to health; $8,998,950 was intended for education; and only $1,200,600 was allocated for housing. The largest portion of the funding, $18,389,550, was set aside for agriculture and forestry. See "The Point IV Program," Foreign Relations, Rockefeller Reports, box 62, Harry S. Truman Library and Museum, Independence, Missouri.

24. Other initiatives included providing scholarships for supporting the education of young women at American colleges and universities. In addition, each year the Iranian Department of Education sent a high-school girl to attend the annual *New York Herald Tribune* Forum for High Schools. See the Archives of the Ministry of Foreign Affairs, Tehran, Iran, box 72, file 23: "Americans' Promotion of Health and Culture of Other Nations," no. 1/9 (June 5, 1953). It is important to note that the main agenda of the Point IV Program was to "help people to help themselves." As a 1949 article from the *Washington Post* reports: "Like the Marshall Plan, [the Point IV] has been a program of helping others to help themselves through cooperative effort," *Washington Post*, June 12, 1949, 3.

25. From 1952 to 1962, King served as a home economist educator in such countries as Egypt, Iran, Lebanon, and Turkey.

26. Bernice W. King, 1954, U.S. Office of Education, Home Economics, Division of Education and Training, lot 9235 (G) LC P&P, box 1 of 3, Library of Congress. The program's extensive research was conducted by King and her crew. She wrote: "The same basic needs were found everywhere. . . . After countless interviews, much digging into grass root needs, close observation of girls' schools of secondary level and homes of the destitute, the very poor, and the average and the wealthy, I was able to dream a dream and was ready to try to make that dream come true."

27. The homemaking programs in Iran were modeled after instructions that by the 1950s had existed in the United States for more than half a century. American homemaking educational programs in themselves dated back to the late 1860s. According to the architectural historian Gwendolyn Wright, most home economist specialists wanted to educate a great many consumers rather than a few good women designers. Moreover, greater standardization in American houses seemed a sign of democratic equality, a presumption that greater similarity between individual dwellings would create a more homogenous community. Therefore, in the American context the concern was not just to break with the unprofessional and unhygienic environment of older houses, but rather ideologically to effect change in larger aspects of culture. Gwendolyn Wright, *Moralism and the Model Home* (Chicago: University of Chicago Press, 1980), 164–66.

28. In addition to these efforts, the Education and Training Division of Point IV offered courses in Tehran that intended exclusively to "familiarize [Iranians] somewhat with life in the United States." This program included informal talks, panel discussions, and films. Attending the program was a requirement especially for those students who were to be sent to the United States for university education. See William E. Warne's personal letter to Reza Djaffari, at that time Iran's minister of education, in the National Archives of Iran, Tehran, box 297019988, folder 014S2API, microfilm no. 121–44 (August 24, 1954). It is also noteworthy that the Cultural Branch (shu'bih farhangi) of the Point IV Program in Tehran organized regular evening gatherings that allowed the interaction of Point IV workers with Iranian officials and their families; see the National Archives of Iran, Tehran, box 290003684, folder 888V5ABI, microfilm no. 8–98 (1952/1331). Other cultural activities took place at various events organized by the Iranian-American Society (Anjuman-i Iran va Amrika).

29. In all likelihood these photographs were taken to be archived at the U.S. Department of Education. There is no evidence of the reproduction of these photographs in any Iranian publications, whether home economics books, women's magazines, or otherwise.

30. Martin Hollis, "The Self in Action," in *John Dewey Reconsidered*, edited by R. S. Peters (London: Routledge and Kegan Paul, 1977), 56–75; the quotation appears on 61. It is noteworthy that at the end of the nineteenth century, the body began to be understood as a mechanical element of industrial productivity and an extension of the factory apparatus. "Scientific management" as promoted by Frederick Taylor, also known as Taylorism, sought to rationalize and standardize the body's motions in order to convert it into efficient labor power. See Anson Rabinach, *The Human Motor* (Berkeley: University of California Press, 1992).

31. John Dewey, *Human, Nature and Conduct*, part 2, section 4 (New York: Holt, 1922.), 128; quoted in Rabinach, *Human Motor*, 62.

32. Foreign Relations, Rockefeller Reports, box 62, Milo Perkings, "Point IV and U.S. Foreign Policy," p. 7, Harry S. Truman Library and Museum. This disciplining of the individual as well as the nation was different from the one at work in earlier colonial contexts where

there was "continuous supervision and control" and where the mechanical body was to be distinguished in political practice from the individual's mind or mentality. See Timothy Mitchell, *Colonizing Egypt* (Cambridge: Cambridge University Press, 1988), 100. The relationship between disciplining the body and creating an advanced state has been articulated by Arjun Appadurai: "The specific projects (however successful) of modern nation-state, ranging from sanitation to the census, from family planning to disease control, and from immigration control to language policy, have tied concrete bodily practices (speech, cleanliness, movement, health) to large-scale group identities, thus increasing the potential scope of embodied experiences of group affinity." See Arjun Appadurai, *Modernity at Large: Cultural Dimensions of Globalization* (Minneapolis: University of Minnesota Press, 2000), 157.

33. In *Experience and Education*, Dewey draws a connection between one's living environment and experience: "An experience is always what it is because of a transaction taking place between an individual and what, at the time, constitutes his environment. . . . The environment . . . is whatever conditions interact with personal needs, desires, purposes, and capacities to create the experience." See John Dewey, *Experience and Education* (New York: Collier Books, 1938), 43.

34. Bernice W. King, 1954, U.S. Office of Education, Home Economics, Division of Education and Training, lot 9235 (G) LC P&P, box 1 of 2, Library of Congress. King's assertion bears similarity to a commentary given by Henrietta W. Calvin, author of the 1918 American manuscript, *Home Economics Courses for Girls and Young Women*: "at no time can he [the returned World War I soldier] replace the woman who is well trained in home economics," quoted in Phyllis Palmer, *Domesticity and Dirt: Housewives and Domestic Servants in the United States, 1920–1945* (Philadelphia: Temple University Press, 1989), 89. Although Point IV specialists did not provide such intense and structured programs for Iranian men, they nonetheless offered instruction for high-school boys in home economics. This included a preliminary manuscript to be later revised, published, and taught in schools for many years to come. Long considered part of a man's homemaking duties, such building-technology subjects as patching cracks in plaster walls, repairing leaky faucets and clogged drains, designing walls and window treatments, as well as fixing electrical appliances were included in home economics courses for boys. The instructions emphasized advanced building methods. The report points out that there is no need for providing lessons on fine woodwork or other traditional crafts or decorative skills. Instead, the focus must be on such practical skills as terminating electricity-related problems. See the National Archives of Iran, Tehran, box 297014855, folder 332R5AP, microfilm no. 108–36 (1959).

35. Abbas Karbasiyan, "Tahlili bar natayij ijrai-i asl-i chahar-i Truman dar Iran" (An analysis of the consequences of Truman's Point IV Program in Iran), *Gozarigh*, no. 701 (Day 1378/January 1999), 64–72; the information appears on 70.

36. This fact was communicated in a letter written by Ezattolah Entezam, the Iranian envoy to the Iranian embassy in Washington, D.C., addressing the Iranian ministry of finance, "*ravabet bazargani-e iran va amrika* (Iran-America Commerce Relations)," box 29, folder 26/2, letter no. 3410 (1330/1951), Archives of the Ministry of Foreign Affairs, Tehran.

37. "The Grand Forum of the Representatives of Philco, Hoover, and Indesit Products," *Tehran Economist*, no. 1239 (Ordibehesht 1957/April 1978), n.p.

38. "Grand Forum of the Representatives of Philco, Hoover, and Indesit Products."

39. Feruz Ahmed, "Iran: Subimperialism in Action," *Pakistan Forum* (March–April 1973): 10–20; the information appears on 11.

40. Arjun Appadurai, "Introduction," in *The Social Life of Things: Commodities in Cultural*

Perspective, edited by Arjun Appadurai (Cambridge: Cambridge University Press, 1986), 32.

41. The architectural historian M. Jeffrey Hardwick, for example, titled his book *Mall Maker: Victor Gruen, Architect of an American Dream* (Philadelphia: University of Pennsylvania Press, 2004).

42. The term "master plan" was first posited in 1955 by Charles M. Haar, a Harvard law professor who also collaborated with architects. It is noteworthy that the Iranian translation of this term is *Tarh-i Jami'* (or "general plan"). For a detailed discussion regarding Haar's definition of "master plan," see Timothy Hyde's chapter in this edited volume. See also Charles M. Haar, "The Master Plan: An Impermanent Constitution," *Law and Contemporary Problems* 20, no. 3 (Summer 1955): 353–418.

43. *Comprehensive Plan for Tehran, First Stage—Concept Development: The Planning Concept—Volume III*, Library of Congress Victor Gruen Collection (LoCVGC), box 45, folder 14, III-B-1-7.

44. These concepts are emphasized throughout the text of Tehran's master plan project: "traffic and transportation planning, whereby new street networks are provided as needed to serve the growing city." See *Comprehensive Plan for Tehran, First Stage—Concept Development: The Planning Concept-Volume III*; LoCVGC, box 45, folder 14, III-A-1-4. Similarly, utilities and their service networks had to keep pace with economic growth: "Housing design, minimum yet satisfactory building standards suited to economic growth and provision of commercial, services, and recreational facilities" (ibid., III-A-3-2). My arguments about Gruen's master plan for Tehran are inspired by George Wagner's sharp analysis of the Fort Worth Plan. See George Wagner, "The Lair of the Bachelor," in *Architecture and Feminism*, edited by Debra Coleman, Elizabeth Danze, and Carol Henderson (Princeton: Princeton Architectural Press, 1996), 183–203; the quotation appears on 193.

45. Ali Saremi, "Iran's Unaccomplished Modernization in Architecture," *Mimar* (farvardin–Ordibihisht 1385/March–April 2005): 31–36.

46. *Huzkhanih* is a summer room located beneath the *talar* (an open archway facing the courtyard). Another summer space is the *sardab*: a large, deep basement also used as a family living area during the day's hotter hours. Although these elements are the main components of the summer area of the house, not all of them are necessarily found in all homes. See Masoud Kheirabadi, *Iranian Cities: Formation and Development* (Syracuse: University of Syracuse Press, 2000), 35–39.

47. This element is known as *badgir*, literally "wind catcher."

48. The word used in this context is *nab*, literally "genuine."

49. "How Do You Sit? Manners of Sitting Are Markers of One's Identity," *Taraqqi* 5, no. 31, series 207 (December 30, 1946): 6.

50. *Tehran musavvar* (Day 1329/December 1950), 56.

51. Ragnar Nurkse, *Problems of Capital Formation in Underdeveloped Countries* (New York: Oxford University Press, c. 1964), 61. Between 1951 and 1952 the content of this book was delivered in the form of public lectures in the United States, Brazil, and Egypt.

52. Nurkse, *Problems of Capital Formation in Underdeveloped Countries*, 61.

53. In his book *House and Home in Modern Japan: Architecture, Domestic Space, and Bourgeois Culture, 1880–1930* (Cambridge: Harvard University Press, 2003), Jordan Sand provides a similar argument regarding the Japanese perception of progress in housing and home ethics in relation to those of the West. See especially 366–67.

54. Pierre Bourdieu, *Distinction: A Social Critique of the Judgment of Taste*, translated by Richard Nice (Cambridge: Harvard University Press, 1984), 345; quoted in Sand, *House and Home in Modern Japan*, 366–67.

55. Nurkse, *Problems of Capital Formation in Underdeveloped Countries*, 63.

56. The study of Islamic injunctions and laws through reasoning has been limited in accord with the principle of "sufficient necessity" (*wajib kifa'i*) to those who have the capability and are "worthy of such duty." These individuals are called *mujtahids*. The act of following the *mujtahids* is called imitation. Shiism does not permit imitation of a dead *mujtahid*. Only a living *mujtahid* can comment on the circumstances that did not exist during the time of the deceased *mujtahids*. This marks the difference between Shi'a and Sunni Islam, when it comes to matters of everyday life. In Sunni Islam, due to a consensus of opinion (*ijma*) that happened in the tenth century, it was decided that submission to one of the four Islamic schools of law (Hanafi, Maliki, Shafii, and Hanbali) was necessary. *Ijtihad* or imitation of a school other than these four was not considered legitimate. Therefore, until recently (when some have turned away from this consensus) Sunni jurisprudence has remained the same as it was in the tenth century. See Allameh Sayyed Muhammad Hussein Tabatabaie, *Shi'a*, translated by Sayyed Hussein Nasr (Tehran: Araye Publications, 2006), 121–22.

57. The concepts of *halal* and *haram* are mostly taken from Jafer ibn Ali Yahya's *Sharay-ih al-Islam fi Masai'l al-halal val haram*, whose interpretation of Islamic law is widely accepted among the Twelver Shiites—that is, those Shiites who recognize the twelve *imams* (leaders).

58. For more information regarding the history and development of *Tawzih al-Masai'l* or *Risalih* since the seventeenth century, see Ahmad Kazimi Mousavi, *Peydaish-i risalihay-i amaliyyeh va naghsh an dar gostaresh hughugh mosbateh Shi'a* (The advent of *Tawzih al-Masai'l* and its role in the betterment of Shiism), *Tahghighat-i Islami* 6, nos. 1–2 (1991): 103–13.

59. Ayatollah Abdol Karim Biazar Shirazi, interview by the author, tape recording made in Tehran, Iran, on February 10, 2007. It is worth noting that those people of an Islamist orientation during the revolutionary years found the New *Tawzih al-Masai'l* captivating, but it is hard to say whether it would have held any interest for those not "committed to the faith."

60. Ayatollah Ruhollah Khomeini, *The New Tawzih al-Masai'l*, edited by Abdol Karim Biazar Shirazi, vol. 1, *Worship and the Development of the Self* (Tehran: Moassisey-i Anjam Kitab, 1980), 52–54.

61. Sand, *House and Home in Modern Japan*, 369.

62. Georg Simmel, *The Philosophy of Money* (London: Routledge and Kegan Paul, 1978), 66.

63. This point is also mentioned by the narrator of the documentary *Iran: A Cinematographic Revolution* in which an excerpt from *Under the Skin of the Night* is featured; see Nader Takmil Homayoun, dir., *Iran: A Cinematographic Revolution*, Tehran, 2006.

64. The original title, *Gharbzadegi*, has also been translated as *Westoxication*.

65. Al-i Ahmad was most famous for coining the term *Gharbzadegi*—variously translated into English as "Westernstruck," "Westoxification," "Occidentosis"—in his book by the same name, clandestinely published in Iran in 1952. Jalal Al-i Ahmad, *Occidentosis: A Plague from the West*, translated by R. Campbell (Berkeley: Mizen Press, 1984), 57–58. This was, of course, part of a larger concern regarding culture and authenticity that appeared in the work of other Iranian intellectuals and commentators. The editor of the popular intellectual magazine *Firdawsi* (vol. 895), for example, wrote on p. 3 in 1969 (1348/20, Janu-

ary 1969) that "we need our own Eastern culture. The very same which the Indians have preserved and the Japanese have safeguarded but which we have lost somewhere. In order to find it, we cannot cling to history. We have to reconstruct it." Quoted in Negin Nabavi, "The Discourse of 'Authentic Culture' in Iran in the 1960s and 1970s," in *Intellectual Trends in Twentieth-Century Iran: A Critical Survey* (Gainesville: University Press of Florida, 2003), 91–108.

66. These terms were highlighted by Khomeini but later used by other politicians, especially the third prime minister of the Islamic Republic, Mir Hussein Musavi. He was a trained architect and constantly used these words as he attempted to convince the government to contribute to housing for the poor. During his speech at the opening of an apartment complex for the poor in the city of Zanjan, he said: "The government should prioritize the building of houses for the *Kukh-neshinan.*" See *Jomhuri Islami* 1117 (21 Farvardin 1362/ March 1983): 16. For Khomeini's description of these two terms, see *Jomhuri Islami*, 1109 (Farvardin 1362/March 1983). Although in the long run these ideas were turned into mere ideological slogans that did little to help elevate the condition of peoples' lives, there is substantial evidence—some of which has already been explored by other scholars (especially Asef Bayat)—that the implementation of these ideas in the immediate aftermath of the revolution garnered great acclaim among the poor.

Selected Bibliography

Adler, K. H., and Carrie Hamilton, eds. *Homes and Homecomings: Gendered Histories of Domesticity and Return.* London: Wiley-Blackwell, 2010.

Ghannam, Farha. *Remaking the Modern: Space, Relocation, and the Politics of Identity in a Global Cairo.* Berkeley: University of California Press, 2002.

Ruth Oldenziel, and Karin Zachman, eds. *Cold War Kitchen: Americanization, Technology, and European Users.* Cambridge: MIT Press, 2009.

Shechter, Relli, ed. *Transitions in Domestic Consumption and Family Life in the Modern Middle East: Houses in Motion.* New York: Palgrave Macmillan, 2003.

7

Boundary Games
Ecochard, Doxiadis, and the Refugee Housing Projects under Military Rule in Pakistan, 1953–1959

■

M. IJLAL MUZAFFAR

O N May 20, 1963, some 150,000 residents of the newly built Korangi housing colony in Karachi sat outside their houses with their belongings, hoisting black flags to protest the eviction of one "Yusuf Bhutock" from his house by the Karachi Development Authority (KDA).[1] At any other location the protestors would have been dispersed with the baton if not the bulldozer. Korangi, however, had special status. It was built by the military government of Ayub Khan, the self-appointed field marshal and president of Pakistan from 1958 to1969, as a model housing project for refugees from India who had crowded the streets of Karachi since the partition of the subcontinent, and the end of British rule, in 1947 (figure 7.1). A clash with those refugee groups now would have delegitimized the project as well the government that had celebrated it. A confrontation would have also been a setback for the two American aid agencies, USAID and the Ford Foundation, that had sponsored the project as an experiment into social "pacification" designed to save Karachi's large migrant and refugee population from communist influence.

These concerns were not lost to the project's designer, the famous Greek architect-planner, and global consultant par excellence at the time, Constantine Doxiadis. In a letter to Colonel Nasser Humayune, the military director of the National Housing and Settlement Agency, and Harry Case, the Ford Foundation representative in Karachi, Doxiadis wrote:

> In the four and a half years of my acquaintance with the urban problems of Pakistan it is the first time that I have seen such an enthusiasm, inspiration and coordination of effort under a unique command for the achievement of a natural goal in this field. The

Figure 7.1. Ayub Khan, field marshall and president of Pakistan, Karachi, 1959. Touring the Korangi project during construction. *Source*: Ford Foundation Archives, New York.

> "Operation Korangi" as I think it should be called has all the charac-
> teristics of a beachhead started by commandos in hostile terri-
> tory—by commandos who have the desire to achieve a national
> goal even by deciding to have greater sacrifices and casualties than
> normally. . . . Even more: it should be turned into the beachhead
> that is going to open the enemy land for conquest.[2]

Doxiadis's statement speaks to the founding claim of authoritarian rule in Pakistan: the framing of a heterogeneous polity as an enemy that must be fought
in the present so that a unified nation could be preserved for the future. More
important, it shows how this task is to be carried out: by casting modernization
as a "natural goal" while framing all politics as unnatural hindrances that must
be fought with unshakable resolve.[3] Described as "natural" process, modernization is imbued with an internal logic and unity. In contrast, politics is equated
with the fragmentation of this unity. The unified logic of modernization is lost
in the arena of political interruptions. Only the para-political and centralized
authority of military rule can carry out the coordination demanded by the modernization process.

Projects of refugee settlement, like Korangi, were a critical component in
consolidating this image. They constituted the representative face of the pro-

claimed coordinated enterprise: custodianship. The refugee formed the transitory figure that needed to be incrementally guided into modernity outside of the political arena. The Ayub government too had framed its rule in similar terms when it launched its "basic democracy" program. The program had banned all political parties with the claim that the public first needed to be trained for modern political participation under a centrally administered program of municipal elections. Continuity of administration superseded the interruptions of politics. This framing allowed the military government to forge an alliance with Pakistan's influential civil bureaucracy, extending the latter's powers and giving the military government a civil face.[4] The basic democracy program projected the transitory status of the refugee onto the entire country, turning the entire national population as refugees into democratic politics.

What, however, set this mode of authoritarian power apart was its construction around the idea of transition. Despite the emphasis on centralized authority, that authority is presented as a transitory custodianship of a figure, a nation in transition, who despite its present derailment into political contestations, possesses the key to modernization. Presenting itself as an emancipatory custodian of a transitory figure, the military government was able to have its cake and eat it too. Architecture and planning served as apt tools to tread the line between authority and custodianship, between centralized power and its often disseminated application. But before we look at the process of refugee settlement, its different framings, and their currency in securing authoritarian rule in Pakistan, let us first consider the historical context that had made refugee settlement such a potent issue in the post-partition national political discourse.

Partition

The partition of India and Pakistan had been both unpredictable and violent, displacing more than twelve million people and leaving over a million dead. One major factor of this toll had been the ensuing unpredictability of the partition itself, concerning not only whether the subcontinent would be divided into a Hindu majority India and Muslim majority Pakistan but also regarding where the exact boundaries of the new nation-states would fall.[5] The struggle for independence had produced entrenched divisions between the two major political parties, the Muslim League and the Congress. The political impasse over the sharing of power had led the Muslim League to present a demand for a separate Muslim homeland, Pakistan, in the Muslim majority areas of the subcontinent. The difficulty and costs, both material and human, of such a division in a heterogeneous population was evident to leaders on both sides. Because of these challenges, the status of Pakistan—whether it was to be a confederated set of provinces within a united India or a separate nation-state—remained undetermined. Initially, the British were open to the resolution of political differences before independence, a path particularly stressed by the second to last viceroy, Archibald Wavell.

The Second World War, however, changed the British posture in India. Marred by the political and financial cost of the war, the British government wanted an expedient decolonization with minimum political costs. Using the political impasse as an opportunity, the postwar British government of Clement Attlee pressed for a quick resolution, sending in a new viceroy, Louis Mountbatten (Lord Mountbatten of Burma), with the explicit mission of quickly untangling British involvement with the deteriorating political situation in India. Mountbatten dismissed the long time line proposed by his predecessor, Wavell, and appointed a Boundary Commission led by a London lawyer, Cyril Radcliff. The commission was to provisionally divide the contested states on "notional division" and then hold appeals from different sides claiming majority in particular areas.[6]

This process, bounded by the commission's deadline to give its deliberations, created a crisis. The demands for separation, which were initially used for political maneuvering and for building popular support, became occasions for staging communal riots, giving legitimacy to the haste for decolonization created by the British. Each push for demarcation, in areas with heterogeneous populations, betrayed its impossibility. Till the last tick of the clock to independence, the exact boundaries of the partition remained unresolved. Even though independence was declared on the preannounced deadline, the question of partition lingered on. The status of cities like Amritsar and Lahore, the traditional capital of the state of the Punjab, which had near equal Muslim and Hindu populations, remained unclear. Major population groups held onto their properties in hope. Rulers of many princely states were given the choice to decide their own fate. This created further confrontations between populations in those areas.

When the Radcliff commission finally produced its adhoc report, the results were astonishingly disastrous. Finding themselves on the wrong side of the border, countless people were turned into refugees in their own homes. Massive population movements were combined with widespread massacres. Trainloads of dead arrived on both sides. Villages perished and burned, the dead disappeared into mass graves. More than a million people lost their lives. These dislocations would come to be best remembered in the postwar political culture on both sides of the border through the photographs of Margaret Bourke-White, the famous American photojournalist known for her uncanny ability to be present before unfolding catastrophes. She had been present at the allied liberation of the Buchenwald concentration camp in Germany in 1945; she had taken the famous image of Gandhi at the spinning wheel hours before his assassination; and she was now present in India before the partition.

In Bourke-White's images of the partition, one characteristic stands out: the juxtaposition of opposing scales, the grand and the immediate, the national and the personal (figures 7.2 and 7.3). Distraught faces are set against grand vistas, blank skies, and historical sites. It is as if the partition had opened a chasm that had swallowed all that mediated between the personal and the national, bringing the former into grating adjacency with the latter without the intervening layers of the social, the common, the familial, and the familiar. Bourke-White stressed this forced coupling by highlighting the overburdened and inadequate means of transportation, infrastructure, or simply the makeshift objects that are employed to make the historical crossing. The inadequacy of the means at the individuals' disposal, to meet this historic and spatial challenge, gives the images an air of incertitude. The refugees appear to us to not only be passing through a catastrophic transition but also as if they would forever remain caught in this moment.

And indeed they would. This transitory status would continue to define the idea of the refugees in national political discourse even when they had reached their destinations. Arguably, the popularity of Bourke-White's images in national politics stems from their ability to resonate the perceived uncertainty of space/time/identity that the partition ushered, an uncertainty that still continues to inhabit the contested border between India and Pakistan, making it one of the most monitored boundaries in the world.[7]

Figure 7.2. Margaret Bourke-White, *Partition of India*, 1947. *Source*: Time & Life Pictures/Getty Images. © Time Life Pictures.

Figure 7.3. Margaret Bourke-White, *Partition of India,* 1947. *Source:* Time & Life Pictures/ Getty Images. © Time Life Pictures.

In Pakistan the figure representing the qualities memorialized by the partition would be the refugee in Karachi. Even though the most intense violence and majority of migration occurred across the border in the Punjab—the divided province to the North—those who migrated there were not considered refugees for long in the political discourse. This perception was molded by the fact that displaced Punjabis still had a "homeland" left in the Pakistani half of the Punjab. The same held true for other ethnic and linguistic groups, such as Pathans in the North West and Sindhis in the South, who were seen to belong to the linguistic majorities in the other three provinces of West Pakistan. The refugees in Karachi, however, had migrated from Urdu-speaking urban areas in India and had no corresponding Urdu-speaking province in Pakistan. Most of them were settled in Karachi, the first capital of Pakistan. They soon acquired the curious status of permanent refugees within the country.[8] This framing was taken on by the refugees themselves to claim a separate political identity. Yet it was also projected onto them by others seeking national leadership, particularly the federal government. Because the refugees did not belong to any of the national provincial majorities, the question of their settlement could be taken up to claim impartiality and nonpartisanship.[9]

The refugee in Karachi represented an impartial and transitory subject. Because she appeared outside of national politics, she rendered the politics of associations and alliances transparent. Her future represented the nation's future. If Bourke-White's images depicted the uncertainty that haunted the refugees during the course of their journey, the projects of their settlement betrayed the political currency this uncertainty held after the refugees reached their supposed destinations. Settlement was no longer a question of providing shelter but of transforming the refugees—and through them the nation itself. The refugee became the future national subject, and refugee settlement, the representative project of national modernization.

As the Korangi project would make evident, the Ayub government also deployed the project of refugee settlement to justify its rule. It framed refugee settlement in Karachi as part of a carefully guided process of national modernization that demanded long-term administrative custodianship rather than political representation. The legitimacy of the Ayub government's leadership hung in this coupling between settlement and modernization. It existed as long as this connection was perpetuated, as long as the project of refugee settlement was incomplete, as long as the refugee (and the nation) was depicted in the process of perpetual settlement. Doxiadis had judged these larger political requirements correctly, describing his designs from the beginning as experimental "processes" rather than concrete plans.[10] Each proposal emphasized the systemic coordination of parts, centralized administrative control, and incremental growth. This approach won him several projects from the Ayub government, including the commissions for a new campus for the University of Punjab and, in 1962, for the new capital of Pakistan, Islamabad.[11]

Ecochard

Korangi, however, was not the first attempt at setting in place a process of refugee settlement in Karachi. Although he was prominent, Doxiadis was a latecomer on this scene. It was Michel Ecochard, the director of town planning of the French protectorate in Morocco, who was first invited to propose a solution for settling refugees in Karachi in 1953. Together with George Candilis, Shadrach Woods, and Vladimir Bodiansky—the other members of Atbat Afrique, the African offshoot of CIAM (Congres International de Modern)— Ecochard had recently designed massive housing projects for different migrant populations around Casablanca.[12] The projects were highly praised at CIAM's meeting in Aix-en-Provence, the first after the war, as a new culturally specific form of modernism. In his report to the United Nations and the Pakistani government, Ecochard himself presented the projects as suitable precedents for Karachi's refugee situation.[13] Despite its apparent suitability, however, Ecochard's project for Karachi was not realized, unable to take hold in the turbulent political climate of Pakistan. Yet this failure highlights, just as importantly as Doxiadis's later proposal, the viability of different models of intervention and change in relation to particular structures of the postcolonial state.

Ecochard had arrived in Karachi as a consultant for the United Nations Technical Assistance Administration (UN-TAA) on the recommendation of Ernest Weissman, an active CIAM member and the head of the Housing and Planning Section at the UN headquarters in New York.[14] Weissman's recommendation proved timely for Ecochard. Even though the Casablanca projects were highly praised in CIAM circles for their cultural "sensitivity," they had received severe criticism in Morocco and France for being just the opposite: overly "functionalist" and not sensitive enough to the "cultural requirements" of the native Muslim populations. When Morocco gained independence in 1954, this criticism became Ecochard's Achilles heal, ousting him to Paris when many colonial administrators remained behind. The Karachi project gave the Casablanca schemes a new lease on life, providing an opportunity to maintain the status they had acquired in modern architectural debates.

These differing perceptions of the Casablanca projects in different circles stem from Ecochard's own framing of culture and function as interrelated yet distinct spheres. Following the conventions of colonial anthropology, Atbat had classified the city's migrant population according to different cultural and religious profiles. Their varying characteristics, however, were seen to be transformable under proper regulation, eventually fitting into a normative model of modern nuclear family that was to constitute the building block of the extended French imperial realm. This process of transformation, however, was to happen incrementally, with cultural habits of the native subjects modified periodically, without causing, as it were, a sudden "break" in their cultural "patterns."

Ecochard's and Atbat's schemes sought to attain this goal by slowly moving the native population through different "functional" arrangements representing different population densities—from high-density lowrises reminiscent of native living arrangements to low-density modern highrises. The Casablanca housing blocks, so appreciated at the CIAM conferences, represented different architectural containers in which functional calculations periodically maintained and transformed perceived cultural practices. Culture, in this mode of intervention, becomes an alibi for a particular model of administrative control that appears indirect and distant but is ever present and all encompassing.

The dual focus on culture and function as categories of design is often taken as a sign of contradictory sympathies of the designers by many historians in their evaluation of Ecochard and Atbat's work. But this is not, as Monique Eleb would have it, a sign of an ethically torn, "schizophrenic" mind-set of a colonial administrator, unable to decide what is more important, colonial science or native culture.[15] Schizophrenia was precisely the mode of administration under "inclusive" French colonialism. Modernity was presented as a project of only periodically calibrating the movements of a loosely defined, varied, and dispersed cultural sphere of the French imperial domain. Perpetuated in the name of protecting native populations from sudden influence of modernization, this dual approach allowed colonial administrators to take both a preservationist and transformative stance, emphasizing the dimension demanded by the circumstances: preservationist if labor reserves were required, transformative if displacement was warranted. The dialectic of culture and function seen in play in the Casablanca housing projects reflects this dual strategy of imperial administration.

For Ecochard the logic of incremental organization employed in Casablanca was apt for the problem of refugees in Pakistan as well. Pakistan too needed a model of cultural custodianship built on a system of administrative management, one that was distant yet ever present, inclusive yet centralized. This model had allowed the colonial government to maintain low investment in public welfare in the name of preserving existing cultural practices. It now allowed a third world government to maintain political and administrative control in the face of limited available resources, to fill the gap between what the government could provide and what it must plan to retain political legitimacy.

Ecochard's initial proposal for Karachi constituted of a series of independent satellite "cities" at Landhi, a site adjacent to Doxiadis's future Korangi project.[16] These cities were to be developed over time, along the main railway line that linked Karachi to the outlying industrial areas. This multiple-city approach, however, quickly changed to a more centralized design, composed of a single large city with multiple subunits, or "neighborhoods" (figure 7.4). Although each of these units were to have a fixed periphery—and a fixed "framework" of roads, shopping centers dispensaries, schools, and gardens—they were meant to accommodate changing types and arrangements of housing. The commercial and community areas were to be located at the intersection of multiple housing sectors, leaving minimal restrictions for different possible organization of houses in large swaths of open green.

What's curious here is that Ecochard does not settle on a particular organization scheme for the houses until the very end (figure 7.5). In fact, the possibility of ever-new reorganization is presented as the main feature of the plan. Following Casablanca, Ecochard expected the new city to grow from provisionary shelter to an intermediary stage of "hutments"—that could be arranged and rearranged in different conglomerations within open green space—to other housing types (medium- to high-rise blocks). As the economic and social profile of the inhabitants changed over time, Ecochard argued, the entire settlement would move toward lower densities and more open space.

The city plan is here composed as an infrastructural field that forms both

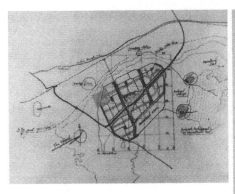

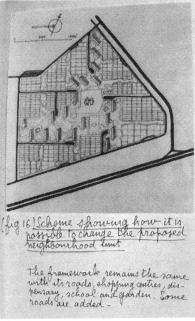

Figure 7.4. Michel Ecochard, Landhi, Karachi, 1953–1954. Site plan of the revised proposal of a single "city" with a "neighborhood" detail showing housing organization possibilities within open space. *Source*: United Nations Archives, New York.

(fig 16) Scheme showing how it is possible to change the proposed neighbourhood limit

The framework remains the same with its roads, shopping centres, dispensary, school and garden. Some roads are added.

Figure 7.5. Michel Ecochard, Landhi, Karachi, 1953–1954. "Evolutive principles" for refugee housing. *Source*: United Nations Archives, New York.

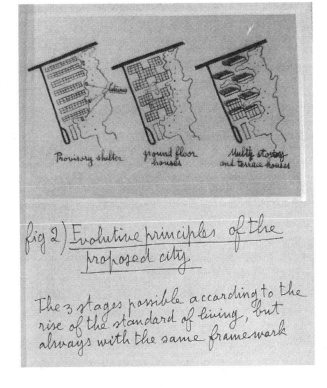

Provisory shelter

ground floor houses

Multi storey and terrace houses

fig 2) Evolutive principles of the proposed city

The 3 stages possible according to the rise of the standard of living, but always with the same framework

the condition of transformation of the houses and their telos, the moment when transforming environment would catch up with the full potential of the framework. The scheme outlines a process of evolution whose final form is already visible. The inhabitants are caught simply in the process of filling in the details.[17] This approach points to Ecochard's background as an archeologist. A graduate of Ecole des Beaux Arts, Ecochard had begun his career working on the restoration of historical buildings in Damascus.[18] There, Ecochard began to formulate a continuity between archeology and planning. For Ecochard, his archeological projects were in fact planning exercises that gave old structures new functions. Working on a restoration of the Azem Palace in Damascus—a project that would lead to the commission for a master plan for Damascus itself—Ecochard asserted that an archeological project "[was] an experiment . . . to bring back to life a building both through visual stimulation and through use of the plan."[19] The plan therefore did not simply authenticate a past and restore a supposed original function to a building; rather, the plan set an experimental path within a new set of forces.

A certain parallel can be established between Ecochard's training as an archeologist and his design approach in Karachi. Ecochard imagined the process of establishing the presence of the state in Karachi as itself an archeological project, only it was an archeology in reverse. Instead of uncovering sedimented layers of the past, the Karachi plan built up the future as sedimented layers of the present. Planning as archeology began like an archeological project with making visible the contours of the site whose contents were yet unknown. In time, planning added new layers to articulate the potential promised by the site. Yet, similar to an archeological exploration, each layer required dismantling the last to dig deeper. The future was to be constructed by a continuous process of dismantling and reassembling. The open green areas surrounding the buildings represented the space of this calibrated transformation.

At Korangi this process came to be articulated in the language of CIAM's famous four functions of "circulation," "work," "living," and "public facilities"— the last modified here as "the care of body and spirit" to include a *jama masjid* (community mosque) and a hospital in the national context (figure 7.6). The four functions announced in advance the profile of modern life whose particular form was to be discovered in time. The city is literally imagined as a palimpsest of these different functional layers, each influencing and nudging the process of culture change toward incremental modernization. Culture is the stuff that happened between the functional layers, incrementally transformed by their dismantling and reassembling in accordance with the requirements and values of modern life.

The houses in Karachi then become spatial frameworks that transform the inhabitants as they traverse the modernization process. The project provided

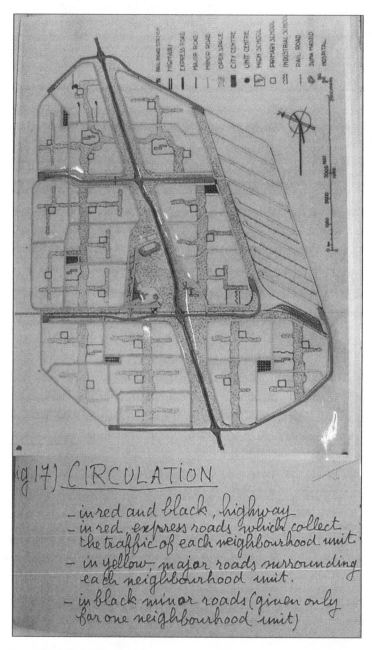

Figure 7.6a. Michel Ecochard, Landhi, Karachi, 1953–1954. Final proposal for the first city showing "circulation," "living," "working," and "body and spirit." *Source:* United Nations Archives, New York.

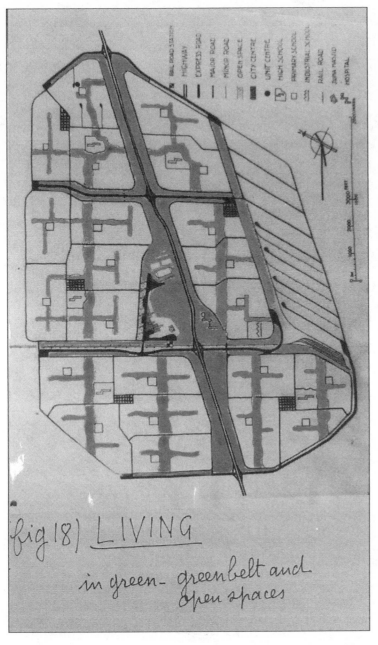

fig18) LIVING

in green- greenbelt and
open spaces

Figure 7.6 b

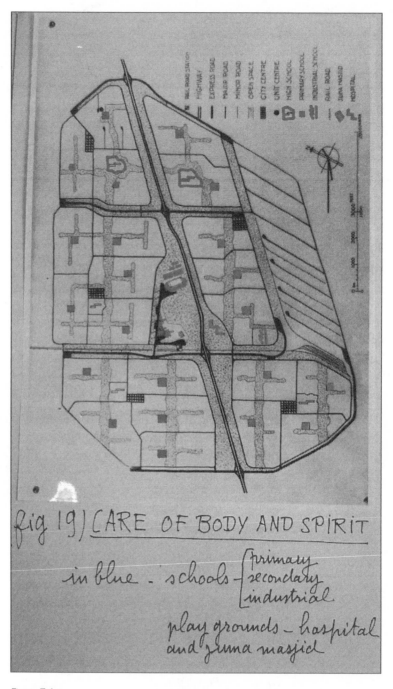

fig 19) CARE OF BODY AND SPIRIT

in blue - schools { primary
secondary
industrial

play grounds - hospital
and juma masjid

Figure 7.6 c

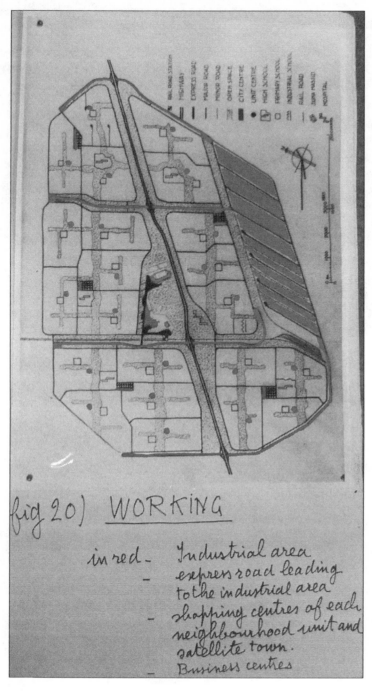

fig 20) WORKING

in red - Industrial area
         - express road leading
           to the industrial area
         - shopping centres of each
           neighbourhood unit and
           satellite town.
         - Business centres

Figure 7.6 d

the comprehensive frame within which these transformations took place. Eco-chard extended this logic to map the entire city of Karachi, mapping its density as indicative of different stages of modernization of the inhabitants and how they could be set on path to the next stage under the guidance of a compre-hensive and visible administrative framework. By setting up a framework for what is not yet there, and may never be, Ecochard's proposal addressed the dilemma faced by the postcolonial state: the difference between the promise and the plan, between what the state can provide and what it must claim to provide to ward off political challenges. Yet Ecochard's approach could not find the same currency in Pakistan as it had in colonial Casablanca. As Paul Rabinow has argued, even in the colonial context of Morocco, the central government did not constitute a homogeneous power.[20] The comprehensive framework of inclusive imperialism was always open to contestations from within. The idea of unified imperial power was primarily advanced by the different elements in the government to justify their positions.

Ecochard assumed that just as it had done in Casablanca, the emphasis on the presence of a comprehensive armature of a central power could serve equally well in negotiating the contestations of governance in the national con-text of Pakistan. In Pakistan, however, the idea of central government had never acquired the historical and ideological weight that different parties could invoke to advance their agendas. A design emphasizing the need for a comprehensive and visible armature of organization, however open, produced the opposite ef-fect, making the very power attained through such a strategy open to attack. In a protracted exchange, Ecochard kept accusing the Refugee Settlement Agency of ignoring the comprehensive nature of the plan and picking and choosing indi-vidual parts for piecemeal implementation. Soon the project came to be framed in the political debate as an idealized scheme beyond the means of a developing nation and disconnected from local concerns and politics.

Doxiadis

The most striking difference between Doxiadis's and Ecochard's plans is their different approach to boundaries. Ecochard had placed particular empha-sis on delineating clear boundaries for his proposed refugee settlements. The proposal by Doxiadis's firm, Doxiadis and Associates (DA), however, purport-ed to an idea of continuous expansion. DA's proposed settlement was to grow linearly over time out of its present site and direct the growth of the entire city of Karachi (figure 7.7). This approach reflected a different idea of consolidating state power than the one proposed by Ecochard.

In setting a predefined scale for the entire project, Ecochard designated the state as the ultimate agent of change. The open interior of the refugee city,

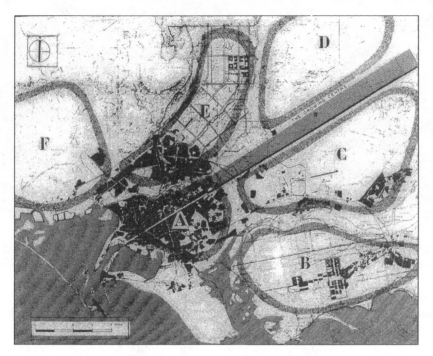

Figure 7.7. Doxiadis Associates, Korangi, Karachi, 1959. Presumed direction of growth (from left to right) connecting other areas of the city. *Source*: Ford Foundation Archives, New York.

enclosed within predefined boundaries, proclaimed all possibilities of change in advance. Indeed, the process of change could take many paths, as Ecochard's multiple housing arrangements made apparent. But all these possibilities were outlined by the state (all houses were to be allocated on a transitory basis). The state designated the end as well as the multiple paths that reached that end. In contrast, Doxiadis's approach, in eradicating the fixed boundaries of the plan, worked toward erasing precisely the scale at which the state made itself visible as the agent of social reform. In Doxiadis's plan, the inhabitant herself is proclaimed as the agent of change. The state's role is deliberately projected to the background, limited to providing only the administrative framework for the inhabitant's self-mobilized emergence into modernity.

Doxiadis's scheme proposed a nestled model of social organization controlled by a disseminated administrative structure, without an identifiable authority (figure 7.8). The population was to be divided into different "community sectors," beginning with the basic unit of "community class I," which included ten to twenty households of similar income levels. Three to seven of such communities grouped together formed the next administrative level of "class

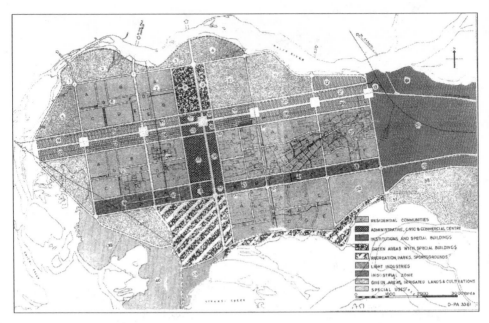

Figure 7.8. Doxiadis Associates, Korangi master plan, 1959. *Source*: Ford Foundation Archives, New York.

II." When an elementary school was added to a grouping of class II, it formed a community of "class III." Each class III community was supposed to be economically uniform, but they could differ in their income level relative to each other. A grouping of different income level class III communities plus a mosque, a teahouse, market, shops, and a cinema, formed a class IV community. Class IV communities were in turn combined to form class V, which formed the basic "community sector" of the Korangi plan.[21]

Even though the structure was hierarchically organized, in Doxiadis's estimation the purpose of this organization was to serve as a basis for "consolidating," and not "centralizing," the structure of public administration.[22] Korangi was to be built through the cooperation of both public and private enterprise. Various private industries pooled together their resources and formed cooperative bodies. These cooperatives were part of the Korangi's board of management and were to fund Korangi's housing sectors according to the needs of their surrounding industries. As a 1959 Doxiadis and Associates progress report on Korangi showed, of the ensemble of housing sectors and community center in the entire settlement, the government was only to build the lowest income housing sectors, and even those only partially. The rest, including major parts of the community centers, including the community mosque, were to be built by providing "incentives" to the private sector at the right moment in the development of the scheme.

Doxiadis hailed his scheme as a structure of "coordinating" public and private interests, a coordination that remained disseminated and largely transparent, providing opportunities of self-mobilization for the inhabitant themselves. Yet "coordination" here serves as a euphemism for managing a certain risk for the government and its allied "private interests." Korangi provided massive labor housing for the surrounding industries. In the past, if the government or the industry provided direct housing to the workers on mortgage, they, instead of paying down the debt, held the debt as employment security.[23] Korangi's nestled spatial organization and administrative structure of coordinated and disseminated authority made it nearly impossible to challenge any policy on a limited scale, while making coordinated evictions expedient. As the city grew, so did the network of mutually dependent spatial relationships and the disseminated administrative structure. The nestled space made the centralized authority of the military government and its allied private interests appear as distant managers of a self-mobilized modernization process, making them both ever present and unidentifiable. What might appear as a contradiction—the dual focus on centralized authority and disseminated application of power—actually formed the very mode through which power was preserved. Such contradictions didn't undo power but made its stable exercise possible.

The dissemination of state authority is premised on the framing of the refugee as a subject in transition between tradition and modernity. Although seen to be dislocated in the modern national landscape, she is not simply claimed as a subject in need of rigid control. Rather, she is presented as subject who possesses the potential of modernization herself. The state simply serves to emancipate this potential. The more the state is able to serve this role from afar, the less it is susceptible to constrain the refugee's capacity to constitute a seamless link between tradition and modernity.

Doxiadis is often accused of abstracting traditional architectural elements—such as the courtyard or windscreens—into standardized elements, rearranged onto grids for logistical convenience, in a way that they lose their social even climatic purpose. Indeed, that was the case in Korangi as well (figure 7.9). As it had previously done in Iraq, Doxiadis and Associates placed the courtyards on the side or in the back of the houses. In its new place the courtyard no longer appears to provide cool air to the surrounding rooms or form a multipurpose social space supposedly shared across gender and age. The courtyard in DA designs only appears to provide space for storage, livestock, or future expansion of the house.

Yet the spatial and symbolic criticism in focusing on what is missed in this ab-

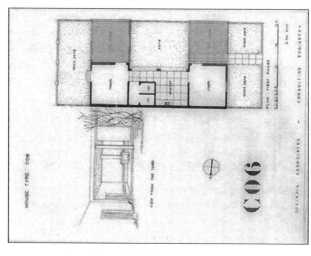

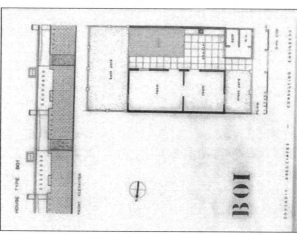

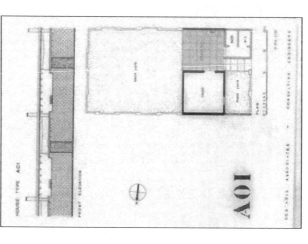

Figure 7.9. Doxiadis Associates, Korangi, Karachi, 1959. Housing plans for different income groups, to be expanded through individual incentive. *Source:* Ford Foundation Archives, New York.

stracting enterprise misses what these abstractions actually do: present culture as a self-regulating and transforming sphere. In Doxiadis's proposals culture is always being transformed by individual agents to bridge the gap between tradition and modernity; it is always already an image of a self-regulating market. For Ecochard, culture also constituted an intervening layer between tradition and modernity. But it was a layer that did not inhere any agency of change itself. It was necessary to preserve culture so as not to expose the native populations too quickly to modern life. Layers of culture were to be dismantled and reassembled by the colonial and the nation-state over time to ensure that all cultural identities slowly transformed toward greater integration and modernization. For Doxiadis, state did not need to claim this role. It was only a custodian of culture that itself bore the potential of modernization as long as it was not hijacked by political contestations. Culture too, like modernization, possessed a self-regulating internal unity and logic that, given the right circumstances, complemented (not opposed) modernization. Moving the courtyard to the side of the house provided precisely such an opportunity of unleashing the potential of modernization within the cultural sphere. The courtyard could now be recognized by the cultural agent herself as an opportunity for expanding the house or for providing storage for a small home-run business.

The houses at Korangi, nestled in the ever-expanding grid, reflected the narrative of culturally driven entry into the market economy. The grid of streets established individual property lots and a permanent structure of ownership. The houses too were based on a uniform grid system. This allowed the minimum inhabitable house provided by the state to differ in size for different "classes" of inhabitants, while maintaining the lot size to be more or less the same (see figure 7.9). This uniformity, Doxiadis argued, provided the poor classes with more potential of investment in the house in the future. The empty portion of the lot thus served, Doxiadis asserted, as a credit-building device as well as a basis for establishing demand for the building industry. As individual owners combined modern living habits with their cultural mores, they expanded their houses and built credit, generating further economic activity, extending both the linearly growing commercial center and housing sectors. The houses allowed the individuals to enter the market economy as cultural agents of change, incrementally making their own choices that tied them in a unique manner to the modern industrial and financial systems. For Doxiadis, this individuated, culturally driven entry celebrated the unique standing of the third world in the globalizing world. Its cultural agents enriched the global market economy, preventing it from taking the form of mind-numbing uniformity that characterized Western modernization.

This view stemmed from Doxiadis's understanding of culture as an organic-biological force, not a process of sedimentation of certain values and practices over time, as Ecochard had imagined. Culture followed the dynamic, shifting, and sometimes aggressive logic of biological evolution. Human settlements were the continuous trace left behind by this force whose operative principles were otherwise hidden from view. Doxiadis kept referring to cities as bodies with arteries, heart, lungs, and nerves that grew with the multiplication of cells. The basic units of this multiplication process were cells called "shells," an elementary cultural unit, filled with multifarious potentials that were tested out against other shells in the wider field of the social realm. New ideas emerged from a shell and came into contact with others outside it. Over time, the destructive ideas were eliminated and productive ones were strengthened, shaping the contours of the larger society.

But this evolutionary process entailed immense waste. Cultural evolution sometimes followed dead and destructive ends. These potentials could be guided, Doxiadis asserted, if we understood and shaped the urbanizing environments in terms of particular programmatic dimensions of "man," "nature," "society," "shells," and "networks" (figure 7.10). These broadly conceived spatial categories could be used to provide cultural force fields across the world with certain developmental pathways. This managerial approach was to be called "Ekistics, the science of human settlements" and was given a home in the 1950s at the Athens Technological Institute. There has been considerable critical attention paid to Doxiadis's programmatic categories, particularly his idea of net-

Figure 7.10. Constantine Doxiadis, holding the 3-D model of Ekistics with spheres representing its basic elements of "man," "society," "shell," "nature," and "networks." Each element is connected to the other four. *Source*: Doxiadis Archives, Benaki Museum, Athens, Greece.

work as a category that not only held its own independent sphere but was also connected to and embedded in all the other categories. This critique, however, has ignored the nature of the space implied *between* the network lines. This is the space of culture, triangulated within the connecting rods of Doxiadis's three-dimensional model of Ekistics.

For Doxiadis the essential quality of culture in the non-Western world was its transitory status. Suddenly brought to the world stage through rapid decolonization and modern communication, culture in this sphere was susceptible to lose its self-correcting qualities and be suppressed in the haste for modernization. In this view Doxiadis could be seen to be in line with other conservative theorists of development that saw the postwar era as being ridden with conflicts of mutually exclusive forces. What sets Doxiadis apart, however, is that instead of seeing this duality as hindrance to modernization, he saw it as providing a particular advantage for developing countries in the networked world of the future.

Transition was the moment when cultural differences and similarities became unhinged and lost their meaning as absolutes. The cultures in transition provided a solution—on the one hand, to the ever-present threat of exaggerated difference that led to global conflicts such as the World Wars, and on the other hand, from the haunting prospect of global homogenization and boredom. Cultures in transition held the potential of both preserving difference while encouraging integration. The goal of development then was not to resolve transition as quickly as possible but to highlight and prolong it. Seen this way, cultures in transition were not only the terrains on which the network lines were to be stretched; they were also the spaces that collectively formed the condition of a stable networked world.[24]

The refugee as a figure in transition was the prototype subject for the project of global integration. Yet this framing also allowed for the sleight of hand that made Doxiadis's proposal so desirable to authoritarian regimes and their sponsors around the world. The transitory subject also provided an alibi for a system of perpetual management, of continuous design and infinite transition. We see this dimension valued in the idea of custodianship sketched out by the Ayub government, a custodianship that wanted to usher in market economics but withhold the supposedly accompanying process of political participation. A particular idea of the pre-political consumer is constructed in the Ekistical world, one who is available for adventures in the market but is declared unsuitable for those in politics. This consumer can best understand the language of culture and for this reason warrants political management. Culture becomes an alibi for pushing entry into the market while delaying entry into politics. The subject becomes the generator of demands but not a patron of democratic politics.

The argument for the cultural entry into modernity presented in the design of the houses at Korangi leaves out the fact that individuated change, when cast primarily in the language of culture, also ensures that the cultural subject forever remained caught in his or her transitory stage. Refugee is a figure that can host the idea of delay in political representation. Both seen as being out of sync with the action in the national political theater and valorized for it, he or she can perpetually celebrate the idea of soft modernization cast in the language of culture.

Returning to Doxiadis's militaristic statement in the aftermath of the Korangi protest, we can now discern another dimension of the curious framing of the public as a certain enemy: in Pakistan, as would be the case in many military postcolonial states seeking U.S. alignment, the shifting status of the public from friend to enemy was a function of scale, not of category. It is the individual that is the subject of urbanism and development while the social is equated with socialist politics. In Doxiadis's proposed program, the object of state intervention is no longer the social but the individual. From the very onset, Korangi is imagined as a project that could prevent the socialization of refugees as a political group.

Doxiadis and the Ayub government did not consider, however, that such delaying strategies could not be continually masked with architecture. As the Korangi protest showed, the very sites of supposed transition could just as easily be turned into sites of social organization, reframing the system of perpetual transition as one of perpetual crisis. It would take almost another decade, a tainted election, and an economic crisis for the political opposition to mobilize the mass protests that would eventually unseat Ayub Khan. Yet the inherent political crisis of Pakistan stemming from the attempts to keep ethnic and linguistic divisions in check through centralized control would continue to resurface. Ayub handed over power to a transitory military government that promised to hold immediate elections. The election, however, resulted in conflicting claims to power that led to the separation of East Pakistan from the western part in 1971.[25] It was not long before the national and international fault lines that brought Ayub into power created another opening for a military coup. In 1977 the socialist civilian government was disposed by a U.S.-leaning military dictatorship just when the Soviet Union began to increase its influence in neighboring Afghanistan.[26]

What is critical to note in these reiterating crises of power is the manner in which the international and the national embed themselves within each other to advance their agendas, rather than imposing them independently. Indeed, power is secured abruptly. Yet its maintenance requires continuous tactical maneuvers. In this realm development is repeatedly advanced as a problem of coordination of different cultural forces by both national and international forces. Architecture is claimed as the behavioral turf on which this coordination takes place. Development is often simply seen as a form of neoimperialism imposed from the outside. An external power imposes its will on a subjugated society. This model of oppressor-oppressed does not adequately explain the mutually legitimizing modes of power in the development arena, just as it does not explain the complexities of colonial governance. It is here that architectural and urban projects, such as Doxiadis's and Ecochard's, provide critical archives for understanding the new and emerging modes of intervention. It is here that they also betray a history of modern architecture's intimate relationship with structures of power in the postwar international arena.

Notes

1. See "K. D. A. Ejectment Drive Cut Short," *Dawn,* May 21, 1963.

2. Constantine Doxiadis, "On the problem of rehabilitation of displaced persons and urban development of Pakistan," undated letter, Ford Foundation Archives, New York.

3. Doxiadis, undated letter; reports for Korangi's progress over the years had carried the title "a project for cultural evolution of a nation." This title was also adopted as the key phrase of President Ayub's speech at the project's inauguration.

4. For a detail discussion of the Ayub government's "basic democracy" program, see Ayesha Jalal, *Democracy and Authoritarianism in South Asia: A Comparative and Historical Perspective* (Cambridge: Cambridge University Press, 1995).

5. For a detailed account of the unpredictability surrounding the partition, see Hassan Amtul, *Impact of Partition*, RCSS Policy Studies 37 (New Delhi: Manohar Publishers, 2006).

6. For a detailed account of the "Radcliff line," see Yasmin Khan, *The Great Partition: The Making of India and Pakistan* (New Haven: Yale University Press, 2007).

7. This continued perception of Bourke-White's photographs as representative images of the partition's uncertainty is evident in their appearance on the cover of many recent studies of the partition. See, for example, see Yasmin Khan, *The Great Partition: The Making of India and Pakistan* (New Haven: Yale University Press, 2007); and Stanley Wolpert, *Shameful Flight: The Last Years of the British Empire in India* (New York: Oxford University Press, 2009).

8. This dislocation of the "Urdu-speaking" population indeed was a curious phenomenon, pointing not so much to the marginalization of a minority but to uncertainty surrounding the status of the central government itself in a politically heterogeneous landscape. Urdu was declared by Muhammad Ali Jinnah, the leader of the Muslim League and Pakistan's first governor general, as the national language because it did not belong to, and hence favor, any of the country's four provinces. But because of this para-provincial status, the language also operated as a mark of marginalization.

9. For a discussion of the politicization of the refugee question in different international context, including South Asia, see Smita Tewari Jassal and Eyal Ben-Ari, eds., *The Partition Motif in Contemporary Conflicts* (New Delhi: Sage Publications, 2007).

10. Doxiadis had first presented his firm's planning approach as an open-ended experiment in his proposals for Iraq. Between 1955 and 1958, Doxiadis had proposed a large-scale national planning program for then contested monarchical government in the country. The

program was carried out with the help of U.S. aid agencies as part of the Cold War foreign policy of "containment" of communist influence. Although Doxiadis's ambitious plan was left incomplete when Iraq's monarchical government was overthrown in 1958, it presented for Pakistan's Ayub government, which was also supported by United States under the containment policy, a viable model for managing the refugee question. For Doxiadis and Associates' designs for Iraq, see Panayiota Pyla, "Rebuilding Iraq, 1955–58: Modernist Housing, National Aspirations, and Global Ambitions," *International Working-Party for Documentation and Conservation of Buildings, Sites, and Neighbourhoods of the Modern Movement* 35 (2006): 71–77.

11. The securing of Islamabad project presented a major validation of Doxiadis and Associates' agendas and approach. Doxiadis publicized the commission heavily in modern architectural circles and publications and media, including dedicating a special issue of *Ekistics* on it. Also see Doxiadis's interview with Deena Clark on NBC's "A Moment with" on March 1, 1968, which focuses on Islamabad as a global solution to the crisis of an urbanizing world, available online at (Part 1) http://www.youtube.com/watch?v=hSQWS9WcCQs; (Part 2) http://www.youtube.com/watch?v=EKvY6iRirJs&feature=related; and (Part 3) http://www.youtube.com/watch?v=hvstRTw2aaU&feature=related.

12. For a detailed history of Atbat Afrique and its projects in Morocco, see Jean-Louis Cohen and Monique Eleb, *Casablanca: Colonial Myths and Architectural Ventures* (New York: Monacelli Press, 2002). Also see Jean-Louis Cohen's "Architectural History and the Colonial Question: Casablanca, Algiers, and Beyond," *Architectural History* 49 (2006): 349–68; "The Whiteness of the Surf: Casablanca," *Any* 16 (1996): 16–19; and "The Moroccan Group and the Theme of Habitat," *Rassegna* 52, no. 4 (December 1992): 58–67.

13. "These proposals [for Karachi]," Ecochard argued in Pakistan, "are not theoretical; these principles have been applied on a very large scale in another country [Morocco]." Michel Ecochard, "The Problem of Refugees in Karachi, First and Second Reports," 1953, United Nations Archives, New York.

14. As a UN consultant, Ecochard's contract was much shorter (six months) than Doxiadis's protracted engagement that not only produced initial plans and reports for the project but also consultancy services for the scheme's construction as well as for setting up parallel research and education institutions. Yet the two modes—the long-term and the short-term—work as complementary vectors, each creating the space and legitimacy for the other. This fact is made evident by the change in Ecochard's position, when he stayed on in Pakistan on several private and government projects after the Landhi project was cancelled. Two large commissions secured by Ecochard from his stay in Pakistan were the projects of Karachi University campus and the museum at the ruins of the 2600 B.C. settlement Muhenjo-daro, now a famous UNESCO World Heritage site. Securing of these projects by Ecochard raised concerns within the UN headquarters in New York on the ethical implications of UN consultants using their "mission" assignments as platforms for expanding their private practices. The concerns, however, were dismissed by Weissman when he argued that Ecochard's prolonged stay in Pakistan, though private in nature, was still providing consultancy service for Pakistan's development program.

15. See Monique Eleb, "An Alternative to Functionalist Universalism: Écochard, Candilis, and ATBAT-Afrique," in *Anxious Modernisms*, edited by Sarah Williams Goldhagen and Réjean Legault (Cambridge: MIT Press, 2000). Eleb sees the dual emphasis on "culture" and density in Atbat's work as a sign of a "schizophrenic" colonial approach to social reform that was unable to resolve the dichotomous demands of tradition and modernity.

What is ignored in this argument is the consideration that colonialism always operates in a schizophrenic manner. Framing modernization as a problem of setting in "balance" the vectors of "tradition" and "modernity" reasserts the authority of the colonial government as an inclusive power and the ultimate custodian of multicultural change. The schizophrenic approach betrayed by late French imperialism in Morocco was particularly pertinent in responding to the emerging national movement and was a critical aspect of French *associanism*, the correlate of British "indirect" rule in central Africa rule that constructed a system of native authority armed with oppressive powers in the name of cultural preservation. For the British policy of "decentralized despotism" in Africa, see Mahmood Mamdani, *Citizen and Subject: Contemporary Africa and the Legacy of Late Colonialism* (Princeton: Princeton University Press, 1996). In a similar vein as Eleb, Nathalie de Mazières has also described "contradictory" tendencies in colonial governance as a shortcoming rather than a mode of power itself. See Nathalie de Mazières, "Homage," *Environmental Design: Journal of the Islamic Environmental Design Research Centre* 1 (1985): 22–25.

16. Landhi, the area east of Karachi, was chosen by the government as the site for refugee colonies as a favor to industrialist interests, such as the Dhada Bhoy family, that wanted easy labor access for their factories in the area. In this context, turning political questions into problems of administration formed the very basis of the government of civil bureaucrats.

17. Surely the scheme is also presented as an example of the social and climatic advances brought about by modernist planning practices (open green spaces promoting health and exercise, allowing prevailing wind to enter the houses, etc.). Instead of criticizing these claims, I have chosen to highlight the particular model of administration embodied in the design that is often ignored in the assessments of architectural modernism.

18. After graduating from Ecole des Beaux-Arts, under a curriculum that privileged the primacy of archeological knowledge, Ecochard's first job was in the Public Works department in Damascus. Although he began as a draftsman, he quickly moved on to work with prominent colonial archeologists on the restoration of important historical buildings, from the temple of Bel in Palmyra to the mosque of Bosrah. These restoration and planning projects launched Ecochard's career as an architect and planner in the Middle East. His next project was the restoration of the Azem Palace in Damascus, a prominent project that led to a series of private commissions in the city, leading to the commission for preparing the master plan for Damascus itself.

19. Quoted in de Mazières, "Homage," 22.

20. See Paul Rabinow, *French Modern: Norms and Forms of the Social Environment* (Cambridge: MIT Press, 1989).

21. Constantine Doxiadis, "Progress Report on Korangi, 1959," Ford Foundation Archives, New York.

22. Doxiadis's undated letter to Ford Foundation, Karachi, "Observation on two report-proposals to strengthen western policy toward developing areas," Ford Foundation Archives, New York.

23. Doxiadis learned this point from a previous UN mission report on Pakistan by Charles Abrams and Otto Koenigsberger, "A Housing Program for Pakistan with Special Reference to Refugee Rehabilitation, prepared for the Government of Pakistan by Charles Abrams and Otto Koenigsberger," September 14, 1957, United Nations Technical Assistance Administration, New York.

24. From this perspective Greece was the new center of this transitory world. Doxiadis argued that as a developing country, Greece not only was experiencing the current historical transition, but because of its particular geographical location, Greece had the added historical experience of always having been in transition between opposing cultural forces of East and West.

25. After years of political contestations, the Ayub government handed over rule to the interim military government of Yahya Khan in 1969. The following election in 1970 resulted in conflicting claims to power. Zulfiqar Ali Bhutto, previously Ayub's foreign minister and now the leader of the opposition party Pakistan Peoples Party (PPP), claimed victory in Western Pakistan, and Mujib-ur-Rahman, leader of the Awami League, claimed power in East Pakistan. The ensuing contestation between Bhutto and Mujib resulted in the continuation of military rule. This in turn led to popular unrest in East Pakistan. Attempts at suppression led to Indian involvement and a war between Pakistan and India. The war ended with East Pakistan claiming independence as Bangladesh in 1971 and Bhutto coming to power in West Pakistan.

26. The Bhutto government's initial socialist policies were greatly feared by the United States as a turn toward the Soviet Union. Bhutto's suppression of opposition and increasingly authoritative measures created a window for a military coup that brought General Zia-ul-Haq to power for the next eleven years. Zia's regime was strongly supported by the United States during the proxy war in Afghanistan against the Soviet occupation. Bhutto was executed by Zia's regime in 1979 on charges of masterminding the murder of an opposition leader.

Selected Bibliography

Abrams, Charles, and Otto Koenigsberger. *A Housing Program for Pakistan with Special Reference to Refugee Rehabilitation.* Prepared for the Government of Pakistan by Charles Abrams and Otto Koenigsberger, September 14, 1957. New York: United Nations Technical Assistance Administration, 1957.

Amtul, Hassan. *Impact of Partition.* RCSS Policy Studies 37. New Delhi: Manohar Publishers, 2006.

Cohen, Jean-Louis, and Monique Eleb. "Architectural History and the Colonial Question: Casablanca, Algiers, and Beyond." *Architectural History* 49 (2006): 349–68.

———. *Casablanca: Colonial Myths and Architectural Ventures.* New York: Monacelli Press, 2002.

———. "The Moroccan Group and the Theme of Habitat." *Rassegna* 52, no. 4 (1992): 58–67.

———. "The Whiteness of the Surf: Casablanca." *Any* 16 (1996): 16–19.

de Mazières, Nathalie. "Homage." *Environmental Design: Journal of the Islamic Environmental Design Research Centre* 1 (1985): 22–25.

Eleb, Monique. "An Alternative to Functionalist Universalism: Écochard, Candilis, and ATBAT-Afrique." In *Anxious Modernisms.* Edited by Sarah Williams Goldhagen and Réjean Legault, pp. 55–73. Cambridge: MIT Press, 2000.

Jalal, Ayesha. *Democracy and Authoritarianism in South Asia: A Comparative and Historical Perspective.* Cambridge: Cambridge University Press, 1995.

Jassal, Smita Tewari, and Eyal Ben-Ari, eds. *The Partition Motif in Contemporary Conflicts.* New Delhi: Sage Publications, 2007.

Khan, Yasmin. *The Great Partition: The Making of India and Pakistan.* New Haven: Yale University Press, 2007.

Mamdani, Mahmood. *Citizen and Subject: Contemporary Africa and the Legacy of Late Colonialism.* Princeton: Princeton University Press, 1996.

Pyla, Panayiota. "Rebuilding Iraq, 1955–58: Modernist Housing, National Aspirations, and Global Ambitions." *International Working-Party for Documentation and Conservation of Buildings, Sites, and Neighbourhoods of the Modern Movement* 35 (2006): 71–77.

Rabinow, Paul. *French Modern: Norms and Forms of the Social Environment.* Cambridge: MIT Press, 1989.

Wolpert, Stanley. *Shameful Flight: The Last Years of the British Empire in India.* New York: Oxford University Press, 2009.

PART III
Engineering and Culture

8

The Design of the Nubian Desert
Monuments, Mobility, and the Space of Global Culture

■

LUCIA ALLAIS

C ONSIDER the following architectural event: between 1960 and 1980 twenty-four Egyptian temples were surveyed, dismantled, and relocated from their original sites on the banks of the Nile to make way for an enormous reservoir lake created by the building of the Aswan High Dam. Designed to render fertile entire stretches of desert and bring electricity downstream to Cairo, the dam was also scheduled to flood the entire region of Nubia, a long and narrow strip that crosses the border between Egypt and the Sudan, sparsely dotted with mud-brick villages, archaeological sites, and Pharaonic temples. Two groups of temples (the island of Philae and the monoliths of Abu Simbel) were moved by a few hundred yards to nearly identical sites. Eleven others (such as the temple of Amada) were rebuilt and grouped in three oases overlooking the new Lake Nasser. Seven more temples (including the fortress of Buhen) were placed in national museums in Aswan and Khartoum. The last five (including the temple of Dendur, now at the Metropolitan Museum in New York) were sent to Western museums as "grants-in-return" for technical and financial assistance. Fifty nation-states took part in these operations, sending more than 150 teams of experts to Nubia and contributing a total of forty million dollars to a trust fund managed by the United Nations Educational Scientific and Cultural Organization (UNESCO).

The coherence of all these operations as one historical "event" was guaranteed by UNESCO's designation of one "campaign"—the International Campaign to Salvage the Temples of Nubia—which was inaugurated at one ceremony (on March 8, 1960) and terminated at another (on March 10, 1980). The word "campaign" connotes both classic territorial conquest and modern political machinery; UNESCO used it to signal a new type of international action that follows a script characteristic of twentieth-century parliamentary diplomacy: the general assembly of an international organization publicized an "appeal" on behalf of one of its member-states to attract and coordinate multilateral action by other nations.

The first it its cultural genre, the Nubian campaign combined the rhetoric of humanitarian intervention with the tone of international philanthropy. "It is not easy to choose between temples and crops," declared UNESCO Director-General Vittorino Veronese in his appeal. "I would feel sorry for any man who is called upon to do so without a feeling of despair." By 1980 his successor, Amadou-Mahtar M'Bow, had closed the campaign by calling it "the first example of international cooperation to an essentially cultural end" and congratulated "the present-day world community" for mobilizing "resources comparable to those used by the sovereigns of Egypt to build the temples" that had been salvaged. In their relocation, M'Bow argued, the temples of Nubia had become emblems of a "movement of worldwide solidarity without precedent in the history of mankind."[1]

Most accounts of the campaign have taken their cue from this grandiose rhetoric, telling the story of a twenty-year architectural "salvage" from an all-too-human "despair." Few have questioned the conflation of architectural salvage with ethical salvation that permeates UNESCO's literature, or its claim to have transformed ancient temples into emblems of a modern political order. Recent debates on cultural restitution have cited the campaign as a historical turning point, a step toward an age of cultural reciprocity between Western nations "rich in the economic sense" and non-Western cultures "rich in cultural values."[2] The political theorist Elazar Barkan has even seen this kind of restitution as evidence of the rise of a new "international morality" in late-twentieth-century diplomacy, an era in which governments increasingly use cultural "rights" to remedy historical "wrongs."[3]

But there is also a spatial coherence to all the transfers of objects and values that were orchestrated during the campaign (figure 8.1). All the displacements of temples have followed a single logic of concentration and dissemination. In Nubia, where visitors are few, the temples have been concentrated in six locations, three temples per site. In Western Europe and North America, which are frequented by millions of tourists, the temples have been dispersed to five major cities, one temple per city. In other words, the number of visitors to the temples has been optimized. Furthermore, the value of the temples in the eyes of the visitor has been increased in this reconfiguration. A 1924 British traveler consulting the *Baedeker's Guide to Egypt* would have found Nubia on its own page, represented as a stretch of Nile dotted on either side by an undifferentiated sequence of sites, none earning more than one of Baedeker's famous stars. A visitor consulting the 1984 edition, on the other hand, found each Nu-

Salvage Priorities Assigned by UNESCO

Relocations Performed

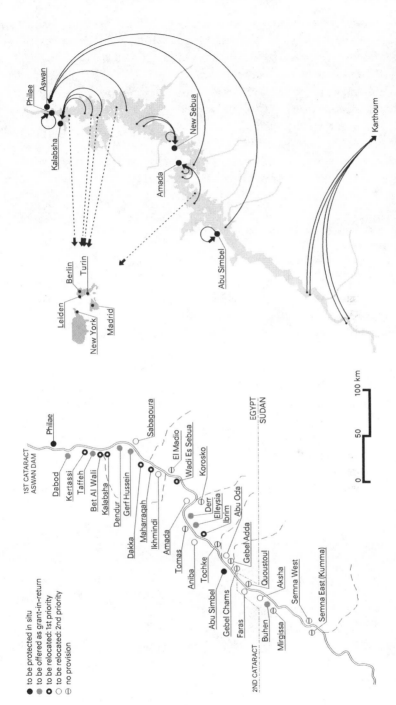

● to be protected in situ
◉ to be offered as grant-in-return
◎ to be relocated: 1st priority
○ to be relocated: 2nd priority
⊖ no provision

1ST CATARACT
ASWAN DAM

Dabod
Kertassi
Taffeh
Bet Al Wali
Kalabsha
Dendur
Gerf Hussein
Dakka
Maharraqah
Ikhmindi
Amada
Tomas
Aniba
Tochke
Abu Simbel
Gebel Chams
Faras
Mirgissa
Buhen
Quoustoul
Aksha
Semna West
Semna East (Kumma)
2ND CATARACT
Philae
Sabagoura
El Madio
Wadi Es Sebua
Koroska
Derr
Elleysia
Ibrim
Abu Oda
Gebel Adda

EGYPT
SUDAN

Aswan
Philae
Kalabsha
New Sebua
Amada
Abu Simbel
Karthoum
Berlin
Turin
Leiden
Madrid
New York

0   50   100 km

Figure 8.1. The movement of monuments. Temples relocated during the International Campaign to Salvage the Monuments of Nubia between 1960 and 1980. Twenty-four were originally identified for relocation, with three levels of priority. Seven more were surveyed but not moved, left to be submerged. Diagram by Lucia Allais. *Source:* Data from UNESCO. © Lucia Allais.

bian oasis represented on the overall map of Egypt's "High Spots," each now earning one or two stars. Between these two dates, the Nubian desert was deliberately and cohesively redesigned. What is the connection between the coherence of the Nubian campaign as an event in international political history and the coherence of Nubia as a cultural space designed by expansion, concentration, and dispersal?

To understand the international campaign for Nubia as a massive design project requires an expansion of the traditional apparatus of architectural historiography, be it only because there is no immediate answer to the question, Who designed the Nubian desert? Neither UNESCO nor the United Arab Republic (UAR, as its Gamal Abdel Nasser renamed Egypt after 1958) ever produced a single plan, and all the actors involved—from archaeologists to engineers, from preservationists to cultural ministers—resisted any description of their agency except in the reactive language of "salvage" and any attribution of authorship except on behalf of "mankind." This puzzling reluctance is partly explained by the looming presence of the Aswan High Dam in Egypt's national history. The dam transformed Egypt by reshaping its geography, dictating profound changes in the lifestyle of the entire nation, and rendering certain practices, diets, regimes, schedules, and settlement patterns obsolete.

Nasser's regime delegated much political power to the dam as a technology, but its economic and environmental consequences far outpaced the predictable features of its design. Thus historians of Egypt increasingly treat the dam as a historical agent in its own right, a pervasive force that penetrated the social order, provoking reforms, triggering mobilities, and creating a space permeated by calculability with little regard to ideology.[4] This suggestive image of the dam's diffuse power further highlights the deliberate, designed nature of the temple concentrations. UNESCO's campaign belongs in economic history as one of the effects of the dam. But it also belongs properly in architectural history, in a long lineage of works by architectural patrons hoping to make history by creating monumental effects.

In fact, the Nubian campaign revived a feature of Egyptian monuments that had been on hold for most of the twentieth century: mobility. Ever since an Assyrian monarch conquered Thebes in 664 B.C. and carried two obelisks sixteen hundred miles home to mark the occasion, the movement of Egyptian monuments has tied the passing of power with the marking of a new place. It is not only that monuments served as emblematic trophies for victorious leaders but also that these leaders used the monuments to inaugurate novel space-making practices in their new imperial homes.[5] Exiled obelisks brought to Rome during the empire became crucial instruments in the birthing of modern European urbanism under the baroque popes—contributing, in architectural historian Henry Millon's formulation, "the idea that an urban complex can be described and bounded by a series of crucially placed stone needles."[6] Similarly, the expansion of post-Enlightenment European nations relied on the periodic repatriation of authentic colonial objects and subjects—sometimes entire streetscapes—to construct the twentieth-century spatial regime the political theorist Timothy Mitchell has called "the exhibitionary order."[7]

So, to ask what spatial politics legitimated the mobility of Nubian temples is to ask, What makes these temples the postcolonial successors of relocated imperial obelisks and exported colonial objects? In this chapter I propose an answer that combines graphic synthesis and textual analysis of UNESCO's data on the campaign, treating its bureaucratic mechanisms as architectural instruments, comparable to a set of design drawings. My goal is not only to make visible the movements of objects, people, and capital that explicate the campaign as an event. I also want to show that this kind of "event" epitomizes the cultural value of architecture in the postwar international order: a practice that helped nation-states interrupt territorial contiguities and historical continuities, offering material, tectonic, and atmospheric integrities instead. Monument mobility, I argue, transformed Nubia into a governable space by suspending in time and space the question of who exactly was being governed.

As a twenty-year occupation of Nubia, the salvage campaign unfolded in five waves of mobility: an influx of foreign expertise; a comprehensive archaeological survey; an investment of foreign capital; the relocation of local populations; and the movement of temples. Each wave is described graphically, in the context of the debates to which it gave rise and the spatial paradigm it inaugurated. This graphic progression tells a simple story in five acts. But behind the scenes of each act lies an intricate network of committees whose task was to solve the growing legal, diplomatic, financial, and architectural problems posed by each type of mobility. The first of these committees was itself itinerant: a Consultative Committee of Experts—archaeologists, architects, preservationists, cultural attachés, engineers, and curators—who traveled up the Nile from October 2 to 11, 1959, visiting each threatened temple and drawing up a "plan for international action."[8] This plan, sketched out during this initial cruise-meeting and implemented over the next twenty years, is what I call "the design of the desert."

Act I: The Influx of Experts

The temples of Nubia were Cold War objects, salvaged during tumultuous decades when Eastern and Western blocks struggled to gain a strategic foothold in the Middle East. This geopolitical tug-of-war is clearly revealed in figure 8.2, which represents the number of expert missions that "directly participated in salvage work." UNESCO itemizes these participations as evidence of its universalism, but when located on a geographic dial from East to West, this data reveals that the Nubian campaign was largely a Western affair. It was also a response to an Eastern project—what UNESCO's data does not show are the four thousand Soviet engineers who were also in Egypt, building the Aswan Dam. Nasser had made the dam the centerpiece of his revolutionary project in 1952, commissioning the Antiquities Department to produce a report on the consequences of the dam for Nubia's temples as early as 1955. But as soon as the dam became a bargaining chip in Nasser's international policies, the fate of temples became dissociated from the project. In 1956 the World Bank, the United States, and the United Kingdom offered to fund the dam, only to retract the offer a few months later. By 1959 the conflict had escalated: Nasser had nationalized the Suez Canal, Israel had invaded Egypt then withdrawn, and Khrushchev had come forward with a funding offer of his own, with no previsions for the temples at all. It was at this late date that the Egyptian cultural minister, Sarwat Okasha, officially approached UNESCO.[9] Thus Nasser leveraged East-West tensions into not one but two nation-building opportunities: with Khrushchev he built the dam; with UNESCO he salvaged the temples.

But if figure 8.2 makes visible the Cold War polarities embedded in the Nubian campaign, it also shifts the focus from the unprecedented nature of UNESCO's achievement to its improbability. Because of Nasser's nonalignment, there were considerable strategic, diplomatic, and ideological obstacles to the temples' survival. Strategically, American politicians debated the relative propaganda merits of saving the temples to show altruism or letting them perish to underscore the irresponsibility of Soviet actions. Diplomatically, most former colonial powers had frozen official relations with Egypt after the Suez crisis. Also surprising, in hindsight, is Nasser's commitment to a project not directly related to his pan-Arabist cultural policies, which favored a revival of Egypt's Islamic heritage over its Pharaonic past. Against these odds, how was the massive international effort in figure 8.2 coalesced?

The answer begins in the organizational history of the United Nations system, where UNESCO seized the predicament of the Nubian temples as an opportunity to claim a role for "culture" in global politics, at a time when "technical assistance" had become the privileged mode of international intervention. "Technical assistance" designates a type of aid that aims not only at immediate relief but also at the transfer of knowledge for long-term economic development. For UNESCO's Cultural Affairs Division, which described its mission as "cultural propaganda" well into the 1950s, technical assistance presented a particular challenge. In short, "culture" had to become "technical." In this context the predicament of the Nubian temples appeared specialized enough to attract technical experts but large enough to be spectacularized as evidence of cultural cohesion on a worldwide scale.

Accordingly, the campaign for Nubia rose to the top of UNESCO's agenda as a merger of two initiatives—one technical, the other general—that were promoted by the chair of the Museum and Monuments Committee, the American archaeologist John Otis (Jo) Brew. Brew was a veteran of the archaeological digs of the Tennessee Valley Authority and had worked to pass federal legislation in the 1940s requiring that all public works in the United States include a budget for "salvage archaeology." He now hoped to internationalize these regulations. In a 1958 pamphlet titled "Emergency Archaeology: Salvage in Advance of Technological Progress," Brew depicted archaeologists as mediators

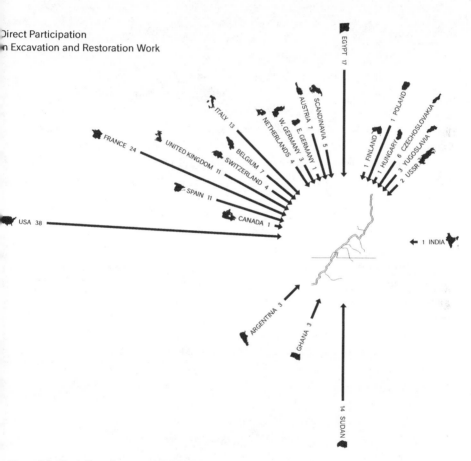

Figure 8.2. The influx of experts. UNESCO collected each country's "direct participation in excavation and restoration work," quantifying this participation in number of missions and experts. Diagram by Lucia Allais. *Source:* Data from UNESCO. © Lucia Allais.

between past and future, bearers of a historical force that hovered redemptively around public works, salvaging the remains of the past.[10]

Brew used the Tennessee Valley Authority precedent cunningly—it was a favorite reference for advocates of international cooperation—and secured a part of UNESCO's 1959 budget to publish a general report on "the consequences of large-scale engineering works as it concerns the conservation of the cultural heritage of mankind." That same year, Brew also planned to inaugurate an International Campaign for Monuments, a global publicity event featuring monuments as vehicles for international understanding. But in a decidedly "technical" turn of events, both the report and the campaign were suspended so that Brew and the Monuments Committee could devote itself to Nubia instead. Thus figure 8.2 depicts not only a strategic gamble for Egypt but also a gamble of cultural politics for UNESCO—a massive show of technical assistance, triggered by a massive push of cultural propaganda, an "appeal."

The appeal took place at UNESCO House in Paris over one long and speech-filled day. The avowed goal was to "create a real psychological shock" in the international community, illustrating the impending flood with images of semisubmerged temples (figure 8.3).[11] But the more subtle achievement was to neutralize the monuments from the Cold War, inscribing their fate once and for all in an abstract narrative about the "history of mankind." Much of this neutralization was performed by the French cultural minister André Malraux, who presided over the launch ceremony with his dramatic vibrato.[12]

Malraux opened his speech by setting UNESCO apart from the sphere of international politics, where nations were involved in "overt or open conflict." He praised the project as a "TVA of Archaeology," "the antithesis of the kind of gigantic exhibitionism by which great modern states try to outbid each other." He then proceeded to outline a Hegelian scheme of world history, where the lack of political "unity" between nations was dialectically countered by the cultural "indivisibility" of their heritage. Thus preservation was an index of progress: a victory of man over nature, of "art" over "history." To illustrate how the Nubian monuments contributed to this worldwide aesthetic rebirth, Malraux spoke only of human forms—"sculpted mountains," "colossal effigies," "colossal death-masks," "the face of Queen Nefertiti"—despite the fact that only few of the temples included full-sized sculpture. This emphasis on sculpture allowed Malraux to rephrase the ethical dilemma of "choosing between temples and crops" in aesthetic terms: as a choice between "men" and "statues." It also aestheticized the relationship between Egypt and other nations: Egyptian art was a "witness to the twentieth century" but the twentieth century could only salvage "an Egypt that never existed." Thus Malraux's famous closing pronouncement inviting humanity to "snatch something from death," which was incanted periodically throughout the fund-raising process, seemed applicable equally to the ancient art of Egypt and the modern practice of preservation.[13]

Malraux's speech set the tone for the rest of the campaign, providing an aesthetic justification to intervene in a country without endorsing its nationalist agenda or its strategic allegiances. His high-profile endorsement of the project as a way out to the "exhibitionism" of international politics is especially significant because he had spent much of the decade theorizing the world as an

Figure 8.3. The impending flood. Trajan's Kiosk, semi-submerged, circa 1960. Since the raising of the first Aswan Dam in the 1930s, most temples—including the entire island of Philae, where Trajan's Kiosk was built—spent half of the year underwater. Images of this periodic flooding were used in UNESCO's early campaign material to "create a psychological shock" and enlist contributions. Photograph by Christiane Desroches-Noblecourt. *Source:* © UNESCO. Used with permission.

"imaginary museum." In his seminal multivolume work, translated into English as *The Museum without Walls*, Malraux described how an imaginary counterpart to the progress of "real museums within their walls" had grown in the modern mind, motivated by an "intellectualization of art."[14] This worldwide inventory worked through mass media, "unifying all the scattered works of art" as if pushed forth by an "imaginary super-artist."

Similarly, in his Nubian speech Malraux presented the Nubian campaign as a step in the construction of a "worldwide storehouse of art" and a sign of the indivisibility of the world's heritage. But the agent of this unity was no longer an abstract metaphysical force. Instead, Malraux addressed the director-general of UNESCO directly, personifying this historical undercurrent in the bureaucracy itself: "At the moment when our civilization divines a mysterious transcendence in art and one of the still obscure sources of its unity, at the moment when we are bringing into a single, family relationship the masterpieces of so many civilizations which knew nothing of or even hated each other, you are proposing an action which brings all men together to defy the forces of dissolution. Your appeal is historic, not because it proposes to save the temples of Nubia, but because through it the first world civilization publicly proclaims the world's art as its indivisible heritage."[15] Oscillating seamlessly between Nubia and his own metaphysics of art, Malraux retained the vivid image of temples "dissolving" into the waters of the Nile, calling forth a new a global aesthetics that would coalesce around the act of defying these "forces of dissolution."

This spatial narrative of "dissolution" cannot be dissociated from the political neutralization Malraux performed on behalf of UNESCO, as it recalls a very particular architectural dilemma that accompanied his story of the "museumification" of the world. To "fill the gaps left by museums," the mass media had created the imaginary museum: no physical space could contain all works of art, but many more could be reproduced in books. Indeed, Malraux believed, photography had the power to create unexpected dialogues across civilizations, granting art a certain scalelessness, removing it from its context while enhancing its objecthood as if from within. Conversely, according to Malraux, curators in real museums had begun to appeal to the photographic inventory that existed in the mind of every museum-goer: increasingly isolating objects, lighting them against increasingly neutral backgrounds, as if to include them in a future catalog. This was why architecture had not yet entered the imaginary museum: because no medium of reproduction had yet been able to detach buildings from their site, while enhancing their value with an atmospheric integrity.[16]

Transposed to the Nubian desert, this spatial dialogue between museums "without walls" and "without gaps" became an architectural feedback loop. Like Malraux, UNESCO believed in the power of mass media to elevate rather than debase the arts, as evidenced by its work as a global publishing house for catalogs and exhibitions. There is in fact a striking resemblance between the trademark visual layout Malraux pioneered in his books—what art historian Henri Zerner called his "filmic technique"—and the way UNESCO's *Courier* publicized the campaign, with vignettes of people, temples, and objects (figure 8.4).[17] Malraux reenacted this montage in person when he visited the site in 1966, facing off with the detached face of Rameses. Intercalated between modern talking heads and ancient sculpted faces, the temples of Nubia entered the imaginary museum. But Nubia was also an actual collection, located in time and space, invested with a specific materiality, and now threatened with dissolution. The physical dissolution of Nubia as a place coincided with its virtual consolidation as an imageable collection. So when the experts in figure 8.2 entered Nubia, they arrived not in modern-day Egypt but in an imaginary spatial continuum: a space where they had been authorized to act as "imaginary super-artists," but where the effects of the museum as a mass medium onto architecture had yet to be tested.

Act II: The Archaeological Campaign

The phrase "TVA of archaeology" stuck. Images of teams of archaeologists busily surveying the banks of the Nile before engulfment were distributed worldwide, broadcasting archaeology as a redemptive act. Figure 8.5 describes the archaeological reality behind this media image: the digging sites assigned foreign institutions between 1959 and 1964, each site a microcosm of international cooperation. What is most striking about this overnight transformation of Nubia into an international archaeological laboratory is that, when UNESCO launched its appeal in 1959, interest in Nubian archaeology was meager at best. Oriental Institute archaeologist John Wilson, who led the American archaeological mission, recalled his initial "dismay" at the appeal: "Nearly twenty-five years had passed with a minimum of fieldwork. The Egyptologists had turned to other lines of research; few of them were now experienced in excavation. Further, when compared to Egypt proper, Nubia was a backward and unpromising area for digging. The preservation of the stone temples was a job for the engineers. The first reaction to the appeal was one of dismay. What could we do?"[18] This rhetorical question highlights how much coordination the "TVA of archaeology" would require, not only between different fields but also within archaeology itself.

Unlike Brew, Wilson was an Egyptologist, trained to dig specifically for objects, not systematically on projects. This branch of archaeology had excluded Nubia from "Egypt proper" for centuries—at least ever since the Napoleonic Expedition published Bourguignon d'Anville's 1765 map, which showed that one ended where the other began. In fact, when Wilson was invited to a meet-

Figure 8.4. The launch of the international campaign. In 1960 the UNESCO *Courier* presented the "temples to be moved" in a grid of vignettes of talking heads ("Patrons of the Campaign") and objects to be received ("Gifts from the Land of Pharaoh") that echoed of André Malraux's graphic montage technique. Photographs by Lucia Allais.

Archaeological Concessions
by Country

32°

POLAND Dabod
ITALY Dehmit
CZECHOSLOVAKIA Kertassi-Taffa
SWITZERLAND USA Beit el Wali
ITALY Kalabsha
ITALY Sabagura
ITALY Kubban
USSR Dakka 22°
ITALY Ikhmindi
AUSTRIA Sayala
FRANCE Tomas FRANCE Wadi Sebua Wadi Allaqi
INDIA Afya USSR
SPAIN Sheikh Daud
SPAIN EGYPT Masmas Aniba Amada W. GERMANY
ITALY Tamit Korosho-Qasr Ibrim ITALY
NETHERLANDS HUNGARY Abdallah Nirqi Ibrim UNITED KINGDOM
USA Gebel Adda Toshka-Arminna USA
USA Ballana Qustul EGYPT
POLAND Faras Serra East Qasr el Wizz USA USA
FRANCE ARGENTINA Aksha Faras to Gemai SCANDINAVIA
GHANA SCANDINAVIA Debeira West Argin SPAIN
USA Dabarosa
Meinarti SUDAN EGYPT
USA Buhen-Kor Qasr Iko SPAIN SUDAN
USA Dorginati Kasanarti SUDAN Cairo
FRANCE Mirgissa Gemai FINLAND
USA Semna Askut USA Aswan
USA Semna South Kumma USA EGYPT
Melik en Nasir W. GERMANY SUDAN
Sonqi ITALY
Ukma SWITZERLAND
Akasha SWITZERLAND
Kulubnarti USA Khartoum

0 50 100 km

Figure 8.5. The archaeological campaign. Concessions for surveying the archaeological sites of Nubia were granted along institutional lines, often provoking collaborations across national boundaries and transforming Nubia into a microcosm of the international order, with a bent toward the West. Diagram by Lucia Allais and Sam Stewart-Halevy. *Source*: © Lucia Allais.

ing of specialists convened by the U.S. Department of State in late 1959 to construct the American response to the appeal, the question "what could we do?" was answered by distinguishing two types of archaeologists: those who would conduct most of the digging, and those who would attract most of the funding. Most of the Nubian sites to be flooded were prehistoric; they contained the "hearths, homes, flint implements and other artifacts of Neolithic and Paleolithic man."[19] This kind of digging was likely to attract so-called dirt archaeologists: prehistorians from research universities "interested in uncovering information . . . just for its own sake." But more resources and publicity, everyone agreed, would be forthcoming if the campaign became "a method for museums to acquire materials." These museums were interested in objects of Pharaonic origin, not in the hearths and homes of anonymous prehistoric men. The difference between uncovering information for its own sake and acquiring material, between *knowing* and *having*, was an institutional divide and a methodological rift.

But even if these two branches of archaeology could be made to collaborate, a number of disputes in the early twentieth century had soured the relationship between Egypt and foreign excavators of any kind. This history is usefully illustrated by the bust of Nefertiti, one of the most famous Egyptian objects of the twentieth century and still a subject of a bitter restitution debate. The limestone bust was brought from Armana to Berlin in 1914 by a German expedition and remained in private hands for a decade, until it was gifted to the Egyptian Museum. As soon as the museum published the object in its bulletin in 1923, the Egyptian government protested that it would never have allowed such an outstanding piece to be exported. To this, the German archaeologists replied that two "outstanding" objects had been found in the 1912 digging season—Nefertiti's head and a limestone altarpiece—and that one piece was conceded to Germany while the other acted as a "counterpiece" in Cairo.

This concept of a "counterpiece" had long been the medium of exchange between Egyptologists and Egypt, designed to ensure a fair trade between access to a site (granted by the Antiquities Department) and the resources to dig in that site (brought by the archaeologist and his patrons). Every archaeological find was divided into two lots, in a "fifty-fifty division of value," and any controversy over an exported object was actually a controversy over the relative value of an object and its counterpiece. As colonial control over the Antiquities Department faded, this fifty-fifty regime was thrown into crisis. Beginning in the 1920s, an increasing number of unique objects found in the Egyptian subsoil were declared national property. In the 1930s Western museums phased out their excavations; by the 1940s demand for access to Egypt had all but died.[20]

So, to bring Egyptologists back to Egypt and make Nubia attractive to them, UNESCO had to negotiate a new balance of archaeological access and cultural reward. The terms of this balance were set out in one document, a "Declaration by the Government of the United Arab Republic," jointly authored by Okasha and UNESCO experts and distributed the day of the appeal.[21] On the surface the declaration was a legal contract in the Egyptological tradition, which restored the fifty-fifty regime. In reality, it did much more: it constructed an elaborate legal and bureaucratic procedure that completely transformed the terms of colonial archaeology, replacing it with a new international regimen for cultural exchange among nations that offered territorial control of a region under the guise of cultural generosity.

To begin with, the declaration promised archaeologists not only half of their finds but also rewards from outside of Nubia: access to archaeological sites "north of the dam" (the place Wilson called "Egypt proper"), as well as gifts from Egypt's "vast collection of antiquities in Cairo." These outside rewards cleverly lured Egyptologists into the campaign by promising to reunite them with innumerable objects they had given up in Cairo as counterpieces over a century's worth of fifty-fifty divisions. However, these outside rewards and digging sites north could only be obtained once the digging in Nubia had been finished. This clause created considerable tension between the two archaeological camps: prehistorians digging in Nubia were skeptical of "squawking Egyptologists" and expressed their skepticism in terms of a debate between science and aesthetics.[22] Egyptologists, eager to begin digging north of the dam, repaid the contempt of dirt archaeologists with zealotry for their own cause, "the revival of Egyptology."[23] The declaration leveraged this disciplinary rivalry into a territorial bind, effectively projecting the fifty-fifty rule onto the geography of Egypt. The difference between Egypt and Nubia became an equivalence, the kind of archaeological equivalence where one object is deserved in exchange for another.

Even the dismantling and moving of temples was to be regulated by this new territorial regime. The declaration invited foreign institutions to take on financial or technical responsibility for the temples—adding that some of the "smaller temples" would themselves be given as "grants-in-return" for these operations. Formally, this implied no relation between archaeologists and engineers. Informally, the Egyptian government advertised the entire procedure as a "package deal": institutions could receive rewards only if they *both* excavated in Egyptian Nubia *and* made a contribution to the preservation of the so-called big temples, Abu Simbel and Philae.[24] In other words, the "package deal" created an archaeological connection where none existed: between a kind of digging that yielded no objects (surveying Nubia) and a kind of object that required no digging (the temples preserved). What looked in the press like old-fashioned archaeology was in fact an elaborate bureaucratic procedure for unifying disparate acts.

Ultimately UNESCO used this archaeological narrative to establish itself
as a mediating agency that enforces international standards. The avowed goal
of these new standards was to "liberalize" the field of archaeology. Whereas
Egyptian sites had been largely monopolized by missions from Western Europe,
now all countries were free to compete for licenses, with UNESCO as arbiter.
Yet this new international regime also put pressure on the nation-states to be
culturally homogenous. Thus the declaration specified that no object deemed
"uniquely representative of Egyptian civilization" could be exported, because all
finds were to be used to "complete" Egypt's national collection. This "completion" clause brought with it an image of national cohesion and also set in motion
a logic of cultural excess: any object *not needed* to complete a national collection could now be described as "surplus," and this is how it was in fact cleared
for export.

Throughout the campaign no object was ever described as being "ex-
changed"; instead, an entire language of gifting was developed. Access to
Northern sites was described as "bonus digging"; temples to be sent abroad
were declared "surplus," and objects to sent abroad, once known as "counter-
parts," were now to be designated as "gifts," "gifts of gratitude," (*don de reconnaissance*) or "grants-in-return."[25] This veneer of generosity enacted a principle
French anthropologist Marcel Mauss called "total prestation"—the principle
that "one gives because one is forced to," that gifting weaves a pattern of bonds
between people and things.[26] In UNESCO's Nubia the desert was the medium
for this weaving. As gifting became a universal tongue, it unified Egyptian objects
despite their dispersal. "The gift of certain monuments," in Brew's words, did
not "cut them off from Egypt's cultural inheritance" but rather constituted an
"extension" of it abroad.[27] To the surplus economy of heritage corresponded
the spatial logic of dissemination.

Act III: The Investment of Foreign Capital

No longer an imaginary museum, Nubia was by 1961 an inhabitable ground
producing material rewards. But the bureaucratic blueprint provided by UNES-
CO forbid any translation between monetary values and cultural objects. How
then could contributions be assessed and temples be disbursed in return? How
would the gifting economy of culture be integrated into the financial paradigm
of development? The question was answered on April 7, 1961, when American
president John F. Kennedy pledged twelve million dollars to the salvage of Nubian temples, to be paid in "U.S.-owned Egyptian pounds" and divided into two:
half for the Island of Philae, half for the "remaining lesser temples" and for archaeology. Kennedy echoed Malraux's aesthetics of unity: "The whole world,"
he wrote, "believes that the ancient and the new components of human culture

should blend in one harmonious whole." He also mapped this aesthetic onto United States–Egyptian relations: "The United States, one of the newest of civilizations, has long had . . . a special interest in the civilization of ancient Egypt . . . and a deep friendship with the people of the Nile Valley."[28]

Most important, Kennedy matched this rhetoric with a financial commitment. This pledge sent ripples around the international political community and remains the single most important event of the entire fund-raising campaign. Its effect was double: it tipped the balance of the fund and established a scalable spending pattern for the campaign to follow. Figure 8.6 shows how UNESCO's trust fund absorbed this pattern in a number of qualitative and quantitative disproportions: in the size of the U.S. contribution (half), in the amount devoted to salvaging the two "big temples" (90 percent); in the proportion of Egyptian pounds (two thirds); and in the fact that the fund only constituted half of the total budget (Egypt provided the other half). Disproportion was actually a basic principle of salvage economics: the principle that salvage should be budgeted *as part* of public works, so amounts needed for archaeology would seem proportionately small compared with the large sums spent on infrastructure. In Nubia, where the temples had been separated from the Aswan Dam budget, the American pledge created an alternative concentration of funds, to which smaller amounts could be attached.

The investment of capital in figure 8.6 was therefore managed as if it were a large-scale engineering project, in three successive settings: in the American political arena, in the Egyptian Antiquities Department, and eventually in a proliferating number of UNESCO expert committees. This sequence had lasting technical and spatial consequences on how the temple movements were engineered and how architecture's monumental value was used to negotiate between the diffuse economics of gifting and the stubborn objecthood of the nation-state. The story of how the Kennedy pledge was secured is a tale of back-door diplomacy, by cultural advocates arguing that political ideology should not get in the way of an elegant financial solution. American archaeologists had first tried to secure government funds by connecting national interests with cultural altruism. When the State Department asked John Wilson to quantify the value of preserving Abu Simbel, for instance, he insisted that the temples themselves "transcended money valuation" and spanned instead from the monuments' "unique value" to the United States's "cultural leadership" in five numbered steps.[29]

But it soon became evident that a type of funding was available—Public Law 480 "counterpart" funds—which was specifically designed to showcase American disinterestedness. Derived from the sale of agricultural surpluses to Egypt, counterpart funds were held in Egyptian banks, to be used for projects of technical assistance agreed upon by both nations. This aid scheme bridged between domestic policy (finding customers for surplus American wheat) and

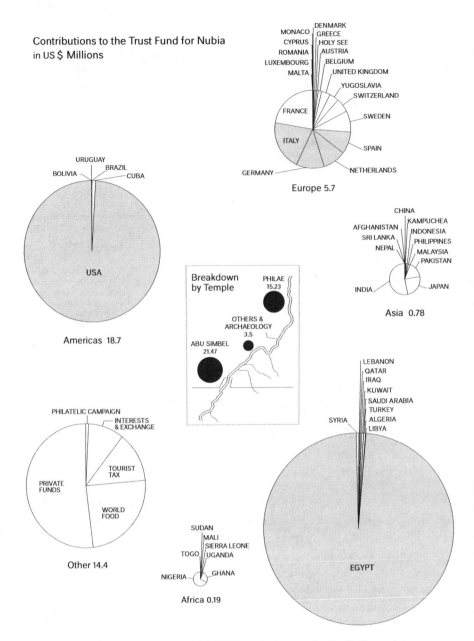

Contributions to the Trust Fund for Nubia in US $ Millions

Europe 5.7

DENMARK
MONACO — GREECE
CYPRUS — HOLY SEE
ROMANIA — AUSTRIA
LUXEMBOURG — BELGIUM
MALTA — UNITED KINGDOM
YUGOSLAVIA
SWITZERLAND
FRANCE
SWEDEN
ITALY
SPAIN
GERMANY — NETHERLANDS

Americas 18.7

URUGUAY
BRAZIL
BOLIVIA — CUBA
USA

Breakdown by Temple

PHILAE 15.23
OTHERS & ARCHAEOLOGY 3.5
ABU SIMBEL 21.47

Asia 0.78

CHINA
KAMPUCHEA
AFGHANISTAN — INDONESIA
SRI LANKA — PHILIPPINES
NEPAL — MALAYSIA
PAKISTAN
INDIA — JAPAN

Other 14.4

PHILATELIC CAMPAIGN
INTERESTS & EXCHANGE
TOURIST TAX
PRIVATE FUNDS
WORLD FOOD

Africa 0.19

SUDAN
MALI
SIERRA LEONE
TOGO — UGANDA
NIGERIA — GHANA

EGYPT

LEBANON
QATAR
IRAQ
KUWAIT
SAUDI ARABIA
TURKEY
SYRIA — ALGERIA
LIBYA

Figure 8.6. The raising of foreign capital. UNESCO created a trust fund in 1963 to receive contributions from member states and calculated its final balance in a combined statement for contributions and other income, all expressed in U.S. dollars. Four categories of capital mobility represented: national (contributed by the Egyptian government to Nubia in a decentralizing gesture); transnational (contributed in dollars by nations directly to Egypt in a bid for bilateral influence); translocal (contributed in Egyptian pounds in a gesture of neutralization); and international (contributed in dollars by individuals, nongovernmental organizations, traveling tourists, and interests and exchanges accrued by the fund). Diagram by Lucia Allais and Sam Stewart-Halevy. *Source*: Data from UNESCO. © Lucia Allais.

strategic interests (enlisting allies abroad) by way of disinterested action (feeding the hungry).[30] It was Jo Brew who first suggested that temples could be substituted for wheat in the equation.[31] The argument was well timed: Egypt's participation in the PL 480 program dated to 1955 and reached a peak after Kennedy renamed the program Food for Peace in 1961. In a classic predicament of the development decades, the building of the Aswan Dam, designed to render Egypt agriculturally self-sufficient, actually increased Egypt's dependence on food imports. Thus Kennedy hoped to use food aid in Egypt to "recognize the forces of Arab nationalism," but turn Nasser's revolutionary project inward by provoking the kind of "neutrality" that comes from "concentrating on internal problems." So although Kennedy pledged his commitment to "international friendship," the funds he committed were designed to neutralize Nasser's international ambitions.[32] In a neat application of Maussian theory, the diplomacy between Nasser and Kennedy unfolded according to a logic of giving and countergiving: Egypt offered surplus temples as gifts; the United States offered to pay for them with a gift of surplus food. Gifting, to borrow French writer George Bataille's expression, became "acquiring a power."[33]

The trouble with tying international policy to domestic politics, however, is that counterpart funds were subject to being appropriated by Congress. Twice, American archaeologists testified in the Senate. Twice, they failed. The first time they argued that counterpart funds were accumulating in Egypt, unspent, and presenting a risk of devaluation in light of mounting tensions with Nasser.[34] "Culture," they argued, was a safe, "noncontroversial" way to spend them.[35] But Congress was skeptical, expressing unfamiliarity with UNESCO and familiarity in contrast with a tradition of personal and corporate philanthropy in American politics. Indeed, the diplomatic channels that had been employed to secure Kennedy's pledge closely resembled philanthropy, involving the First Lady on the American side and the Aga Khan on the Egyptian side. Even the U.S. archaeologists were encouraged to testify in Congress as private citizens.

The strategy backfired, however. In September 1961, Congress suggested that private sponsorship should be sought, rather than government expenditure. This first refusal was reported around the world, prompting a major mobilization of private fund-raising.[36] But American archaeologists continued to press politicians. Inverting their strategy, they embarked on a publicity tour to argue that monument salvage would succeed where "food for peace" had failed: by rendering visible America's influence in Egypt. Playing on growing fears that Nasser was reaping the public relations benefit of U.S. food aid, they ventured that most Egyptians thought bags of U.S. surplus wheat came from Nasser's land reclamation project—worse yet, from the Aswan High Dam.[37] In contrast, archaeologists argued, the Kennedy pledge had been publicized so broadly that the United States was effectively working in a paradigm of monuments-for-peace.

But by 1963 the climate of cooperation between the United States and the United Arab Republic had soured, while Egyptian-Soviet friendship had escalated to symbolic heights. After all, the Aswan Dam had the monumental upper hand, and the Congress had refused to appropriate the funds a second time. In May 1964 the U.S. State Department resolved to adopt a process where no vote was necessary. The funds were finally secured by "appropriation waiver authority," through the U.S. Agency of International Development (USAID), which certified that the funds would contribute to "balanced economic development" of Egypt through "increased tourism."[38] When the United States finally succeeded in spectacularizing technical aid, it was by channeling agricultural funds into a nascent global culture industry. The hungry Egyptian, original target of American influence, was replaced by a new cultural constituency: the international tourist. In 1964 this tourist was still theoretical; only in 1971 did the Food and Agricultural Organization develop a Lake Nasser Tourist Development Programme, and only in the mid-1970s, when Egypt inaugurated its Open Door economic policies, was the American investment fully realized.[39] Ironically, this ten-year delay vindicated UNESCO's rhetoric about the timelessness of Egyptian art: the Nubian temples were able to incubate political value because, as cultural objects, they apparently existed in an alternate timeframe, leaving national ideologies untouched while offering a common platform of financial investment.

As the Nile waters rose steadily over the 1960s, the Nubian desert was materially and visually transformed into an incubator of cultural value. Visitors found the temples spread out in a disassembled form, as collections of numbered and classified blocks, arranged in alleys and grids on the sand (figure 8.7). As soon as Kennedy had made his pledge, the Egyptian Antiquities Department had begun to dismantle all the temples at once, using a traditional method of disassembly that was dictated by the abundance of Egyptian pounds. Indeed, local funds were best used to pay local workers to conduct labor-intensive procedures, while the machinery required for more adventurous techniques could only be purchased with convertible currency. Thus all relocations were performed by manually taking temples apart—in more than half the cases, *sawing* them apart—rather than through more advanced means. (Perhaps most famously, the colossal temples of Abu Simbel were sawed apart instead of being jacked up hydraulically.) Once stored, these temples could safely wait to be funded for reconstruction, temple by temple.

As monuments were stored in this disaggregated state, their value was dissociated from their objecthood. After UNESCO appointed a series of committees to raise funds for reconstructions, some Western nations were eager to turn individual temples into symbolic objects. Germany took on the relocation of Akasha, and France of Amada, hoping to make them emblems of bilateral

Figure 8.7. The disaggregation of temples. Dismantled blocks of the temples from the Island of Philae, stored on Elephantine Island. Photograph by Condotte and Mazzi Estero. *Source:* © UNESCO. Used with permission from UNESCO.

solidarity. Yet it was not the value of temples as objects, but rather the value expended in their assembly and disassembly, that became the paramount source of symbolism. For instance, the Kennedy pledge had been calibrated to cover the entire cost of Philae Island, known as "the Pearl of Egypt," which housed a diverse and much prized collection of temples of different styles and periods— a microcosm of Egyptian architecture on an island. Saving this stylistic diversity would, Kennedy and his advisers thought, have fittingly advertised America's global patronage in an age of multiculturalism. But when the American funds were redirected to cover a third of the cost of the Abu Simbel monoliths instead, the tectonic metaphor for the salvage was inverted. Instead of allowing one nation to claim a composite architectural object as symbol, one monolithic architectural object became the collective symbol of a multitude of nations. Against the "dissolution" threatened by the natural forces of the Nile, the campaign brandished aggregation as a cultural act.

When a committee was convened to decide which nations would receive the temples "in return," architecture proved able, again, to bridge between the economic disproportion of the fund and the political objecthood of the nation in UNESCO. The United States earned the temple of Dendur in March 1965; a year later Ellysia was granted to Italy; and a year after that, the Netherlands and Spain were granted Taffah and Debod, respectively.[40] Eventually Germany received a monumental gate that was found disassembled in the subsoil of Kalabsha. There is a gross disproportion between the amounts spent by each of these five nations to receive these temples, but their spending pattern is consistent: these are the nations that contributed the largest amounts of local currency (the United States and Spain) or oversaw most of the engineering operations (the Netherlands, Italy, and Germany) for the "Big Temples."[41]

That the value of these five exiled temples lies in their reassembly rather than in their objecthood is evidenced by the widely divergent standards with which they are conserved. At the Metropolitan Museum of Art in New York, for example, an immense amount of effort went into the design of the architectural and atmospheric conditions around the temple of Dendur. Brought to New York as part a broad effort of cultural renewal and concentration, the temple became a prized fund-raising asset for the city's cultural elite. In contrast, three European temples went to admittedly secondary locations, in a gesture of cultural decentralization. Only a small portion of the temple of Ellysia could be salvaged to be sent to Turin; in Leiden the temple of Taffeh acts as an actual gate between rooms. In Madrid the temple of Debod is exposed to the outside air. In contrast to these regional attractions, the Kalabsha gate in Berlin is treated as a national treasure, one that legitimates the continued presence of the Nefertiti bust.[42] What these museums are conserving is not the value of temple as an object but its state of reconstitution—the value that was expended by its material reaggregation into a recognizably Egyptian form.

Act IV: The Relocation of Nubian Populations

From without, the extraction of temples unified Egypt as a cultural entity. But from within, the reorganization of temples coincided with a complete emptying of Nubia's living culture. Figure 8.8 shows the resettlement of 120,000 Nubians to the distant oases of New Nubia and New Halfa, performed by the

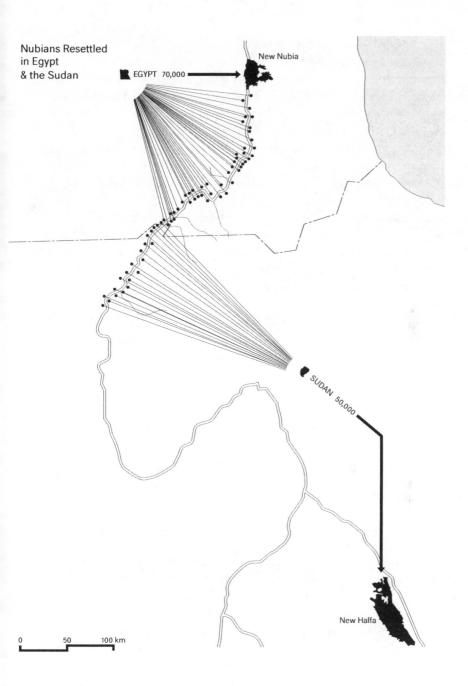

Figure 8.8. The resettlement of Nubian populations. The Nubians had already relocated twice in the century, but the Aswan High Dam interrupted the seasonal rise of the Nile, which organized their striated settlement patterns. In New Nubia villages were divided into three ethnic zones and given names that echoed their original names, such as New Kalabsha. In New Halfa the villages were simply numbered and given no names. Diagram by Lucia Allais and Sam Stewart-Halevy. *Source*: Data from UNESCO and Fahim. © Lucia Allais.

Egyptian and Sudanese governments. Although UNESCO had no control over this process, Nubians and temples were often paired as the human and archaeological prices to be paid for the dam. And although most Nubians traveled much farther than most temples, theirs was considered a "local" mobility, while the movement of temples was seen as international. But if the modern Nubian was largely absent from the cultural literature, his transient ancestor was ubiquitous as the protagonist in Nubia's cultural history. From Nubia's past as "a corridor to Africa" to its present as a "vast archaeological camp," UNESCO introduced Nubia to a worldwide public as a proto-international land, defined by a history of mobility.[43]

The foundations for this new cultural identity had been laid by the first and second archaeological surveys of 1907 and 1929, which had "refuted the commonly held belief that ancient Nubia was culturally dependent on Egypt."[44] The new scholarship went much further in translating Nubia's history of enslavement into a history of hospitality and drawing from this legacy a portrait of a region exemplary of modern cultural autonomy and resilience. This historiographic revision resonated with the concurrent formulation of the main tenet of UNESCO's multiculturalism: the notion, articulated by anthropologist Claude Levi-Strauss in his landmark 1952 essay "Race and Culture," that human societies are built for "optimum diversity," that there is no cumulative civilization into which cultures are collected, and that therefore the mission of international organizations was "to preserve the fact of diversity, not its historical content."[45] The promotion of diversity itself as a value worthy of "preservation" encouraged UNESCO to think of architectural conservation as a political mission that promotes human diversity. But this abstract, formalist notion of diversity also diverted attention from the fact that the United Nations has little power over the rights of global minorities such as the Nubians, especially when faced with national governments. In this sense, UNESCO's worldwide dissemination of Nubia's cultural identity helped to masquerade the incredible social concentration that was occurring in Nubia at the hands of the United Arab Republic and Sudanese governments.

The Egyptian Nubians had already moved their villages twice in the twentieth century. But whereas earlier dams had merely raised the level of the waters, this time the material link between Nubian lifestyle and the Nile Valley was totally severed. Interrupting once and for all the river's seasonal rise, the Aswan High Dam put an end to the periodic deposit of silt that fed the Nubians' agrarian cycle, organized their striated settlement patterns, and provided the aggregate for their mud-brick architecture. The new oases replaced the Nile with artificial lifelines of wells and railroad. Expansive courtyard houses became concrete prefabricated housing. The resettlement also erased the geographic grain of Nubian culture, which progressed along the Nile into three different ethnic groups, each with corresponding language, religion, and architecture. They were divided into national groups and relocated in ethnically zoned new towns.[46]

Precisely at this moment of geographic estrangement, mud-brick architecture was popularized as authentically Nubian, becoming a model for a new vernacular modernism throughout the Middle East.[47] In the 1970s the Food and Agriculture Organization (FAO) recommended that rest-stops built along Lake Nasser follow "the Nubian style." Even UNESCO disengaged the material specificity of Nile valley culture from Nubians themselves, by encouraging a purely constructive connection between the sandstone of the temples and the Nubian subsoil. Preservationists were even urged to collect Nile silt for use as mortar in reconstructions. Thus figure 8.8 depicts a disassociation of Nubia's cultural fiber from its social fabric. Emptied of its cultural traditions, but reinjected with cultural authenticity, the desert made room for tourists to navigate Nubia as an international land, inheriting its history as a place where remnants of material cultures are deposited along the trails of a transient past.

Act V: The Movement of Monuments

While UNESCO themed Nubia with a history of mobility, architectural preservationists were in a decidedly more sedentary mood. As early as 1959, when Pietro Gazzola, the Italian architect and lead preservationist of the campaign, was sent on a reconnaissance mission to identify threatened temples, he prefaced his report with a "Statement of Principle" that expressed a fundamental objection to moving temples at all: "As far as the principle of transfer is concerned, I must begin by stating my negative scientific opinion against any monument relocation: for reasons of history and of architectural authenticity. However, in absolutely exceptional cases, such relocation is inevitable, and can nonetheless be acceptable."[48]

For Gazzola it was only under the terms of an "exception" that relocation was acceptable. The limits of this exception were geopolitical. Gazzola rejected the notion that temples could act as "ambassadors" abroad, frankly wishing that "no government would avail itself" of the Egyptian offer of export. "The times for moving monuments out of their national borders," he concluded, "have thankfully passed." But aside from this historical rationale, which set the twentieth century apart from the excesses of colonial times, Gazzola also articulated a more recent periodization: "The most advanced modern techniques, and the experience we have recently gained from the destructions of war, have changed nothing to what remains, fundamentally, a problem of principle. . . . The transfer of any monument, as perfectly executed as it can be with contemporary techniques, is still an imperfect solution." As an advocate of preservation, Gazzola was torn between the impulse to distance himself from a history of forced relocations and the opportunity to build on the experience of rebuilding after World War II. Indeed, the European reconstruction had produced major advances in preservation techniques—from the rebuilding of monuments out of piles of rubble, to the adaptive reuse of gutted shells, to the displacement of entire buildings out of the way of new infrastructure. But however radical these transformations, they had all been performed for the sake of preserving a monument's place within urban footprints. For Nubia to be salvaged, an entire set of relationships had to be redesigned.

The debates over how to perform the relocations began as soon as the floating commission started traveling up the Nile with Gazzola's report in hand, discussing the nature of "the Nubian landscape" as a "monumental environment."[49] The discussion pitted those who wanted to preserve all monuments as close as possible to their sites against those who wanted to move them far north. Gazzola led the charge for the first camp, invoking the need to maintain the "integrity" between object and its site. Opposing this view was Walter Emery, a British Egyptologist who questioned whether tourists would travel to a "desolate Nubia" purely for its temples. In some ways Emery was more intransigent than Gazzola. Because the "Egyptians chose sanctuary sites through a ritual conception," and since this ritual meaning would disappear with the flood, the experts were free to "transfer all the temples to an island near a tourist site." The director of the Egyptian Antiquities Department, however, warned that the point was not to "satisfy tourists." Instead he reoriented the discussion toward the problem of how to translate a "cultural framework" into a physical landscape.

One compromise solution for translating "culture" into "environment" while "continuing to attract tourists" was proposed by Christiane Desroches-Noblecourt and supported by the chairman of the High Dam project: to group the monuments in two "oases" along the new lake, reproducing both the distance of each temple to the Nile and its angle toward the sun. Given this guarantee, Gazzola conceded that temples could be moved "in exceptional cases," so long as new sites were "aesthetically analogous" to the original locations. But this aesthetic analogy forbad any relocation to radically different environments in Western museums. Again, Gazzola cited the criterion of "integrity" against foreign dissemination. It was the delegate for the Egyptian Cultural Ministry, Anwar Shukry, who put an end to the debate. He rephrased the dilemma in terms of visual and spatial excess: "Egypt would be very happy to preserve all the temples in Nubia. . . . Yet if, in order to preserve them, they had to be grouped around the two oases, these temples would be very numerous. In such a case, the Egyptian government would be ready to concede several of them, which would serve as extraordinary ambassadors for Egyptian culture abroad."

By performing an imaginary sequence of design moves involving concentration, crowding, and dissemination, Shukry portrayed the temples as too "numerous" and translated the language of surplus into a spatial logic. Sending temples to European museums was legitimate, because *crowding* temples was more inauthentic than *moving* them.

By the time the floating commission arrived at Abu Simbel, the desert had been effectively redesigned. The temples had been made mobile, even if by way of an exception, and most of the features of figure 8.1—the concentration in oases, the dissemination abroad, the need for an "aesthetic analogy"—had been agreed upon. Over the next three years Gazzola reworked the terms of his "aesthetic analogy" into a theoretical doctrine. In this, he was joined by British conservationist Harold Plenderleith, with whom he oversaw the technical criteria for the campaign. Both men were invested in the codification of international norms of preservation—Gazzola as principal author of the 1964 Venice Charter and founder of the International Council of Monuments and Sites (ICOMOS), Plenderleith as director of the International Center for Conservation in Rome (ICCROM). Both men were keen to ensure that the campaign was understood as an exception to a nascent set of preservation rules. They began by appending a statement of "principles" to the official record of the campaign, which made a distinction between the "concrete" concessions needed to accomplish the project and the "theoretical" lessons that preservationists should draw from it. But they also provided one basic criterion for relocation, which operated at the scale of every masonry unit: "Every stone, even if it is not decorated, has in itself an absolute value. It should be preserved at any cost."[50]

As the movement of the temples became increasingly dependent on various forms of cutting, dismantling, and disaggregating, Gazzola and Plenderleith articulated this "absolute value of each stone" in increasingly fine grain. In late 1961 they distributed the "sacred value" of a monument throughout its entire tissue. "It is imperative," they wrote, "to consider the primordial value that each stone contains in itself. The sacred value that a monument holds in its entirety distributes itself over everyone of its elements."[51] The more mobile monuments became in the desert, the more finely aggregated they became in preservation discourse. In 1962 each stone type was sent to the ICCROM laboratories in Rome and assigned an "identity card" that detailed its material substance and chemical behavior. Concurrently, Plenderleith composed a document titled "Ideas that should be taken into consideration in re-erecting ancient monuments," which began with the only principle that was never violated in the campaign: "Stones consist of granules in connective tissue." The aesthetic analogy between old and new site had shrunk to the scale of the stone grain, unifying a diverse architectural collection—which included diverse architectonic forms, from rock-cut chapels to axial Pharaonic temples and freestanding kiosks—as if a single material tissue flowed among the temples and between their sites, and as if Nubia's desert, as a monumental environment, was composed entirely of tiny pieces of stone. It was by concentrating expert attention on this "connective tissue" that preservationists worked rather literally to defy what Malraux called "the forces of dissolution."

How this shrinking of value to the scale of a grain of sand was then reexpanded to the vast expanse of the entire desert became evident in 1964, when a new committee of architects, landscape architects, and engineers was appointed to compose the "basic principles" for the design of the "oases." These principles operated at the level of the entire monuments:

1. New sites should be selected as far as possible in the vicinity of existing sites.
2. When temples are grouped to form a precinct, they should be separated so as to be visible only one at a time, and the original orientation of each temple is to be maintained.
3. Landing quays should not be placed immediately before any temple but sited at a distance, preferably in a place where they are concealed.
4. Rest houses and other installations should likewise be hidden and should be sited so as definitely not to be a part of the temples complex.
5. The false analogy of an open-air museum could be harmful: the atmosphere of a temple precinct is to be sought and maintained and might be enhanced eventually by the judicious introduction of trees.[52]

The new monumental environment would be designed by orchestrating the visual intervals between monuments. The oasis of "New Kalabsha," for instance, was designed to gather four temples on a small island, carefully calibrating each position to make structures "visible one at a time," while reproducing the view of the Nile as foreground or background for this visibility (figure 8.9).

But it is the fifth principle, against the "false analogy with an open-air museum," that signals the major spatial innovation of the relocation campaign. This "open-air" analogy had been used liberally in the early days of the appeal. "The greatest open-air museum in the world is about to disappear," decried Desroches-Noblecourt in a 1960 call to arms.[53] In the accompanying article, she took the reader on a "tour" of Nubia. Because "the temples were set at almost regular intervals," they could be conceived as "floors in a museum," with the Aswan Dam as a "door." Desroches-Noblecourt proceeded through Nubia as if it were the Louvre, where she had been trained. She took readers through a sequential enfilade of successive periods, from Old to New Kingdom and onto the medieval period. But unlike the Louvre, as a typology, the open-air museum made a connection between monuments and local inhabitants. Thus

Kalabsha Island (as built)

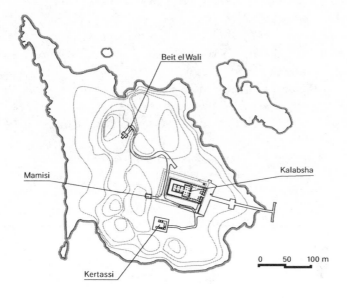

Beit el Wali

Mamisi

Kalabsha

Kertassi

0   50   100 m

Potomac Island:
Smithsonian Proposal

Metropolitan Museum:
Indoor Pavilion (as built)

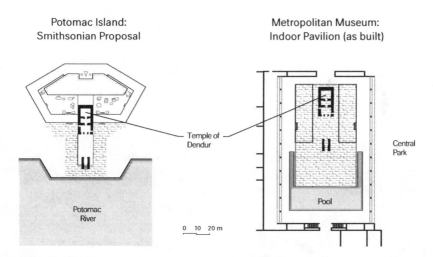

Temple of
Dendur

Central
Park

Pool

Potomac
River

0 10 20 m

Figure 8.9. The new oases. The principles for relocation dictated that temples could be concentrated but should remain "visible only one at a time" and any tourist facilities be "hidden" behind
landscape elements. The role of the Nile as a horizon line in this visibility was maintained but fragmented, temple by temple. Conversely, temples in export locations were to be isolated and their
"material integrity" was to be engineered at the scale of a grain of sand. Drawing by Lucia Allais and
Sam Stewart-Halevy. Source: Data from UNESCO. © Lucia Allais.

Desroches-Noblecourt predicted that at "the Kalabsha oasis," the visitor would "encounter a reconstitution of that Nubian life and husbandry which he thought were lost forever."

It was this kind of reconstitution that the committee forbid in 1963. Although Nubian life among Pharaonic architecture was probably as old as the temples themselves, the temples were to be "isolated" and the "atmosphere of a temple precinct" maintained. Taking the place of Nubian locality, however, was a different guarantee of authenticity: the so-called "sanctity of each stone" that had been articulated by Gazzola and Plenderleith as the ethic that governed the movement of temples.

Nowhere is this transformation of the open-air typology more evident than in the work of a commission appointed by President Lyndon Johnson in 1965, to field proposals from American museums hoping to receive the temple of Dendur. The Smithsonian Institution in Washington, D.C., proposed to rebuild the temple on the banks of the Potomac, in an explicit open-air analogy to the Nile. In contrast, the Metropolitan Museum in New York argued that its advanced environmental technology could engineer an interior climate more similar to Nubian conditions than any outdoor site in the United States. This environmental discourse located value of the temple at the particulate scale of the sandstone, its "friability," "porosity," and "absorbability"—and its likely deterioration outside of Nubia. The Metropolitan Museum experts even pointed out that the Smithsonian proposal would have required impregnating the stone in a chemical process that may have posed a threat to the very fabric of the object, by bringing the external environmental threats to the inside of the stone itself.[54] Against this, "only the detached surroundings of a specifically tailored interior" would do.[55] The Met eventually reconstituted the "atmosphere of a temple precinct" by maintaining the temple's axial sequence of gates, augmented with tinted glass and reflecting pools. This new setting completely erased the desertic realities of sun, sand, and light. But the integrity of monuments—now defined as a granular continuity with their environment—had been preserved. If preservation worked by "aesthetic analogy," in other words, this was an analogy that operated both from within (embedded in the temple's connective tissue) and from without (surrounding the temple as an object).

As an orchestration of the gaps between *and* within monuments, figure 8.1 describes the invention of a space akin to Malraux's imaginary museum: not the cumulative space of a Louvre enfilade but an art book on the Nile. Nubia became a cinematic montage of sites, dramatically lit for modern photographic memory. Ultimately architectural preservation acted as a mass medium not unlike photography—a technique that rendered architecture scaleless and siteless, reproducing buildings away from their original site while retaining an element of their original atmosphere. Preservation became an international norm by codifying itself as a reproductive medium, and its mode of mediation was material integrity.

The Aggregate of Global Culture

To return to the historical stakes of this whirlwind of mobility, Did the Nubian campaign really inaugurate a new age of cultural reciprocity among nation-states? If so, it is not an age regulated by a nebulous "international morality." The post-Nubian era is one where cultural values can be calculated quite precisely, and architecture is implicated in a process that political theorists have called "the bureaucratization of world politics."[56] Theorizing international organizations along Weberian lines, these scholars argue that organizations within the UN system exert a "rational-legal authority" on the world stage. Under the pressure to appear politically neutral, agencies like UNESCO create "rules for the world" by inflecting their bureaucratic authority with a three-part combination of "morality, delegation, and expertise." It was this hybrid authority that UNESCO wielded in Nubia to create a new spatial paradigm. Certainly the relocation of monuments would not have been possible without the "moral authority" of cultural figures like Malraux, who attracted publicity by sheer force of rhetoric; the "delegated authority" of archaeologists like Brew and Wilson, who opened channels of negotiation despite strained diplomatic ties; and the "expert authority" of preservationists like Gazzola, who made disciplinary compromises for the sake of technical success. Each wave of mobility represents a step in the establishment of this rational-legal spatial regime.

It is both more accurate and more evocative to say that the Nubian campaign opened a new space for cultural action, by weaving material and architectonic values into patterns of mobility for knowledge, people, and capital. This space is regimented by the presumed neutrality of culture and is a product of the radical expansion of political culture across the globe in the postwar. But it still bears the architectural specificity that it acquired during the massive reorganization of the middle valley of the Nile between 1960 and 1980. It is a museum both "without walls" and "without gaps," the result not of removal but rather a total dispersal, an infiltration of norms and values into the fabric of even the finest of cultural aggregates. Contrary to the image that museumification has come to invoke, the expanding space of postwar cultural neutrality is not an immaterial expanse regulated by a modernist grid. It is rather like a desert, an isotropic field where objects can be globally relocated, but also a material system where value is engineered at the granular scale. In this space UNESCO continues to act as a teacher of norms, encouraging both the nebulous morality of consolidation (the principle that cultural objects belong naturally in cohesive national collections that cannot be broken apart) and the equally vague promise of an expansive liberalization (the idea that museums are neutral spaces wherein all cultures are substances that circulate freely and equally). Most important, UNESCO continues to conceive of its rules and norms in architectural terms, as a kind of cultural aggregate, an invisible cement that holds together the space of global culture and prevents its dissolution.

Notes

1. Vittorino Veronese, "An Appeal Launched on 8 March 1960 by the Director-General of UNESCO," and Amadou-Mahtar M-Bow, "Introduction" in *Temples and Tombs of Ancient Nubia: The International Rescue Campaign at Abu Simbel, Philae, and Other Sites*, edited by Torgny Säve-Söderbergh (London: Thames & Hudson; Paris: UNESCO, 1987), 76–77; 9–13.

2. "Often the country that is poor in the economic and industrial sense is rich in cultural values. . . . Thus there can be a real exchange, a two-way action, which will enable all the countries to give and to receive, to enrich each other." In Rudolf Salat, "Cultural Values and International Cooperation," in "The Proposed Program for UNESCO 1961–1962," *UNESCO Chronicle* 6, no. 11 (1961): 413–16. Elazar Barkan cites the campaign as a precedent in "Amending Historical Injustices," his introduction to *Claiming the Stones, Naming the Bones*, edited by Elazar Barkan and Ronald Bush (Santa Monica: Getty, 2002), 38.

3. Elazar Barkan, *The Guilt of Nations: Restitution and Negotiating Historical Injustices* (Baltimore: Johns Hopkins University Press, 2000).

4. See Timothy Mitchell, "Para-Sites of Capitalism" in *Rule of Experts* (Berkley: University of California Press, 2002), 19–122; Ahma Shokr, "Hyrdopolitics, Economy, and the Aswan High Dam in Mid-Century Egypt," *Arab Studies Journal* (Spring 2009): 10–31; and John Waterbury, *Hydropolitics of the Nile Valley* (Syracuse: Syracuse University Press, 1979).

5. On obelisks, see Peter Tompkins, *The Magic of Obelisks* (New York: Harper and Row, 1981); and E. Ann Matter, "Review of Giovanni Cipriani's *Gli obelischi egizi: Politica e cultura nella Roma barocca*," *Sixteenth Century Journal* 26, no. 2 (1995): 397–98; and Brian Curran, Anthony Grafton, and Pamela O. Long, eds., *Obelisk: A History* (Cambridge: MIT Press, 2009).

6. Henry Millon, "The Visible Character of the City," in *The Historian and the City*, edited by Oscar Handlin and John Burchard (Cambridge: MIT Press, 1963).

7. Timothy Mitchell, "Orientalism and the Exhibitionary Order," in *Colonialism and Culture*, edited by Nicholas Dirks (Ann Arbor: University of Michigan Press, 1992), 289–317.

8. "Plan of Action," UNESCO/SN/R.EXP/SR, November 12, 1959, p. 42, UNESCO Archives, Paris.

9. Letter of Sarwat Okasha to the director general of UNESCO, April 6, 1959, UNESCO Archives, Paris.

10. John Otis Brew, "Emergency Archaeology: Salvage in Advance of Technological Progress," c. 1960, Brew Archives, Harvard University Archives, Cambridge, Massachusetts. This was originally "The Repercussions of Dams on Historical Monuments and Prehistoric Remains," in *Athens Proceedings of the IUCN, Technical Meeting*, unpublished typescript, vol. 2 (1959), 187–92; later republished in Fred Wendorf, *A Guide for Salvage Archaeology* (Santa Fe: Museum of New Mexico Press, 1962).

11. "Meeting of International Experts on the Safeguarding of the Sites and Monuments of Ancient Nubia Cairo," November 12, 1959, UNESCO/SN/R.EXP/SR, Brew Archives, Harvard University Archives, Cambridge, Massachusetts.

12. André Malraux, "Speech delivered at the launch of the International Campaign for the Salvage of the Monuments of Nubia," *UNESCO Courier* (May 1960): 8–11. On Malraux's rhetoric, see William Righter, *The Rhetorical Hero* (New York: Chilmark, 1964).

13. Malraux, "Speech delivered at the launch of the International Campaign for the Salvage of the Monuments of Nubia."

14. André Malraux, *Le Musée Imaginaire de la Sculpture Mondiale* (Paris: Pléiade, 1952). André Malraux, *Museum without Walls*, translated by Stuart Gilbert and Francis Price (New York: Doubleday, 1967), 160. The translation of "imaginary" into "without walls" was approved by Malraux.

15. Malraux, "Speech delivered at the launch of the International Campaign for the Salvage of the Monuments of Nubia."

16. "Reproduction, though not the cause of the intellectualization of art, is its most effective tool," from Malraux, *Museum without Walls*, 82. The comment on architecture appears in a footnote about the way that photographic plates must "compensate for a depth they do not possess." He continues: "It is the impossibility of solving a problem of this nature that has—thus far—prevented the museum without walls from including architecture within its realm," from Malraux, *Museum without Walls*, 148n1.

17. Henri Zerner, "Malraux and the Power of Photography," in *Sculpture and Photography*, edited by Geraldine Johnson (Cambridge: Cambridge University Press, 1998), 116–30. See also Rosalind Krauss, "Postmodernism's Museum without Walls," in *Thinking about Exhibitions*, edited by Reesa Greenberg (New York: Routledge, 1996), 344–46.

18. John A. Wilson, *Signs and Wonders upon Pharaoh: A History of American Egyptology* (Chicago: University of Chicago Press, 1964), 195.

19. "Summary Meeting on UNESCO involvement in the Safeguarding of the Sites and Monuments of Ancient Nubia," September 18, 1959, CUL (59) 4, p. 5, Brew Archives, Harvard University Archives, Cambridge, Massachusetts.

20. On Nefertiti's long history, see Dominic Montserrat's "Ninety Years of Nefertiti," *Apollo* 485 (2002): 3–8. On colonial archaeology, see Elliot Colla, *Conflicted Antiquities* (Durham: Duke University Press, 2007); Donald M. Reid, "Indigenous Egyptology: The Decolonization of a Profession?" *Journal of the American Oriental Society* 105, no. 2 (April–June 1985): 233–46 and "Nationalizing the Pharaonic Past," in *Rethinking Nationalism in the Arab Middle East*, edited by Israael Gershoni and James Jankowski (New York: Columbia University Press, 1997), 127–49.

21. "The Declaration by the Government of the United Arab Republic Concerning the International Action To Be Taken to Safeguard the Monuments and Sites of Ancient Nubia," reprinted in UNESCO, *A Common Trust* (Paris: UNESCO, 1960), 27–28.

22. Letter from Brew to William Y. Adams, April 24, 1967, Correspondence, Brew Archives, Harvard University Archives, Cambridge, Massachusetts.

23. William S. Smith, "The Rescue of the Monuments of Nubia," delivered to the U.S. Committee of the International Council of Museums, May 25, 1960, Boston, p. 3, CUL (60) 8, Brew Archives, Harvard University Archives, Cambridge, Massachusetts.

24. National Committee for the Rescue of the Monuments of Nubia, "Interim Report to the Executive Committee, from executive secretary John Wilson," April 4, 1960, box 9,

folder 1086h, Brew Archives, Harvard University Archives, Cambridge, Massachusetts.

25. The gifting vocabulary was inaugurated by the Consultative Committee, who decided to change the French word "contrepartie" into the English "grant-in-return" then back into French as "gifts of gratitude." Brew described the temples as "originally declared 'surplus'" in a letter to Wilson on August 5, 1963, 10/54b, Brew Archives, Harvard University Archives, Cambridge, Massachusetts. Publicly, Veronese concluded his inaugural speech with Herodotus's phrase "Egypt is a Gift of the Nile." In UNESCO's literature the passage from "counterpart" to "gift" was effected in a few months; a 1960 pamphlet spoke of "Objects to be Offered as Counterpart," and by October 1961 the *Courier* showcased "grants-in-return" under the title "Gifts from the Land of Pharaohs"; see *UNESCO Courier* (October 1961): 22–23.

26. Marcel Mauss, "Essai sur le Don," in *Sociologie et Anthropologie* (1912; reprint, Paris: Presses Universitaires de France, 1950), 145–280.

27. UNESCO/SN/R.EXP/SR: 3, Brew Archives, Harvard University Archives, Cambridge, Massachusetts.

28. John F. Kennedy, "Letter from the President to the President of the Senate and the Speaker of the House," April 6, 1961, Press Release PR(61)5, April 7, 1961, Brew Archives, Harvard University Archives, Cambridge, Massachusetts.

29. The three intermediary steps were "the arts and humanities," the "peaceful consensus of nations," and "improved relations with the UAR." See letter from Wilson to Max McCullough, January 8, 1963, Correspondence, Brew Archives, Harvard University Archives, Cambridge, Massachusetts. See also "Minutes of Meeting convened by the State Department at the National Gallery of Art," March 24, 1960, 9/1086m, Brew Archives.

30. On American Food Aid, see Harriet Friedmann, "The Political Economy of Food," *American Journal of Sociology* 88, "Marxist Inquiries: Studies of Labor, Class, and States" (1982): S251–S286; and Michael Wallerstein, *Food for War—Food for Peace* (Cambridge: MIT Press, 1980).

31. Brew wrote: "This would seem to be an excellent opportunity to use for good purpose some of the considerable amount of money which has accumulated in Cairo under Public Law 480"; letter from Brew to Thayer, January 2, 1963, 10/54d, Brew Archives, Harvard University Archives, Cambridge, Massachusetts.

32. By "concentration on internal problems," Kennedy meant "raising the standard of living of the people and so forth." See John F. Kennedy, *Strategy of Peace*, 217–19, cited in Douglas Little, "The New Frontier on the Nile: JFK, Nasser, and Arab Nationalism," *Journal of American History* 75, no. 2 (September 1988): 501–27. The United States was not alone in making its contribution in local currency rather than convertible dollars. France and the United Kingdom took the campaign opportunity to resolve asset disputes with Egypt. There were also "in kind" contributions, as when the World Food Organization made a donation of more than 3.5 million dollars by feeding the entire Philae construction site for three years. See UNESCO 20C/85/Appendix 1 (May 31, 1978), Brew Archives, Harvard University Archives, Cambridge, Massachusetts.

33. Georges Bataille, *La Part Maudite* (Paris: Minuit, 1967), 129.

34. As John Wilson put it: "These funds exist there with the problem of what the disposal of them might be." The problem of "excess funds" became apparent in the 1960s, leading to the designation of certain countries as "excess-currency countries." Eventually

this problem led to the end of the Food for Peace program. See Lisa Martin, *Democratic Commitments: Legislatures and International Cooperation* (Princeton: Princeton University Press, 2000), 142.

35. Mutual Security Act of 1960: hearings before the Committee on Foreign Relations, United States Senate, Eighty-sixth Congress (Washington, D.C.: United States Government Printing Office, 1960), 576. In private, the archaeologists saw the threat of devaluation as "a good argument for people who would not otherwise be interested in a cultural matter." Brew, Memorandum to the Executive Committee, September 19, 1961, 9/1086f, Brew Archives, Harvard University Archives, Cambridge, Massachusetts.

36. Assistant Director General René Maheu himself confidentially suggested that "a campaign in the private sector" be started. U.S. National Committee for UNESCO, "Minutes of Meeting of Executive Committee," October 14, 1961, 9/1086e, Brew Archives, Harvard University Archives, Cambridge, Massachusetts. In fact, the largest portion of "other" contributions to the Abu Simbel Fund consists of private contributions (including the highest amount, US$1.6 million, from the USSR).

37. Jean-Jacques Dethier and Kathy Funk, "The Language of PL 480 in Egypt," *Middle East Report* 145 "The Struggle for Food" (March–April 1978): 22–28. Recent analyses have questioned the negotiating power that the United States really derived from its PL 480 sales: "There is little evidence that U.S. food aid policy usefully served U.S. diplomatic interests." See "Public Law 480: 'Better Than a Bomber,'" *MERIP Middle East Report* (March–April 1987): 22–28.

38. Letter from Brew to Wilson, August 14, 1964, 10/54a, Brew Archives, Harvard University Archives, Cambridge, Massachusetts.

39. P. Bernecker and E. H. Plank, "Lake Nasser Tourism Development Programme: A Report prepared for the Lake Nasser Development Centre," FI/UAR/58/2, Food and Agriculture Organization of the United Nations (FAO), Rome, 1971. See also "Lake Nasser Development Centre, Aswan: Egypt: Project Findings and Recommendations," FAO, Rome, 1975. On tourism in the Middle East, see Robert Vitalis, "The Middle East on the Edge of the Pleasure Periphery" *Middle East Report* 196 (September–October 1995): 2–7; and Rami Farouk Daher, *Tourism in the Middle East* (Buffalo: Channel View, 2007).

40. UNESCO / 15C / 58 Annex 1, p. 10, Brew Archives, Harvard University Archives, Cambridge, Massachusetts.

41. France serves as the exception that confirms the rule. It is the only nation that moved the Amada temple "as one block." It is also the nation that spent the second highest amount of local funds but, instead of a temple, requested a bust from the Cairo warehouses in return.

42. See Cyril Aldred, "The Temple of Dendur," *Metropolitan Museum of Art Bulletin* 36, no. 1 (1968): 5–80. David Gissen, "The Architectural Production of Nature, Dendur/New York," *Grey Room* 34 (Winter 2009): 58–79; *Debod: Tres decadas de historia en Madrid* (San Isidro: Museo de San Isidoro, 2001); and Silvio Curto, *Il Tempio di Ellesija* (Milan: Electa, 1999).

43. Louis Christophe, "Nubia Today: A Vast Archaeological Camp," *UNESCO Courier* (October 1961): 21.

44. "Lake Nasser," *A Dictionary of Archaeology*, edited by Ian Shaw and Robert Jameson (London: Blackwell, 2002), 349–50.

45. "Human societies define themselves by a certain *optimum* of diversity, above which they cannot go, but below which they can also not descend without danger." See Claude Levi-Strauss, *Race et Histoire, Race et Culture* (Paris: Albin Michel/UNESCO, 2001): 119. Levi-Strauss famously repudiated this text in a 1971 lecture given on the occasion of another "year of the fight against racism," titled "Race and Culture," which was eventually published in 1983 as preface to Levi-Strauss's *Le regard éloigné* (Paris: Plon, 1983).

46. Ethnographic surveys have shown that attempts to transplant aspects of Nubian village life to these inland oases—duplicating place names, installing modern amenities in vernacular architecture, building a factory for employment—could not mitigate the radical change undergone by the Nubian social system. The relocation was closely monitored by anthropologists from the Ford Foundation's "Ethnological Survey of Nubia." See also Hussein Fahim's *Dams, People, and Development* (New York: Pergamon, 1981).

47. For the role of these Nubian relocations in a broader history of architectural globalization, see Lucia Allais, "Global Agoraphobia" in *Global Design History*, edited by Glenn Adamson, Giorgio Riello, and Sarah Teasley (London: Routledge, 2011).

48. Pietro Gazzola, "Transfert des Temples et autres monuments et ruines: Considérations de caractère architectural et archéologique," UNESCO/SN/R.EXP/6, Le Caire, September 28, 1959, ICCROM Archives, Rome. Translation by the author.

49. "Preservation of Monuments," UNESCO/SN/R.EXP/REPORT, 7, UNESCO Archives, Paris.

50. Centre international d'études pour la conservation et la restauration des biens culturels, conseil provisoire, "Avis du centre de Rome sur la Mission préliminaire en Nubie concernant le déplacement des temples," prévue au paragraphe 53 du rapport 55 Ex/7, December 8–10, 1959, Rome, CP4/RES.1, pp. 1–2, ICCROM Archives, Rome.

51. Pietro Gazzola, "Projet de sauvetage des monuments existants dans le territoire de la Nubie Destinés à être innondés à la suite de la construction du au barrage d'Assouan" (196), 5–6, ICCROM Archives, Rome.

52. "United Arab Republic Consultative Committee Concerning the Safeguarding of the Sites and Monuments of Nubia: Third Session," January 24–February 3, 1962, Cairo, 6, UNESCO/Nubia/2CE/9, UNESCO Archives, Paris.

53. Christiane Desroche-Noblecourt, "The Greatest Open-Air Museum Is about to Disappear," *Museum* 13, no. 3 (1960): 156–94.

54. The competition between the Metropolitan Museum and the Smithsonian unfolded in the spring of 1966 as fragments of the temple of Dendur were circulated in conservatories on the East Coast to test the feasibility of "impregnating" the sandstone to make outdoor exhibition feasible. The ultimate assessment was that the modern chemical substances that would have to be used to protect the ancient sandstone would have been vulnerable to the forces of deterioration: "We now know that air pollution, moisture and change of temperature will not prove harmful to the temple, but that the risk of weathering and abrasion will be even greater than suspected. The stone is extremely soft and its friability is increased by dampness. There is no means of hardening it that would not itself be affected by air pollution, freezing, and so on. The final conclusion remains the same; the temple cannot be placed outdoors without exposing it to considerable damage." Letter from Henry Fischer to Douglas Dillon, October 14, 1966, folder "Dendur Acquisitions 1965-66," Metropolitan Museum of Art Archives, New York.

55. "Only in the detached surroundings of a specially tailored interior can it again be seen to full advantage, without distracting and inappropriate background, and be seen bathed in an illumination that brings out every detail of the reliefs that cover its outer walls." Letter from Henry G. Fischer to Harry McPhearson, December 22, 1965, folder "Dendur Acquisitions 1965-1966," Metropolitan Museum of Art Archives, New York.

56. Michael Barnett and Martha Finnemore, *Rules for the World: International Organizations in Global Politics* (Ithaca: Cornell University Press, 2004), 1–44.

Selected Bibliography

Barnett, Michael, and Martha Finnemore. *Rules for the World: International Organizations in Global Politics*. Ithaca: Cornell University Press, 2004.

Mitchell, Timothy. *Rule of Experts: Egypt, Technopolitics, Modernity*. Berkeley: University of California Press, 2002.

Preziosi, Donald, and Claire Farago, eds. *Grasping the World: The Idea of the Museum*. Burlington, Vt.: Ashgate Publishing, 2004.

Säve-Söderbergh, Torgny, ed. *Temples and Tombs of Ancient Nubia: The International Rescue Campaign at Abu Simbel, Philae, and Other Sites*. London: Thames and Hudson; Paris: UNESCO, 1987.

Stubbs, John H. *Time Honored: A Global View of Architectural Conservation: Parameters, Theory, and Evolution of an Ethos*. Hoboken, N.J.: John Wiley and Sons, 2009.

9

Decree, Design, Exhibit, Consume
Making Modern Markets in France, 1953–1979

■

MEREDITH TENHOOR

ARIS, 1969: A battle raged in neighborhoods, newspapers, and government offices about the future of Parisian urbanism. The wholesale
food markets at Les Halles, located in the geographic and symbolic heart
of the city since the eleventh century, were about to move to the southern
suburb of Rungis, and nothing had been chosen to fill the void they would
leave behind. Liberating Paris from the spatially demanding food trade would
not just unclog traffic in the city's formerly paralyzed central district; it would
also create an important opportunity to modernize Paris. But not everyone
desired modernization. Small-scale food vendors worried they would go out
of business. Nocturnal flâneurs wondered where they would catch a glimpse
of picturesque Paris or nurse bowls of onion soup at 3 a.m. And journalists,
architects, artists, curators, and politicians fretted over the planned destruction of architect Victor Baltard's beloved nineteenth-century iron and glass
market buildings.

Modernization nonetheless won out: Baltard's pavilions were bulldozed
when the critics went on their August vacation in 1971, leaving behind a gaping
hole in the center of the city. Ground broke on President Georges Pompidou's
cultural center in the market's former parking lot at the plateau Beaubourg in
1972, and the hole at Les Halles was filled by the Forum des Halles shopping
center and a regional train hub in 1979. Even before the colored ductwork on
the Centre Pompidou was complete, commentators critiqued the city's changes. Paris had cut out not only its stomach but its heart. The Centre Pompidou
was an elite cultural "machine" that was no substitute for the worker-oriented
market commonly known as the "Louvre of the People." Paris had not just been
modernized; it became postmodern: filled with shopping malls, transit centers,

216

and tourists rather than family-owned businesses, gastronomy, and nineteenth-century architecture. Critics from Jean Baudrillard to Guy Debord to Albert Meister railed against the sterile culture of image and spectacle symbolized by the changes in Central Paris, claiming that the French State had replaced a visceral and vivacious culture of Les Halles marketplaces.[1] This wide-ranging criticism of the transfer hit enough of a nerve that even today Parisians and casual historians mourn the loss of the markets at Les Halles; indeed, their lost authenticity is somehow supposed to return the site, which is currently being replanned at the behest of the Parisian mayor.[2]

The nostalgia that many feel for the old Les Halles might not only be for the urban energy and architectural distinction of the district, but for the lost worlds of work and commerce that Les Halles seemed to exemplify. For the transfer from Les Halles to Rungis not only changed the urban fabric of Central Paris, it also touched the pocketbooks, bellies, and work lives of residents of the entire Parisian metropolitan region. The Les Halles–Rungis transfer was part of a nationwide attempt to generate new forms of post–World War II French consumerism: the logic of politicians who promoted it was that simplifying the process of food distribution would lead to lower food prices, which would then leave room in household budgets for the purchase of nonessential consumer goods, which would in turn fuel the postwar economy. Indeed, the transfer occurred on the eve of an economic era that is often called post-Fordist: one in which growth is driven heavily by culture, leisure, and tourism; one in which labor is service work that mobilizes social connections and competencies more often than "material" or industrial labor; and one in which it is increasingly difficult to imagine a space outside of the capitalist marketplace for nonproductive activities.[3] The "postmodernization" of Central Paris was a symptom of a larger "post-Fordization" of the political economy of everyday life.

While the Les Halles–Rungis transfer is not in any way solely responsible for these widespread social and economic changes, it is a case where the government attempted to plan economic modernization through both regulation and territorial transformation. Its architects had to design not just a functional wholesale market, but a physical model for an economic and social system that did not yet exist. Together, architects and administrators planned a market that not only was highly efficient but one that also might compensate for the losses that accompanied modernization. And surprisingly, the forms and programs that they developed in the Parisian suburbs were then recycled and reinvented in Paris, when Les Halles became a shopping mall ten years after the markets' transfer. To understand the significance of Les Halles's transformations, it is necessary to take a detour that critics of the 1970s did not bother with: to head past the city center to the suburbs of Rungis, the sprawling complex of loading docks, rail lines, pneumatic tubes, computer circuits, heavy trucks, and concrete buildings, where Paris's food is bought and sold and where prototypes of the city's postmodernity were invented.

Decrees: The Political Origins of the Les Halles Transfer

Les Halles's move to the suburbs arguably had more to do with hunger than urbanism. Lingering memories of wartime deprivations and a desire to avoid them in the future led the French prime minister Joseph Laniel to attempt to give the state a further measure of control over the food supply so that it could be better managed and regulated. On September 30, 1953, in consultation with the French Council of State, Laniel issued a decree that nationalized formerly local wholesale food markets, creating a network of National Wholesale Markets (*Marchés d'intérêt national*) in France.

The decree argued that the creation of a unified national network of markets was necessary to modernize the French food system, lower food prices for consumers, and assure the highest prices for producers. Lower prices would primarily be achieved by eliminating profiteering middlemen. Thanks to technological advances in packaging and transport, food products previously highly variable in price, age, and quality could be normalized and standardized, making it easier to sell them at high volume. Nationalization would protect consumers from speculation and allow France to compete with countries that had more sophisticated food-distribution systems.[4] Although the decree did not refer to this directly, remaking wholesale markets was also necessary because they were important components of the food-distribution system. In post–World War II France only 5 to 6 percent of food was distributed to consumers through supermarkets; the figure was 70 percent in the United States.[5] Anticipating huge postwar population increases, up to twelve million in the Parisian region by 1990, politicians realized that more food had to be brought into the city. They also wanted this food to cost less than it had previously; making fresh fruits and vegetables affordable was necessary to improve the health of the French population. And, possibly hedging against a loss of the colonies, they hoped to use the system of markets to increase exports of French food, something that would be possible if it were packaged in standardized formats and able to be sold from a single point of purchase.

French National Wholesale Markets were modeled on wholesale "terminal" markets that had been built in Philadelphia, New York, Stuttgart, Cologne, and Munich. These markets were connected to rail lines and other forms of transportation to facilitate the transport of food and were largely located in the peripheries of cities, where land was cheaper and transportation connections were simpler. Because of their peripheral location, these markets were also invisible to consumers. Architecturally, they did not need to be invested with the aesthetic qualities of earlier markets that had occupied a place of pride in the center of growing cities.[6] They were typically uncomplicated industrial buildings, a sort of cross between an airplane hangar and a train station.

National Wholesale Markets were established in the French provinces before being organized in the capital. This was politically and materially more feasible and allowed the system of wholesale markets to gain momentum while plans were solidified for remaking Les Halles. Lyon's market was one of the first to be rebuilt as a modern wholesale market in 1963, and it was followed by markets in Nice, Toulouse, and Lille. Integrating Les Halles into the system of National Wholesale Markets would be an order of magnitude more complicated than it had been to make modern markets in smaller French cities. Although Les Halles's problems were clear to all who tried to do business there (market pavilions were unsanitary and in disrepair; delivery trucks clogged narrow neighborhood streets, paralyzing the entire Halles district during most of the day; and food distributors who wanted to expand their operations had no room to do so in the crowded district), there was nonetheless great opposition to making changes in the district. Workers resisted moving to the suburbs. Property large enough for building a modern market was expensive and scarce within reasonable commuting distance of Paris, and the existing markets at Les Halles were extremely culturally entrenched.

Strong justification for a move, one that would speak to the needs of Les Halles's workers first and foremost, was necessary. This justification came in the form of a study from the venerable public polling institution, the Institut Français de l'opinion publique. In 1958 the Prefect of the Seine published a lengthy report by the institute detailing the threats to workers, businesspeople, and French stomachs that would result from leaving Les Halles as it was; it was graced with an introduction by the eminent Parisian historian Louis Chevalier.[7] It showed that it took an average of three hours per day for food store owners to travel to Les Halles, make purchases, and return to their stores to begin the workday. This was a considerable amount of time, given that shopkeepers made this trip an average of five times per week. The inconvenience was only tolerable to store owners because the products sold at the market were relatively inexpensive. If nothing was done to remedy the situation, the study suggested, the market would fall out of favor with large-scale food vendors, who were increasingly moving their business operations outside of the market, and the valuable real estate in the center of Paris would be lost to the unprofitable and inefficient business of food distribution.

The city of Paris demonstrated little inclination to push the transfer forward; in order to achieve the transfer of Les Halles, the state would have to use the power it granted itself to nationalize markets in the 1953 decree. In 1959 a decree from the newly elected Charles de Gaulle's administration made Les

Halles a part of the National Wholesale Market system. That August a fire in
the grain storage building at Les Halles killed six people and helped to turn public opinion in support of the transfer. In 1961, after much debate, the ministers
of the interior, finance, public works and transport, agriculture, construction,
and national commerce signed a decree authorizing the creation of a *société
d'économie mixte*, a company funded by both private and public capital, charged
with studying and developing a new market.[8]

The public-private partnership, called the Société d'économie mixte pour
l'aménagement du Marché d'Intérêt National de Rungis (the Public-Private Partnership for the Development of the National Wholesale Market at Rungis, or
SEMMARIS) was first headed by Camille Nicolle, an agricultural engineer who
had run markets and businesses in Egypt and Algeria before returning to France.
Nicolle assembled a team of secretaries and assistants, and the team began to
seek a place for a new wholesale market. After considering a number of possible sites on the periphery of Paris, where parcels of land large enough for the
new market were available, they chose to develop the market in the commune
of Rungis. Located approximately ten kilometers from the southern border of
Paris, in a largely agricultural area adjacent to Orly airport, Rungis was one of
the last communes immediately outside of Paris with enough open land to accommodate the crème de la crème of National Wholesale Markets.

Control of the SEMMARIS was soon given to the charismatic public ser-
vant Libert Bou. Bou had begun his career as an administrator of wholesale
markets in Algeria during the French occupation, and had worked to develop
the network of National Wholesale Markets in France. Once appointed, he
further clarified goals for the market, attempting to translate the language of
political decrees into an actionable plan. (He was so forceful that journalists of
the time referred to him as "Rungis Khan.") Following the goals laid out in 1953,
Bou hoped to organize high-volume sales by rapidly communicating information
about prices and quantities of food for sale. Doing this would create a means
of regulating and simplifying the 1953 decree's "best prices" for the consumer
without overburdening their food budgets. Bou insisted that Rungis should be
a "closed system": nothing could be bought or sold at the market, or physically
pass into its interior, without being entered into the market's records, making it
possible to track inventories and prices across multiple private businesses.

The market would impose minimum standards for sales volumes of participating businesses, eliminating smaller-scale business that supposedly raised
prices to cover their higher costs. It would place limitations on the sale of
goods, which would eliminate speculation on food prices. And although a national program to improve the food supply would seem on first glance to have
little to do with urban Paris, the effects of the 1953 decree would register in
Paris most potently. As Bou and his colleagues noted countless times in their

letters to each other, one of the chief benefits of making Les Halles into a National Wholesale Market would be improved traffic and hygiene in Paris, and of course the higher real estate prices that could be commanded in the newly gentrified Central Paris. Transformation of the food system thus laid the groundwork for a reshaping of urban tissue.

Designs: Making a Modern Market at Rungis

Although Bou had many ideas about how Rungis should be organized, the market's architects were responsible for rendering Bou's goals in space. Many public works projects of this scale were overseen by engineers, but in the case of Rungis an architectural firm with an in-house engineering team had total responsibility for the design. The firm was that of Henri Colboc, a young graduate of the Academy of Beaux-Arts and a Rome-prize laureate, and his partner, the engineer-architect Georges Philippe. Colboc and Philippe had participated in several large-scare postwar reconstruction projects, such as the new port at Le Havre and the construction of industrially produced housing.[9] Colboc's wife, Genevieve, active in local politics, knew Libert Bou socially, and Colboc and Philippe's firm was awarded a contract to build Rungis without a public bidding process.[10]

Colboc's firm finalized initial plans for Rungis market in 1964. The market was divided into zones, with separate sections for the sale of fruits and vegetables, dairy products, fish and seafood, and flowers, as the markets had been arranged at Les Halles. (At this point meats were excluded from the market because planners intended to build a new slaughterhouse at La Villette.) The market also featured a series of administrative buildings, banks, and other commercial services; a large area for the incineration of trash; train and truck stations for the arrival of merchandise; an area to be urbanized and developed for retail commerce; a sector with storage warehouses for agricultural businesses; and finally, a zone for leisure, hotels, and restaurants (figure 9.1).

The market buildings themselves were simply designed, and looked similar to those at other terminal markets (figure 9.2). Built of reinforced concrete and capped with skylights, they consisted of a central open hall, surrounded by exposition areas for products, with stores behind them. Loading docks lined the outside of the buildings. Offices were located above the stores and faced a hallway that overlooked the central hall. Below the stores were individual storage spaces, stairs, bathrooms, and other services. Although the market pavilions were carefully planned, there was little time or funds available to consider how they might be adorned. Genevieve Colboc, herself an architect, was dismayed that the buildings were so plain and felt that they were caricatures of functionalist "hard" architecture of postwar France.[11]

Figure 9.1. A model of Rungis Market, photographed from the northeast. Courtesy of Georges Philippe.

Figure 9.2. Photograph of market buildings at Rungis, 1968. *Source: Techniques et Architecture* 30, no. 3 (1969): 88.

The most crucial facet of the market's design was not the form of the buildings, nor the arrangement of the market into zones, but rather the ways in which
the buildings might facilitate various forms of communication and movement.
Precisely because Rungis was intended to unclog Parisian traffic, its planners insisted on connecting it to all possible forms of circulation: to highways, including
the Périphérique, or Paris beltway; to rail lines; and even to the recently completed airport at Orly. As one of Rungis's planners, the agricultural engineer
Philippe Barre, explained: "These markets are stations for merchandise: in effect, they constitute the point of arrival and departure for these food products
which are not really meant to stay in one place, but to be in transit in the best
possible conditions: of speed, price and comfort."[12] The less time food spent
in the market, the better: its perishability could be controlled, and it could be
consumed most quickly. This commitment to maintaining the effortless movement of food through the complex is part of what differentiated Rungis from
Les Halles, where passing a crate of vegetables from one side of the market to
the other could be an enormous challenge. At Les Halles transportation was
managed largely by *forts*, the strong men who carried food purchased from the
marketplace to trucks and whose deft ability to maneuver through tight spaces
allowed the marketplace to function. At Rungis the *forts* would be replaced by
trucks, rail lines, and fork lifts, so that the only strongman labor required at the
market would be that necessary for removing food from trucks and depositing
it onto loading docks. Facilitating movement through design, the architects of
Rungis built a new model of market labor for post-Fordist France.

The other category of labor that would be transformed at Rungis was the
business acumen of wholesale food distributors and purchasers, who previously used long lunches and informal social networks to make educated guesses
about the relationship between supply and pricing. At Rungis, thanks to the
closed nature of the market and the public nature of pricing data, this work
would also largely be turned into data, where it could be shared with anyone,
regardless of his or her personal connections. Business relationships would continue to be important in making and negotiating deals, but information about
supply and pricing would cease to be a carefully traded secret.

Rungis's architects and engineers focused their design energy on perfecting
electronic systems to support these two transformations of labor. To facilitate
tracking and controlling the movement and prices of commodities in the marketplace, they installed televisions for displaying price information and specials
into the roof trusses of the interior of pavilions and created a closed-circuit
television network for the market. They installed large signboards, commissioned from the same company that had built the airline arrival and departure
signs at Orly airport, to show prices, rather than arrival times, of moving vegetables (figure 9.3). A pneumatic tube network ran through the market, allow-

Figure 9.3. Price display board at Rungis. *Source: Techniques et Architecture* 30, no. 3 (1969): 85; photograph by Bernard Devaux.

ing data captured on paper to be sent quickly between the markets' different sectors. These design features were intended to make the "normalization" of previously highly variable food prices possible. Like the elimination of the *forts,* they enabled not just labor but also food to become less burdened by material constraints. By designing away its variability and perishability, food, the most organic of commodities, one constantly in a state of decay, could be made into mere information to be managed.

The architects' and planners' desires to dematerialize and disembody labor in the market are most clear in the selection of photographs featured in a special issue of the French magazine of engineering and architecture *Techniques et Architecture* celebrating the market's opening in 1969.[13] Images are shot from the air, emphasizing the vastness of the complex. They feature thickets of rail lines, curving highway cloverleaves, expanses of pavement, concrete awnings, loading docks, and the aforementioned price display boards and television systems; Rungis could almost be mistaken for the set of Jean-Luc Godard's 1965 film *Alphaville.* The just-built market, unsullied by the boxes of rotting eggs and vegetables that would soon adorn it, looks as sterile as a computer control room. The only image of a worker at Rungis is, in fact, situated in such a room: it shows a disembodied female hand and shoulder operating computer machinery (figure 9.4). This hand stands in marked contrast to the full-body photographs of *forts* and fishmongers laden with food that comprised most picturesque documentation of Les Halles in its heyday. The foodless, bodiless images in *Techniques et Architecture* suggest that labor at Rungis was imagined to be a mere matter of operating machines. It could be done by women with manicures, rather than by the burly *forts* of the old Les Halles.

Advertisements in *Techniques et Architecture* further explain the logic of the new marketplace. One, for GE computers, shows a series of melons moving along a conveyor belt, holding a sign that says "priority to ripe melons." The implication is that the work of sorting and classification that food distributors considered to be the value they added to the food system could be automated; computers could become the middlemen. Another telling advertisement is for SFTP pneumatic tubes, which were installed in the market's administration building (figure 9.5). It features "L'homme réseau," the network man, a handsome executive seated at a desk with a large pneumatic tube capsule at his fingertips. The advertisement states: "From his office, he distributes, receives, controls. His network is secret, integrated into the infrastructure of offices. His network is fast, efficient, precise. It transmits any paper, document or object. His network is secure." The suggestion is that physical movement through the complex, something its designers took great pains to make so efficient, is actually no longer a barrier thanks to the pneumatic tube network; the real work

Figure 9.4. An image of labor at Rungis. *Source: Techniques et Architecture* 30, no. 3 (1969): 112.

Figure 9.5. Network
man, in an advertise-
ment for SFTP pneumatic
tubes. *Source: Techniques
et Architecture* 30, no. 3
(1969).

of the market can be done from an administrative building, performed by an
executive who does not handle vegetables. The tube network seems analogous to the network of National Wholesale Markets itself, and perhaps even a
metaphor for the nation, in that it imagines that it is possible to control a highly
complex, materially challenging system by simply managing and mastering the
operating of networks.

Because it was so idealized, Colboc, Philippe, Bou, and Barre's imagination
of immaterial food and labor at Rungis seemed to have a double valence. It was
at once specific to the National Wholesale Market in Rungis, but it also made
the marketplace into a metaphor for the commercial sphere of France as a
whole. This double burden was something inherited from Les Halles. Since at
least the eighteenth century, its major architects had been responsible not just
for designing functional space for selling food, but also for creating an operating model of political economy in stone, iron, and glass.[14] As Rungis's designers struggled to manage the material challenges both of moving food through

space and those associated with making this movement into usable data, they expanded the definition of architectural design to encompass a set of skills quite different from those that market architects of the nineteenth century, such as Baltard, had needed when they designed marketplaces. At the same time, they gave up some of the capacities that architects such as Baltard had claimed for themselves in previous renovations of the markets, such as the mastery of decoration and symbolism. As a space invisible to consumers, and largely unadorned, Rungis had no traditionally imagistic architectural value save that of moving food. Colboc and Philippe's vision of this market, free of material labor, was both chilling and seductive.

Exhibits: Attempts to Create a Social Marketplace

As Rungis neared completion in 1968, its planners were appropriately concerned about how labor shake-ups of the time might rock the market. Even if Rungis was intended to be a place of intellectual rather than material labor, planners were not so naive as to think that they could erase class tensions entirely, and they became concerned that the market would neither meet the needs of its workers nor of the local population. Recognizing that something was missing at Rungis, they developed a series of eccentric schemes to try to shore up the market's cultural life. Surprisingly, their attempts to improve the atmosphere of the market involved recuperating some of the culture that had been lost in the transfer from Les Halles.

In their plans for Rungis, architects had designed a series of small food kiosks and full-scale restaurants to try to replicate the ambiance of those previously found at Les Halles's perimeter. As they explained in *Techniques and Architecture*, "The human side of things, without which business would not be business, and which can't be done by computer—has not been forgotten. Twenty five kiosks, each with their own unique ambiance, will offer a corner to rest, drink, eat, and continue to discuss business."[15] These restaurants were only the beginnings of ambitious plans to make Rungis into an idealized modern space for both work and leisure. The *Schéma directeur*, the land use plan for the Parisian Region that had been adopted in March 1968, indicated that there should be space for culture, leisure, and green space in the parcels of land owned by the SEMMARIS adjacent to Orly airport.

Developing this land presented an opportunity to pacify workers, promote Rungis's modernity, and attract tourists to the area. In 1969, Rungis's planners turned their attention to developing this "zone of hotels, leisure, and tourism", or ZHL. They created a second public-private company to finance it, called the Société d'économie mixte pour l'aménagement et du gestion des annexes du Marché d'Intérêt National de Rungis (the Public-Private Partnership for the

Planning and Development of the Annex Zones of the National Wholesale Market at Rungis, or SAGAMIRIS). The SAGAMIRIS, active until the late 1970s, offered an opportunity to try out new spatial forms for work and leisure under emerging post-Fordist economic conditions.

As they planned the ZHL, the leaders of the SAGAMIRIS understood that they had to attend to the cultural needs of two primary groups: workers and tourists.[16] In their estimation, workers would need places to relax, such as a gymnasium and a cinema. Tourists, who might visit the market after arriving at the recently constructed Orly airport adjacent to Rungis, should have a way to appreciate its technological achievements as well as the bounty of the food that was sold there. After conducting extensive studies of worker satisfaction and consumer desire in the Parisian suburbs, programs were proposed for the ZHL. It would contain restaurants, exercise parks, cinemas, tennis, bowling, and even a museum and cultural center for tourists and workers. There would be a hotel with 208 rooms and conference facilities, all with modern fixtures. There would also be a coffee shop, a panoramic restaurant, two bars, a series of shops, and plenty of escalators to allow everyone to navigate the complex.

Concurrently, Georges Monnet, a former minister of both agriculture and culture who was the president of the yearly agricultural exposition, the Salon de l'Agriculture, had been working on plans for an exhibition to showcase the agricultural richness of the entire French nation. Monnet wanted to create a kind of "museum of gastronomy," a permanent Salon de l'Agriculture that would showcase food products from all of France, highlighting their diversity and richness. He called it the Exposition Permanent des Régions de France (Permanent Exhibit of the Regions of France, or EPRF). He realized that Rungis might make an ideal location for such an exhibition and assembled a committee to explore creating it there, as part of the ZHL.

Monnet found inspiration from an agricultural exhibition in Moscow. A clipping in his archives summarized the goals Monnet would claim as his own: "The intention of the creators of this permanent exposition is to facilitate knowledge amongst farmers from all over the Soviet Union of what is produced in other regions and to help them feel part of a grand collectivity. It naturally will find its place in the exercise of the function of the federal capital of Moscow. It is also a center where the most progressive cultural methods can be initiated."[17] Monnet, a staunch supporter of Charles de Gaulle, backed de Gaulle's program for restructuring the administration of France into regions, and he used these regions as a kind of organizing principle for the EPRF. By giving a particular identity to what was largely an arbitrary administrative district, Monnet hoped that the EPRF might help to ease the transition from familiar departmental divisions to the new scheme. He would effectively remake the semantics of terroir, making it speak of the potentials of de Gaulle's system for the management of the nation.

Monnet commissioned an extensive study of precedents for this type of exhibition in other countries, which examined international expositions in Montreal and Osaka, as well as exhibitions with a regional theme. In February 1968 he published the results of his study in a pamphlet promoting the EPRF project, which featured letters of support from all the ministers of de Gaulle's administration concerned. Raymond Marcellin, the minister of urban planning and territorial development, imagined that learning about development would be a fun leisure activity. He wrote: "I approve of this project, which corresponds essentially to the Parisian population's need for leisure, and of the interest that it has for the totality of French regions and for our foreign guests to have a constantly updated demonstration of the economic and social evolution of the country."[18]

In the same pamphlet Olivier Guichard, the minister of territorial development, also hoped that the EPRF could be a tool for envisioning the benefits of growth: "For each region . . . and for the territory of the nation in its totality, *development* is the essential condition for a healthy increase in economic activity, the beginning of a better life for everyone. In order to promote the most effective solutions, all citizens have to be informed of what has been accomplished, and to be able to visualize growth."[19] Demonstrating that even something as ancient as the food supply could be modernized, the exhibits at the EPRF would make statecraft palpable, and even tasteable. Only eight kilometers from Paris, the EPRF's planners imagined that it would attract a number of commuters and tourists; thousands of parking spaces were planned, as were links to the RER and SNCF train lines, which passed nearby.[20]

The SAGAMIRIS integrated the EPRF into their plans for the ZHL. The zone would be comprised of a vast green park, filled with gardens, fountains, and facilities for playing sports. There would also be cultural facilities, temporary expositions that would continuously attract a large audience, which would demonstrate technical and scientific achievements. The second part of the ensemble would house the EPRF itself, whose exhibitions would be grouped into nine regional sectors: Paris, Haute and Basse Normandie, Nord and Picardie; Alsace, Lorraine, Franche-Comté; Bourgogne and Champagne-Ardenne; Rhône-Alpes, Auvergne; Provence-Côte d'Azur-Corse, Languedoc-Roussillon; Aquitaine, Midi-Pyrénées, Limousin; Bretagne, Pays de Loire, Centre, Poitou-Charentes; as well as the Overseas Departments. Each group of regions would contain:

- An illustrated tableau of economic activities, including agriculture, industry, and tourism, with animated models and photographs.
- An exposition of agricultural and industrial products.
- Workshops demonstrating different activities, notably artisanal production.
- A presentation of urban organizations (of existing structures and plans

for growth), of notable natural and historical sites, as well as monuments and architectural ensembles that would be shown in reproductions or reconstructions.

* Documentation of demographic, economic, and political data, which would be constantly updated.[21]

The expositions would be housed in a grand hall, and the building would also contain meeting rooms, offices, and a welcome center for tourists and business travelers. A key feature of the complex was establishments that would promote the specific gastronomic culture of each region, allowing visitors to associate administrative districts with taste.[22] In keeping with the high-tech image of Rungis, there were even plans for new computerized systems of tracking and organizing survey data from tourists. For food professionals visiting the EPRF, planners proposed a digital database that would showcase purveyors, distribution networks, and supply chains. The unspoken assumption was that such business networks would eventually become so vast and complicated that professionals would need to rely on computers rather than on market savants with particular and embedded knowledge for information about how to make purchases in different regions. Perhaps business could be conducted by computer in a museum, instead of in a restaurant?

When de Gaulle's decentralization proposal failed in the senate, leading to his resignation in April 1969, agendas for the museum shifted accordingly. They moved away from the "regional" focus and toward promoting territorial development more broadly. By 1971 the EPRF's planners hatched more ambitious plans. The exposition was slated to discuss the "future of the French" (including education, teaching, future professions for young people) as well as the "life of the French" (which would include housing and urbanization, transportation, public works projects, arts and culture, consumption). Planners envisaged that the exposition should be constantly animated and full of activities that could be enjoyed at all hours of the day. They proposed creating a vast hall capable of exhibiting any type of wine or cheese, selling regional and artisanal products, installing restaurants, bars, a cabaret, cinema, shooting gallery, toy stores with childrens' play areas, and a business center.

At this point in the archival record, the memorial functions of the museum become clear. Jean Maze, a member of the development team, even proposed the following: "To humanize our building, we should reconstruct one of the Baltard pavilions of the Halles Centrales. . . . Where better than at Rungis? . . . The extraordinary success of the pavilions [as temporary cultural spaces after Les Halles's transfer to Rungis] leads us to think that the one pavilion saved from the bulldozers, with its basement caves, would be an enormous attraction . . . we should equally examine the possibility of creating there a little 'Museum of

Les Halles' which too would naturally be found at Rungis."[23] Maze even pasted an architectural drawing of one of Baltard's market pavilions from Les Halles into his dossier. But Colboc and Philippe, who were also in charge of designing this part of Rungis, had something more futuristic in mind. Their drawings for the complex, filled with fantastically angled forms, conveyed all of the expressiveness that Genevieve Colboc claimed had been missing from the more sober buildings at the Rungis market (figure 9.6). Formal embellishment, if not necessary for Rungis market's masters of intellectual labor, was appropriate for tourists and leisure-seekers.

But by late 1972 the EPRF project had to be, in the words of Libert Bou, "put to sleep." The SAGAMIRIS, out of funds, could no longer continue to finance it. Instead, a complementary and more easily realized commercial development took center stage: a panoramic restaurant referred to as the "pont-restaurant" was built to connect the market and the ZHL. A simple modern building designed by architects Paul Vimond and C. Petit, it featured a wide expanse of windows and was constructed of 8,500 cubic meters of precast and reinforced concrete (figure 9.7). The restaurant would showcase captivating views of Orly's airplanes, automobile traffic on the highways, as well as the activity of trucks and trains at the market. Although its primary purpose was to serve food and drink, there would be a selection of twenty small exhibition centers where people could present, sell, and taste French food products. This was a rather severe deviation from Monnet's plans. He had not simply wanted to exhibit regional food products for their inherent cultural value, but also provide a means of promoting food as a leisure, rather than as a sustenance activity—much as it had been for flâneurs at Les Halles. The restaurant as built lacked this agenda as well as the EPRF's extensive displays of computing muscle and its architectural pizzazz.

If one could not resuscitate the lost commercial culture of Les Halles by remaking it into a tourist destination, another option was to simply fabricate these kinds of experiences elsewhere. Perhaps more easily reached sites, like the supermarket and the shopping mall, were more realistic places for Parisians to experience growth and leisure, and "taste development," as the EPRF's planners had imagined. Indeed, Colboc and Philippe managed to enact many of their dreams for the EPRF at a shopping mall, called the Belle-Epine, which they designed and built adjacent to Rungis on a parcel of land owned by the SEMMARIS. The second shopping mall constructed in the Parisian region, the Belle-Epine opened its doors in 1971 with a selection of restaurants and shops designed by the same exhibition designer, Slavik, who had been retained to make the exhibits in the EPRF. Ironically, the exhibition meant to memorialize and modernize a lost marketplace ended up itself being transformed into a market.

Though peculiar and unfeasible, plans for the EPRF are important because

Figure 9.6. Drawings by Colboc and Philippe for the permanent exhibit of the regions of France, likely from 1971. *Source*: Archives Départementales du Val-de-Marne, Créteil, France, archive 2447 W, box 667.

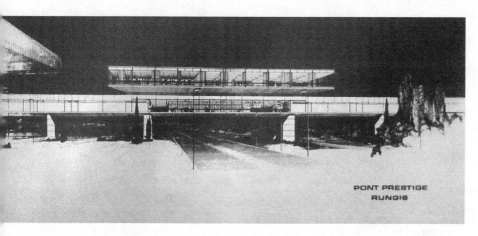

Figure 9.7. Vimond and Petit's plans for a panoramic restaurant at Rungis. *Source*: Archives Départementales du Val-de-Marne, Créteil, France, archive 2447 W, box 667.

they demonstrate the ways in which the administrators of Rungis's market were attentive to the cultural importance of the former markets at Les Halles. Rungis's planners expended great efforts to design a market that would solve material and physical problems at Les Halles, such as its extreme congestion and reliance on expensive and straining manual labor. But they also recognized that the culture of commerce at Les Halles played a significant role in popular memory, and they debated how to generate new and compelling market culture at Rungis. As Les Halles moved to Rungis, ideas about which aspects of Les Halles's market culture belonged in a museum, which belonged in a workplace, and which belonged in a marketplace were debated in these wild and impossible plans. In them we can witness some of the stranger attempts to resuscitate facets of "everyday life" lost to urban renewal.

Consume: Remaking Les Halles

After the markets at Les Halles moved to Rungis, the empty market pavilions at Les Halles were appropriated for a variety of culturally oriented purposes. The Société d'études pour l'aménagement des Halles (SEAH) helped to coordinate several exhibitions that received more visitors than the city's current modern art museums. A popular ice-skating rink and an architectural teaching center were installed at Les Halles, and it became a center of micro exhibitions, happenings, and popular culture until the pavilions were bulldozed in 1971. Despite the success of these initiatives, planners argued for maximizing the potential of redevelopment in such a centralized district. Economic studies and polls, including one by the Institut Français de l'opinion publique, were commissioned to determine what uses might best fit the site. They showed a dearth of shopping spaces and a glut of disposable income and proposed the construction of an urban shopping mall, which could be placed above the underground train station that was planned. Plans drawn up for this shopping center sampled forms innovated at early Parisian shopping malls, such as Parly II and the Belle-Epine.

When the Forum des Halles shopping mall opened in September 1979, the former Les Halles district contained a regional express train hub for managing the circulation of people; the exhibition spaces at the Centre Pompidou for showcasing contemporary art; and the shopping center at the Forum des Halles for leisurely consumption. This hybrid of programs neatly echoes those planned at Rungis ten years earlier: a series of buildings for managing the circulation of food and money were to be accompanied by a museum never built and a shopping mall that was only too easy to realize. The idealized programs of work, leisure, and exhibits planned for Rungis were a potent yet invisible prototype for the developments that later became hallmarks of the urbanism of Central Paris.

Rungis transformed how food was sold and distributed in France, with wide-ranging effects on food consumption, the economy, and urban space. Politicians intended to modernize the market by removing inefficiencies in the food-distribution system, "clarifying" it so that the benefits from efficiencies could be shared. As their decrees were translated into space, it became clear that clarification would also generate loss. The modernization of the food distribution system in France thus had urban casualties, and attempts to compensate—haltingly and partially—for them are key parts of the designs for both Les Halles and Rungis. If Les Halles also borrows from Rungis in this sense, the "spectacular" 1970s urbanism we are now familiar with in Central Paris is marked by attempts both to benefit from efficiencies and to recuperate what is lost to them.

Notes

I wish to thank all of my colleagues in the Aggregate group for their ideas and enthusiasm, with special thanks to Timothy Hyde for his insights and patience. I am grateful to Edward Eigen, Sarah Whiting, M. Christine Boyer, and Stan Katz for comments that have led to important revisions to this text, and to Eric Anglès for his invaluable assistance with translations and revisions. The research for this chapter was supported by the George Lurcy Cultural and Educational Trust and the Center for Arts and Cultural Policy Studies at Princeton University.

1. See Guy Debord, *La société du spectacle* (Paris: Buchet Chastel, 1967), reprinted as *Society of the Spectacle*, translated by Donald Nicholson-Smith (New York: Zone Books, 1996); Jean Baudrillard, *L'effet Beaubourg: Implosion et dissuasion* (Paris: Éditions Galilée, 1977), reprinted as "The Beaubourg Effect: Implosion and Deterrence," translated by Ro-

salind Krauss and Annette Michelson, *October* 20 (Spring 1982): 3–13; and Albert Meister, *La soi-disant utopie du centre Beaubourg* (Paris: Gustave Affeulpin, 1976), interpreted in English by Luca Frei, *The So-called Utopia of the Centre Beaubourg* (London: Bookworks, 2007).

2. For a dossier on this most recent replanning effort, see the special section, "Les Halles: Politics, Planning, and Urban Space in Paris," in *French Politics Culture and Society* 25, no. 2 (August 2007): 46–140, edited by Rosemary Wakeman.

3. Although the literature on post-Fordist labor is broad, I am specifically referring to the work of a group of theorists of "immaterial labor": André Gorz, Luc Boltanski and Eve Chiapello, Brian Holmes, Yann-Moulier Boutang, and Paulo Virno. See, in particular, Luc Boltanski and Eve Chiapello, *The New Spirit of Capitalism*, translated by Gregory Elliott (London: Verso, 2005).

4. Decree No. 53-959, September 30, 1953, aimed at organizing a network of national wholesale markets. The decree was published in the *Journal officiel de la République Française* (October 1, 1953): 8,617–18.

5. Libert Bou and Jacques Millon, "Les Marchés de gros français devant l'évolution des techniques de commercialisation des denrées alimentaires," *Techniques et Architecture* (Numéro Spécial) (December 1964): 120–25, 122.

6. It is notable that designs for early national wholesale markets were published only in technical magazines rather than in avant-garde architectural journals.

7. Emile Pelletier and the Institut Français d'opinion publique, *Les Halles Centrales de Paris: Enquête de L'institut Français d'opinion publique* (Paris: Imprimerie Municipale, 1958). It is worth noting that Chevalier vehemently opposed the destruction of Baltard's market pavilions but not the transfer of the wholesale food market.

8. Decree No. 61-836 of July 22, 1961, appointed a commissioner of the Parisian National Wholesale Market to establish a technical and financial program for a new market to serve the Parisian region. The major funding was provided by the Caisse des dépôts. Shares were held by the Prefect of the Seine, by a private group of wholesalers, and by the CGT, the major French union.

9. Colboc and Philippe had each toured the United States earlier in their careers, visiting buildings by Mies Van der Rohe and Frank Lloyd Wright as well as Henry Ford's factories in Detroit and terminal markets in Philadelphia (Georges Philippe, interview with the author, Paris, France, June 2007).

10. Pierre Colboc, interview with the author, Paris, France, July 2007.

11. Ibid.

12. Philippe Barre, "Les mouvements des marchandises à Rungis," *Techniques et architecture* 30, no. 3 (1969): 86–88, 86. Translation mine.

13. *Techniques et architecture* 30, no. 3 (1969): 50–78.

14. This history is recounted in detail in Meredith TenHoor, "Architecture and Biopolitics at Les Halles," *French Politics, Culture, and Society* 25, no. 2 (August 2007): 73–92.

15. *Techniques et architecture* 30, no. 3 (1969): 85, translation mine.

16. "Une exposition permanent des régions de France à Rungis," date unknown, likely 1971, archive 2447 W, box 667, Archives Départementales du Val-de-Marne, Créteil, France.

17. P. George, URSS PUF, 1962, p. 424, archive 2447 W, box 667, Archives Départementales du Val-de-Marne, Créteil, France.

18. Raymond Marcellin as quoted in "Une exposition permanent des régions de France à Rungis."

19. Olivier Guichard as quoted in "Une exposition permanent des régions de France à Rungis," 9 (italics in the original).

20. Ibid., 13.

21. Ibid., 11.

22. Ibid.

23. Jean Maze, "Exposition Permanente des Régions de France: Quelques réflexions et suggestions," date unknown, archive 2447 W, box 667, Archives Départementales du Val-de-Marne, Créteil, France.

Selected Bibliography

Baudrillard, Jean. "The Beaubourg Effect: Implosion and Deterrence." Translated by Rosalind Krauss and Annette Michelson. *October* 20 (Spring 1982): 3–13.

Boltanski, Luc, and Eve Chiapello. *The New Spirit of Capitalism.* Translated by Gregory Elliott. London: Verso, 2005.

Debord, Guy. *Society of the Spectacle.* Translated by Donald Nicholson-Smith. New York: Zone Books, 1996.

Meister, Albert. *La soi-disant utopie du centre Beaubourg.* Paris: Gustave Affeulpin, 1976. Interpreted in English by Luca Frei. *The So-called Utopia of the Centre Beaubourg.* London: Bookworks, 2007.

Moati, Philippe. *L'avenir de la grande distribution.* Paris: Jacob, 2001.

Petitjean, Marc. *Metro Rambuteau.* Paris: Centre Pompidou, 1990.

10

Marginality and Metaengineering:
Keynes and Arup

■

ARINDAM DUTTA

Why are the good so boring?
The wicked full of fun?
And citizens in conflict,
how do we govern them?
How can we hit the target
while aiming East and West?
And how make people toe the line
when I know what's best?

—Ove Nyquist Arup

I T may be hard to determine the exact lag in time when hindsight acquires the gray weight of circumspection. Nonetheless, it may not be entirely inopportune to claim that one of the facets of the commercial extravagance of the recently deceased Gilded Age—the burst of financial speculation from the mid-1990s onward to the implosive doldrums of 2008—was the string of commissions meted out to a roster of "signature" architects with more or less one distinct mandate: to churn out iconic, formally arresting, often sinuous objects whose atypicality would create new points of visual focus for the urban environment. The icons were of a piece with dominant neoliberal ideology. In policy (or lack of thereof) terms this iconicism relied on two major funding doctrines: the use of sovereign or federal moneys to privilege particular "primary" cities within each nation-state as privileged attractors of global investment; and for "secondary" cities, given the directed retreat of public money for infrastructure support, to use the "cultural" heft from these icons to raise real estate values (and revenue).

In the process this finite roster of auteurs has come to acquire a kind of brand identity equivalent with haute couture impresarios whose status in the consumerist universe they clearly envy: Rem Koolhaas, Zaha Hadid, Frank Gehry, Norman Foster, Herzog and de Meuron, and Daniel Libeskind. And yet to term these auteurs as "authors" of these technologically intricate follies of the new global urban realm would be an overstatement. Name a major iconic commission of the past two decades—whether it be the CCTV tower, the Bird's Nest, or the Water Cube built for the Olympics in Beijing, or that city's gargantuan new airport, the V&A extension, Seattle's Central Library, MIT's Simmons Hall. Note that very little of their signature flourishes would have been realized without the hybrid consulting expertise of a single firm whose practice now straddles across *every one* of the countries in which these architects may be located or may receive commissions: Arup Associates. Arup's global presence on the building engineering front increasingly means that in the current spate of iconic architecture, it does not matter *which* so-called star or signature architect sketches out *what* scheme for *where*. What is reasonably probable is that Arup will design and build it and will be a key arbitrator in modifying design to impinging conditions, whether in terms of budgetary management or local bylaws, technological feasibility, or environmental parameters. The "signature" here is markedly a corporate one: the architect is merely a boutique practice reliant upon—if not in effect nestled within—a much larger global delivery operation to service its clients.

Arup's professional reputation is exactly as pronounced as the prevalence of this genre of urban object, and it goes beyond so-called architecture to embrace "public art," manifestations as much of the Potemkin structures of speculative finance: from the twenty-meter-high *Angel of the North* sculpture in Newcastle-Gateshead to the Anthony Caro–initiated Millennium Bridge in London. Not to forget, also, the enduring collaboration between Arup's Advanced Geometry Unit and Anish Kapoor, to which is owed both the latter's *Marsyas* in the (also Arup-designed) Tate Modern turbine hall for the 2002 Unilever series, "The Bean" in Chicago, and the ArcelorMittal Orbit Gallery at the London Olympics.

Architectural, artistic, and technological frames of the imagination may be said to be underpinned by a kind of "economic rationale" that guides presumptions about the use of materials as the organization of society. For instance, the "modernist" assumption in aesthetics and engineering that dictated on the one hand an "honesty"—organic or industrial—of material usage and on the other rationalism in plan disposition is epistemically congruent with basic dicta in economics regarding the scarcity of resources, characterized by John Maynard Keynes as the "classical" tendency for thrift. Modernist proposals from Ebenezer Howard's Garden City to Frank Lloyd Wright's Broadacre, from Toni Garnier's Cité Industrielle to Le Corbusier's Ville Contemporaine contained elaborate prescriptions, implicit and explicit, as to the basis and limits of income, ownership, and hierarchy of labor—all of these economic propositions being without exception steeped in the classical view. Arup's origins in Britain as technological consultant to key modernists in the immediate prelude to the Second World War, guided by the protean sensibility of Ove Arup, might well be cast in this classical bias.

Arup's expertise in the new global iconicism of the 1990s might be described as diametrically opposed to the modernist and engineer's assumption of thrift: these speculative structures, in both form and content, indicate a shift as much in the theologies of the aesthetic as in technological concerns on optima. In fiscal terms this reversal has been generally attributed to the rise of monetarist doctrine and unilateralism in monetary policy practiced by the United States and the United Kingdom after the 1970s.[1] In that period that the role of the aesthetic might be undergoing a kind of displacement was observed at the very beginnings of this era in the various debates on "postmodernism." Various theorists of the time noted how in "post-Fordist" capital a certain mobilization of the aesthetic might be seen to be translating the modus of the *agonistic* basis of political consent to one of *pleasure*, more specifically, libidinal desire. Arup's transformation from a largely "supportive" engineering firm into a global turnkey operation—its business comparison should be drawn with Halliburton or McKinsey or PricewaterhouseCoopers rather than SOM or KPF—in many ways exemplifies a similar shift from the classical framing of technology. This chapter looks at the history of Arup to discern how the shift in monetary and fiscal outlooks is necessarily caught up with corresponding shifts in aesthetic and technological conceptions: the infrastructural mandate to *design pleasure*, or venues for pleasure, as it were, and the subsumption of the aesthetic as the privileged vehicle of pleasure rather than of an agon.

Arup's international growth, riding on the back of British financial investment abroad—into a company today boasting nine thousand staff working in eighty-six offices in more than thirty-seven countries and ten thousand projects running concurrently—rests significantly on its ability to operate as a unique kind of "para-statal" presence offering technological and legal consultancy to different levels of different governments. Examples are its 2004 report to the Blair government to "determine if the current statutory requirements for publicizing applications for planning permission, listed building and conservation area consent are effect and *value for money*"; its full-service master plan for Dongtan Eco-City, a "sustainable" urban counterpart to deflect criticism for Shanghai's Pudong; and more recently, the services rendered to Indian Railways, the world's biggest corporation in terms of the number of employees, to upgrade its aging colonial infrastructure and facilities in line with India's new economic presence on the global stage.[2] The iconicism that we have laid out above is literally the "front end" of an infrastructural transformation whose impetus is to transform the modalities of governmentality as such: the manner in which the delivery of goods and services by the state produces the rationale for transforming subjecthood itself. We may use Rem Koolhaas's description of Arup's expertise quite against his grain: Arup's "metaengineering" consists in that its remit goes well beyond the mere manipulation of statistics and materials to that of accountancy, financial consultancy, and, most important, the drafting of legislation, in Koolhaas's words, "a form of emancipation—now exploring in a kind of science fiction, *meta-engineering* as a total answer to everything."[3] What we have here is a technopolitics that operates in enclaves somewhat remote from the normal realm of politics but nonetheless will heavily determine the course of our future politics.

To understand the convergence between authorial signature, corporate intervention, and the libidinal economy, between the governmental impetus for territorial restructuring and the iconic, let us take as an instance a piece of Arup's home territory, the South Bank of the Thames River in London. Since the late 1990s, several projects have been constructed on the ancient bank of the Thames: the Millennium Bridge and the Tate Modern, the London Eye, and the headquarters of the Greater London Authority and the mayor of London (City Hall). Standing on this bank, one can look across the river where these edifices appear to indicate an iconic kinship with the Swiss Re Bank (the "Gherkin") on the one hand, and opposite the Eye, the rococo Embankment Place over Charing Cross station. Arup designed each one of these buildings. The South Bank is also home to Royal Festival Hall, for which the architects had initially approached Ove Arup on the eve of the Festival of Britain but were overruled by the London County Council. Arup designed the pathways and bridges for the festival. In the mid-1960s, when the Royal Festival Hall was integrated into the more comprehensive South Bank Arts Centre, including the Queen Elizabeth Hall and the Hayward Art Gallery, Arup was the firm called on to design the new complex.[4] Arup's relationship with the planning of this site dates back to 1972, when it organized its first Thames-side Symposium to consider options for future development of the area, following it up two decades later with a full-fledged "strategic" plan in 1995.[5]

Let us then go to the following pronouncement by one of the greatest economic minds of the twentieth century, the content of which may appear peculiar to those unfamiliar with his biography, economists and architects alike:

> Taking London as our example, we should demolish the majority of the existing buildings on the south bank of the river from the County Hall to Greenwich, and lay out these districts as the most magnificent, the most commodious and healthy working-class quarter in the world. The space is at present so ill used than an equal or larger population could be housed in modern comfort on half the

area or less, leaving the rest of it to be devoted to parks, squares and playgrounds, with lakes, pleasure gardens and boulevards, and every delight which skill and fancy can devise. Why should not all London be the equal of St. James's Park and its surroundings? The river front might become one of the sights of the world with a range of terraces and buildings rising from the river. All our architects and engineers and artists should have the opportunity to embody the various imagination [sic], not of peevish, stunted, and disillusioned beings, but of peaceful and satisfied spirits who belong to a renaissance.[6]

Those familiar with the theoretical preoccupations of this writer will recognize the signature emphasis on *pleasure*. The extract is from an article titled "Art and the State" by John Maynard Keynes, published in the BBC's print organ, *The Listener*. It would be important here to note the date of this publication: August 26, 1936. Within five years of this writing, as Hitler's bombers relentlessly pulverized the silhouette of the city, proposals for the replanning and reconstitution of the city would become the wartime theme du jour, notably by the MARS Group (in which Ove Arup and Berthold Lubetkin were participants) and the "townscape" enthusiast A. E. Richardson, among others.[7]

In 1936, however, this architectural speculation had quite a different import. The exigency that drew forth Keynes's proposal for architectural reconstruction was not the depredations of war but the political aftermath of the Depression. In a way the very invitation from editor J. R. Ackerley to write for the *Listener* speaks to Keynes's extraordinary status in British intellectual life beyond his credentials as an economist, an image consecrated in the popular mind by his transatlantic radio conversations—the BBC's first—with Walter Lippman in June 1933. For this issue of the *Listener*, Keynes was explicitly positioned as the spokesman for British *cultural* policy in an invited international debate on state patronage of the arts; the other invited interlocutors being Goebbels's appointee Staatskomissar Hans Hinkel, Ugo Ojetti from Italy, Victor Lazareff from the Soviet Union, and George Duthuit from France, with Kenneth Clark as the respondent.

This chapter is not the place to rehearse in detail the biographical background by which Keynes came to hold this preeminent cultural position, particularly his membership in the Bloomsbury circle and involvement with the British avant-garde, not to mention his marriage to the Russian ballerina Lydia Lopokova. What is more critical for our purposes is to quickly sketch out how Keynes's aesthetic sensibilities in many ways prefigured his approach to economics, particularly the manner in which both of these draw on a bowdlerized kind of Freudian "pleasure principle." Keynes biographer Robert Skidelsky has pointed out that it was not coincidental that his seminal *General Theory of Employment, Interest, and Money* was published the day after his Arts Theatre opened in an alleyway opposite his berth in King's College, Cambridge, in February of 1934. They were, in fact, "two projects, linked by a common feeling, converging at a single moment in time."[8] One of the first plays that Keynes envisioned staging at the Arts Theatre was Henrik Ibsen's *The Master Builder*.[9]

Much of our understanding of Keynes's aestheticism draws from the work of economists and economic historians. Because of this, the *content* of this aestheticism of approach has remained more or less obscure in the eyes of that audience, forming something like an anecdotal or alluring background to the more rigorous elements of the theory. This parochialism may be said to work to their detriment. Those who otherwise spend their time claiming and declaiming the porosities between Keynes's theory in its poetic essence and what his acolyte Joan Robinson called "bastard Keynesianism" or the "hydraulic" flows of John Hicks's pliable IS-LM model might consider that arts policy was the *only venue*—through his establishment of the Fine Arts Council—in fact, where Keynes actually spelled out his conception of state intervention in spheres other than monetary or fiscal policy.[10] If one surveys the archives in this area, the argument that we are about to embark on becomes clear: that for Keynes, *the aesthetic is an exceptional and paradigmatic instance of the motivational forces that drive economic behavior.* To understand this, it would be critical to recapitulate the salient points of the *General Theory* in its relationship both to the genealogy of economic thought in the half-century preceding, particularly within the ambit of the Cambridge school, and the challenges put to it by the political tides loosed by the international rise of Soviet influence on the one hand and the devastation wrought by the Depression on the other.[11]

The *Listener* debate is of a piece with the ideological conflicts shaping up within European capitalism of the interwar years. As arguments for greater state controls, monopoly even, over economic activity from the Communist parties gathered traction after the Depression, especially in relation to the financial sector, Britain's Labour Party stepped up demands for the nationalization of land, voicing a sentiment that went against the bedrock presuppositions of Anglo-Saxon economic thought on the inviolability of private property.[12] It could be argued that Keynes, no particular votary of the landed interest, nonetheless balked at the prospect of legal alienation of land for its psychological effects on economic behavior rather than on moral grounds, a conundrum that he worked out in the *General Theory* through his "euthanasia of the rentier." Keynes's rearguard motions against a Soviet-type state inveighed expectedly against the constraints that Sovietism produced against the economic energies produced by what he believed to be a "natural" pecuniary motive.

The 1926 *Essays in Persuasion* represents a landmark piece of inoculation against Soviet ideology, where the dampening effect of totalitarian control is countered by speculations as to the appropriate "unit of control and organization" of human society. Keynes argues in favor of a suborganizational level below that of the composite state, "semi-autonomous" bodies on the level of the Bank of England, the universities, and railway companies—entities that are curiously squared off against what he perceived as the tendency of large joint stock corporations to "socialize themselves . . . to approximate to the status of public corporations rather than that of individualistic private enterprise."[13] This devolution would have the benefit of acting in the interest of the downtrodden while not going to the extreme of awarding them full-fledged political power. "How can I adopt a creed which, preferring the mud to the fish, exalts the boorish proletariat above the bourgeois and the intelligentsia who, with whatever faults, are the quality in life and surely carry the seeds of all human advancement?"[14] That qualitative discernment was the exclusive province of the elite is quintessential Bloomsbury, Lytton Strachey, Virginia Woolf, and others having argued: that aesthetic refinement, *including socialist thought*, essentially requires a life of leisure and contemplation unburdened by the harries of toil.

While retaining this hierarchy of taste, Keynes then proceeded in his masterful defense of "marginalist" economic theory—the domain set out by Leon Walras, William Stanley Jevons, and Alfred Marshall only in the half century preceding—by attacking the theory itself. The enemy to Anglo-Saxon theory here was, apparently, Anglo-Saxon *habit*, and its great bedrock upon which economics had established its core of sound economic behavior: *thrift*. The earning expectations from savings reduced the money supply, since the higher interest rates that savings demanded militated against the cheap availability of money. The propensity to save was therefore directly inimical to investment. Against that habitual bedrock, Keynes promulgated his theory of encouraging the "propensity to consume," a vaguely psychological tendency that occupies two of the chapters of the *General Theory*.

Much speculation thus goes into the short term: the set of decisions by which a person will invest money now instead of hoarding it for the future. It is here that the state makes a curious entry: as facilitator of enhanced spending in the short term by controlling the interest rate and the cheapness of money through open-market operations, thus positively modulating the "animal spirits" and passions that drive economic engines such as the stock market. In his early, anti-Soviet polemic, Keynes had fended off communism's censoring of the innate entrepreneurial spirit and the "love of money." Now, Keynes pointed to this "love of money" itself as the key problem but in a completely different sense. The problem here was the herd behavior in open-market conditions that, in conditions of uncertainty, leads to risk-averse behavior, hoarding money where it should be spent.

Then Keynes had advocated for greater media transparency of economic operations—"publicity of information—as a resort to reduce uncertainty. The Keynes of the *General Theory* argues exactly in the opposite direction. Now uncertainty is posited as a *good* thing in that it fuels the erratic and risk-intensive behavior that is crucial to the vibrancy of the market. The famed section on "animal spirits" thus argues against a kind of informational transparency that would reduce all markets to "nothing but a mathematical expectation," thereby dimming the energies stemming from "spontaneous optimism . . . [and] prospects of investment [that] have regard . . . to the nerves and hysteria and even the digestions and reactions to the weather."[15]

Recount the commonplace organic associations in popular culture of the period relating the Depression to a form of economic malaise and contemplate now the audacity of Keynes's counterintuition in suggesting that what was commonly perceived as the contagion was itself the cure. With this description of behavioral randomness and profligacy as the principal fuel of invigorative economic behavior, the state was saddled with a very different managerial task. Individual cautiousness about the future created long-term obstructions for those very individuals to acquire the level of wealth that they could, leading to a sort of chronic economic underperformance. In this situation, Keynes's proposal was to have government's greater control over the money supply substantially remove the frame of decision making about money from individuals, while leaving actual production and realization of profits to laissez-faire and entrepreneurial energies. In a manner of speaking, then, individuals have complete political and economic autonomy and yet are given no better reasonable choice; they are as if condemned to consume as the device that realizes their freedom. In the short term, Keynes argued for a monetary policy aimed at easing negative expectations for the future rather than seeing money merely as a circulating equivalent. By increasing liquidity—literally *writing* money out of nowhere—the central bank would both ease the conditions of risk under which investors chose to spend, and create, through the multiplier effect, a stimulus for new economic activity.

In this move Keynes reconciled within the doctrine an irrefragable anomaly that had proved irresolvable within the ethical frameworks of the political economy: public works. In the old models, the continuing necessity for the state to undertake economic roles otherwise best left to business was both seen as a corrective to cure the inefficiencies of laissez-faire doctrine and to militate against it, therefore continually posing a historical contradiction in the otherwise separate public and private spheres as delineated in Anglo-Saxon dogma. The Keynesian theoretical resolution of this contradiction was simple: in the conditions of near full-employment, which was the state's duty to ensure, state intervention in employment increasingly loses its efficacy, since the heightened consumption stemming from this giveaway that was key to the growth of employment was minimal compared with growth that would stem from relaxing concerns over liquidity. Public works—defined as the state's direct intervention into the investment market—was irrelevant in this situation, not because it presented a contradiction but because it was inefficient: "If the Treasury were to fill old bottles with bank-notes, bury them at suitable depths in disused coal-mines which are then filled up to the surface with town rubbish, and leave to private enterprise to the well-tried principles of *laissez-faire* to dig up the notes again . . . there need be no more unemployment and, with the help of the repercussions, the real income of the community, and its capital wealth also, would probably become a good deal greater than it actually is. It would, indeed, be more sensible to build houses and the like."[16]

Keynes's views on savings and hoarding were significantly influenced by the theories of anal eroticism espoused by a future entrant into the Bloomsbury group: Freud. Just as in Freud, the relationship to certain motor and neural reflexes bear import for the formation of social "character"; with Keynes, the mechanisms of neoclassical economics, with their emphasis on equilibrium, acquire an organicist supplement in the form of a *managed disequilibrium*.[17] This is the principal import of the *General Theory*: money becomes the agent of disequilibrium. It is both equivalent (as commodity) and nonequivalent (notional, textual supplement mobilizing certain "portmanteau . . . propensities" or desire). The throwaway anti-Semitism about the Jews' "love of money" in *Essays in Persuasion* reflects a conventional understanding of money where it continues to be treated, in line with Marshall and the other neoclassicists, as an exogenous variable entering the commodity sphere as a quantitative equivalent, to which either prices or the money supply adjusts. By the time of the *General Theory*, it has become a "costlessly created" governing element producing real social effects and assets.[18] By consciously assuming control of this miraculating, *causative* power of money (rather than hewing to it as equivalent), the state's paternalism is displaced into a thaumaturgical power.

This was Keynes's ideological masterstroke—the state thus comes to simulate both the conditions of total control and the complete absence of control. The coup de grace against the Marxists was that the state had been restored to a preponderant position, extending its power when criticism of laissez-faire had veered to exhortations for the state's complete monopoly over economic activity. It is this double dynamic that plays through Keynes's contribution to the BBC's *Listener*, written six months after the publication of his *General Theory*, and makes the latter's political import explicit. The principal challenge from the rise of dictators on the continent was the ability of art to preempt political dissatisfaction. In some ways Britons should try and emulate the otherwise "bombastic . . . sometimes extremely silly" pageantry of the authoritarian states of Russia, Germany, and Italy; these events have the potential of satisfying, even if "extremely dangerous, [but if] rightly guided . . . the craving of a public to collect in great

concourses and to feel together . . . [providing] an alternative means of satisfying
the human craving for solidarity." And right there, we find the classical perora-
tion on the hierarchy of the arts, seasoned in the contemporary air of discourse
about the proper frames of the public and its self-governance: "Architecture is
the most public of the arts, the least private in its manifestations and the best
suited to give form and body to civic pride and the sense of social unity."[19]

With radio upending the classical hierarchies of the arts in providing a tool—
again the glance to the propaganda machines being assembled on the continent
is palpable—only architecture retained its primacy as a device for building the
public morale and collective emotions that theater and opera had offered in the
past. By 1943, as buildings were being pulverized at unprecedented rates, it is
hard to conceive of Keynes as seeing this as anything less than a positive opportunity, given the long section in the *General Theory* using buildings to instantiate
his views on depreciation and reemployment of capital. In the following passages, the overlay between *economic* demand and demand produced from aesthetic
and public desire is palpable, and it is impossible not to equate "architecture"—
described as a stage for all manner of subsequent activity—in the formulation
below to the primacy of the state's prerogative over monetary control:

> The life in this country in the realm of the arts in the realm of
> the arts flows more strongly than for many a year. Our most signifi-
> cant discovery is the volume of popular demand. . . . But the lack of
> buildings is disastrous. The theatres, concert galleries, and galleries
> well suited to our purpose, taking the country as a whole, can be
> counted in a few minutes. That is where money will be wanted
> when in due time we turn to construct instead of to destroy. Nor
> will that expenditure be unproductive in financial terms. But we do
> have to equip, almost from the beginning, the material frame for
> the arts of civilization and delight.[20]

Elsewhere, he writes: "If I had the power today, I would surely set out to endow
our capital cities with all the appurtenances of art and civilization on the highest
standards . . . convinced that what I could create I could afford—and believing
that money thus spent would not only be better than any dole, but would make
unnecessary any dole. *For with what we have spent on the dole in England since the
war we could have made our cities the greatest works of man in the world.*"[21] And
yet the selection of the South Bank as the specific venue as the place to adorn
the capital city bears an implicit relationship to a key elision within Keynes's
thought that we would be remiss in passing over. Recall the famous sections of
the *General Theory* on the "euthanasia of the rentier."[22]

Keynes compares the land rentier to the "oppressive power of the capitalist to exploit the scarcity-value of capital," in their collectivist power as the votaries of "interest" to militate against investment and therefore against the rise of an authentic individualism—its heroes being "the intelligence and determination and executive skill of the financier, the entrepreneur et hoc genus omne," in economic affairs. The euthanasia so announced, that putative blazon for social justice, was in fact a recourse to protect the "existing system" of property rights while hinting at its future obsolescence, by dint of its eventual unprofitability in the face of the increased mobility of money.

The selection of the South Bank as the architectural stage for the reinvigoration of culture and its attendant enthusiasms performs precisely an analogous double move, if one considers it with reference to the specificities of ownership and what has been called the "landed interest" in Britain. It is here, one would argue, where the deepest ambiguities of Keynes's thought are and would be further revealed given its vicissitudes in the decades to come. If one compares the degree of monopolization of landed property, Britain as a country is more feudal than Pakistan. Fewer people own more tracts of accumulated land than those of Britain's former colonies which, following Britain's specific mode of administration therein, have retained a similar neofeudal character. Of the sixty million acres of land in the United Kingdom, the investigative journalist Kevin Cahill has assessed forty million acres of productive land as belonging to just 189,000 families, or about a third of a percent of the population, with obvious implications given the significant agricultural subsidies going into this sector.[23]

The lands of the towns of Bayswater, Kensington, Belgravia, Westminster, Chelsea, and so on, collectively making up the city of London, are no different, showing a consistent pattern of undervaluation for taxation purposes and 125-year leases that militate against the sale of property showing its "true" value. Both the Crown and the Duke of Westminster, whose interests are protected by his real estate firm Grosvenor Estates, own three hundred acres of land each, which in addition to those of a few other families, comprise most of the land in the city other than those given over to railways and the like. In the period leading up to 1945, the "landed interest" of the hereditary peerages and the Crown, protected by the Tory interest, continually fended off calls for nationalization by Labour in the face of sustained economic stagflation, with the Liberal Party—Keynes's party—occupying the middle ground.[24] In this context the various wartime "townscape" proposals made for the reconstruction of London, emphasizing its traditional squares and gardens as the basis for its rejuvenation, can be said to have been explicitly formulated with the Tory interest in mind.[25] Karl Marx had it right a century earlier: "The Tories in England long imagined they were enthusiastic about the monarchy, the church, and the beauties of the old English constitution, until the day of danger wrung from them the confession that they were only enthusiastic about ground rent."[26]

The preservation agenda was directly a front of the landed interest and continues to be so today. Both Keynes's 1936 proposition to use the South Bank and the Abercrombie plan's "four rings" proposal to decentralize the "crowded center" of London, also proposing the construction of a South Bank complex, implicitly maneuvered around the intransigence of the landed interest in central London, thus abnegating the opportunity arising from wartime destruction used by government in places such as Rotterdam to appropriate private properties for coherent reconstruction. The "radical" plan by the MARS Group equally elided this question at issue, making no mention of the legacies of land in its "close" studies of land use.[27] For Keynes the South Bank proposal was thus literally the recourse to using other incentives instead of augmenting the state's coercive arm through the nationalization of feudal land.

Roger Fry, a member of Keynes's Bloomsbury cohort, uncannily presaged Keynes's sentiments on economic instincts in *The Great State* of 1912, when he wrote: "A great deal of misunderstanding and ill-feeling between the artist and the public comes from a failure to realize the necessity of this process of assimilation of the work of art to the needs of the instinctive life . . . [as patron of art] the Great [socialist] State will live, *not hoard*."[28] Crucially, Keynes imbued the arts with an objective directly linked to the economic function of the state, as a direct psychological trigger for the cheerful propensities and capacities to enjoy the present, essential attributes of the propensity to consume. In other words, the arts were to be a key venue for the manufacture of desire in which the state was to have a key role. The analogy of investment in architecture to making money available to public investment—formerly squirreled away by rentiers and self-denying economic "prudence"—is more than palpable. This is more than substantiated by the fact that architecture and the restriction of the role of government in managing the money supply are played off against the efficacy of governmental intervention manifesting itself in public works or the "dole." If in the decade preceding, Le Corbusier had incongruously pitted architecture against revolution, we can almost imagine Keynes to be distinctly affirming, very much against the Keynesianism that would soon follow in his name: "public works can be avoided."

Thus Keynes's principal rejoinder in terms of policy against the art-based propaganda emanating from the dictatorships on the continent was to place the Arts Council of Great Britain directly under the Treasury, therefore, in theory at least, removing it from political intervention or control of any kind. The mechanisms inherent in this particular arrangement set the administrative paradigm for what came to be known as Keynesian social democracy in general through the "arm's length" management of governmental services and goods. The result was an aesthetic culture formed significantly along Bloomsbury lines, with appointments to the council strongly monopolized by Eton and Oxbridge graduates, directing an official, latitudinarian modernism in its support of the arts that would in the long run inveigh against the radical art expressions of the "angry young" generation of the postwar.[29]

If the Labour government's Festival of Britain—almost exclusively held on the South Bank—proved to be "popular," this was the British public voting with its feet. The subsequent politics of the Labour governments in the British post-war period was a politics relentlessly stymied by the neofeudal preservationism of its landed interests, with successive Tory governments quashing and dilut-ing moves toward comprehensive economic restructuring, including moves in town and country planning, initiated by successive Labour governments. This combative politics, in policy terms, was tacitly played out through a variety of economic proxies—insurance, building bylaws, lending policy, rents, income, entrepreneurial cultures, and infrastructural developments—none of the in-transigent stakes of which allowed anything like the 'carrots' approach lead-ing to Keynes's "euthanasia."[30] Indeed, the centralized land acquisition policies inherent in, say, Alison and Peter Smithson's Golden Lane Housing project of 1952, precisely forms the background for the introduction of modernism into Britain, an introduction that was consistently belayed, even defeated, by the demand for "preservation" of England golden. Furthermore, "redistributive" governmental intervention in postwar Europe continued to be stymied by the equations of hydraulic Keynesianism, with its strong objections to inordinate deficits on the one hand and opposition from the right, with its exhortations against state prerogative as inherently totalitarian, on the other. The *theoretical* riposte to welfarism within Keynesianism thus mirrored the *moral* objections to welfarism—inveighing against "handouts" and so on—posed by the right.

If modernism was realized, this was only in the singular architectures of the New Towns and school and county buildings built on the margins of a market in property significantly unchanged since the war. The modeling of neoclassical economic doctrine on the assumption of the scarcity of resources, nonetheless, transposed onto the aesthetics of postwar construction a commensurate ethics of scarcity, an "economic" paradigm implicitly posed toward an architecture as if produced in bulk, quite unlike its traditional, bespoke mores. The stark-ness of the Smithson's Hunstanton School could be construed as producing the manifesto for this tendency, and on these questions Ove Arup and his firm weighed in heartily, through both policy advocacy and the work of his firm, as well as discussions on standardization and optimization that characterized the dominant discussion of the period. Compare Ove's argument below to that of Keynes's above; the difference therein, I would argue, is the difference between Keynes's own reservations on the role of the state and the *Keynesian* theology of "embedded" liberalism in the design of the postwar state, whose adherents, willing and unwilling, would range from acolytes such as Joan Robinson to conservative skeptics such as Richard Nixon ("We are all Keynesians now"). Here is Ove: "There must somehow be power to direct or influence production. The centre of gravity must be shifted from private enterprise to public service. . . . Organization of industry and communications, the planning of towns and agriculture, the extension of social services are all problems which, so far as I can see, cannot possibly be left to private initiative, but which everybody now realizes ought to be tackled in the interest of humanity."[31]

Both Ove's involvement with the housing projects of Lubetkin and Tecton, with Maxwell Fry and the MARS Group (as its only engineer), and his demonstrated expertise and wartime contributions in building air-raid shelters, trenches, and the like, made him an ideal client for the tasks of postwar development. His commitment toward "total design" engaged his firm in a plethora of projects—from bus stations to factories to apartment buildings to schools and colleges, both in Britain and its colonial protectorates in sub-Saharan Africa, through Arup's association with Fry and Jane Drew. Arup's portfolio in this period also shows a significant interest in heritage and preservation, exemplified in both the design of Coventry Cathedral and restoration of York Minster.[32] Arup's early international operations, other than the United States, were largely constrained to Britain's neocolonial theaters of interest: Australia, Botswana, Nigeria, Zimbabwe, Pahlavite Iran (where it designed and executed the curved surface geometry of one of the Shah's "secular" monuments against a rising political tide) and Hong Kong (through which, following the footsteps of the old colonial engine the Hong Kong and Shanghai Bank, it was to enter China).[33]

With a few exceptions—the HSBC building being one—its clients were dominantly governments, generally the only economic actors with the wherewithal to commission the large-scaled projects for which Arup cultivated its reputation. Much of Ove Arup's own sensibility can be said to be thus a corollary of the "trade union baronage and Wykhamist intelligentsia" that characterized postwar dirigisme.[34] Commensurate with the financial modus of their inception, the principal engineering and architectural questions of the firm revolved around economies of scale. In its early phase, Arup fully implicated itself in the technological repercussions of this economic impetus, working against the grain of the technological secretiveness of firms on the one hand, thus wastefully duplicating efforts and on the other, against the panaceas of "prefabrication." Key research problems of the time undertaken by the firm revolved around, for instance, the scale considerations that went into the design of doubly curved surfaces, which necessitated different assemblies of formwork for each construction, as opposed to plane or singly curved surfaces where formwork could be reused.

The accompanying architectural debates about "structural honesty" in building in this period can be said to impeccably mirror the "scarcity" assumptions at the core of economic thought during the postwar high period of interventional Keynesianism. Ove's thought and writing of the time—as versed in philosophy and Kant as statics and material behavior—is marked by his arguments against architects' conflating their preference for aesthetic "simplicity" with structural honesty, a critique posed pointedly against much modernist dogma of the period. The culprits of this form of myth-making were often the same buildings in which Ove was giving his lectures, the Illinois Institute of Technology buildings, the steel hinges of MIT's Kresge Auditorium, and the internal columns of Coventry Cathedral—the last being an Arup project itself. This from the *Listener*, Keynes's mouthpiece, on July 7, 1955: "The aesthetic programme of the modern movement is hidden away in an excessive admiration for all things technical, for new structural forms and materials, for making full use of all the latest technical innovations long before they are *economically justified*, and for the 'honest expression'—whatever that may mean—of the structure. So much enthusiasm for the means of building is suspicious, it shows that there is more in it than meets the eye."[35]

It is important to keep in mind here that while this disassociation is markedly similar to Reyner Banham's deflation of modernist rhetoric, the far more technologically adept Ove, unlike Banham, was in fact arguing for greater autonomy of the aesthetic from the technological. The "machine-aesthetic" is markedly a false premise; for Ove, architecture is *not* bound by any particular technological constraint. In a paper given at Leicester University Arts Festival in 1969, he described the crux for the architect as being "definitely on his own, in an ocean of complete permissiveness and an almost infinite choice of means."[36] Thus the architect faced with a problem will receive no help by looking up a book on architecture; while the engineer who has forgotten a formula for stresses in a beam may always do so. If architecture is conditioned by precedence, it is only by reference to totality: "what we build is always a whole, an entity—a building, a precinct, a town with roads, etc.—and all these entities interact and influence each other."[37] Art as bearing an unverifiable relationship to precedent, science as a verificatory practice, each with its respective relationship to the sublime: Kantian epistemology—Ove's initial interest was philosophy—has mysteriously reemerged in a description of professional domains.

It is here that a politics of science manifests itself. That it does so by pointing to a moment of extravagance or exorbitance—architecture's indeterminability—in a condition of scarcity should alert us to the fact that this scientific politics (a conflict of the faculties) operates by dint of an alibi that surreptitiously enters to claim the ground of judgment: political economy. "A beautiful structure is rarely the same as the economical structure."[38] Let us consider what is tacitly at stake here in revisiting the classical differentiation between verifiability and unverifiability, between structure and ornament. In describing the aesthetic qualities of the IIT or MIT buildings, Ove did not question the aesthetic qualities of these choices. He emphasized that they merely reflected a certain preference for "simplicity," a simplicity that he concurred had an essential relationship to "beauty." The argument for "structural honesty," by contrast, other than being without substance, obfuscated in Ove's view the essential primacy of aesthetic choice, unnecessarily dissembling itself with the mask of what was in fact only contingent science.

Here the politics of the faculties presents itself by way of a reversal. In divesting architecture from certain kinds of privileging metaphor drawn from science as illegitimate, the norms of architecture are being reverted to traditional forms of rhetoric: simplicity, ordonnance, comfort, "order, balance, space, form." By contrast, engineering—although lower in the hierarchy of the professions—*is without metaphor*, without displacement. The relationship between generality and particularity is a determined one. True modernism lies in engineering, while architecture is still a classical endeavor: "Architecture cannot be said to have progressed from old times till now . . . [although] few would argue that modern architecture is a marked improvement on the architecture of earlier epochs . . . [by] contrast . . . there is steady progress in the achievement of engineering aims, and a very much greater agreement about what is good and bad engineering."[39]

This is *exactly* the argument that the modern movement's apologists such as Siegfried Giedion had sought to make about Henri Labrouste and Gustave Maillart; and the Athens Charter could be equally considered an effort toward "greater agreement" in the international practices of architecture. Here, Ove's philosophical imprecision merely mirrored the architectural field's own philosophical imprecision, leading to a hermeneutic runaround around the content of the term "economy."[40] Indeed, there is something of a structural homology that can be posited between the vicissitudes of the debates on surface and expressive excess in architecture and industrial design in the era of "embedded" liberalism and the implicit tensions between the "scarcity" assumption and the (inflationary) Keynesian "propensity to consume." If "function" appears in the former as a constitutive element for "form," the latter is equally beset by the problems of defining the semiotic equivalent for the concept-phenomenon "money."[41]

It is conceivable that even less than technologically aware readers will be aware of the tremendous reductiveness accorded to engineering in this jerry-rigged asymptote. Architectural students will remember their structures courses to be restricted to a study of physical "moments" in the abstract: arrows indicating compression, tension, shear, deformation, and so on that respond to certain Newtonian calculations of mass and weight. When these calculations

are brought into the field of material performance, engineering has to negotiate with a complex set of determinants that further complicate the calculation
from both physical and social considerations. Questions of "turbulence, material fatigue, changes of state, friction, viscosity, heat transfer, etc." confront legal
frameworks, price structures and availability, budgetary considerations and so
on—the aggregate of which is translated in popular parlance as "economy."
The economic historian Philip Mirowski has questioned if the "design" process
in engineering could claim to be a "science" at all: "they often look up certain
calculations based on crude empirical techniques rather than explicit physical
laws, and then arbitrarily multiply the requirements by ten for safety's sake."[42]
Like English common law or Ove's definition of "architecture," engineering is
as much an accommodation of a history of logical inconsistencies, a characteristic of what economists describe (and are unable to explain further) as "path-
dependent" behavior.[43] More important, the content of engineering is, no more
or less than architecture or any other profession, driven by the impetus to socialization in one form or the other. To accept the economic metaphor in engineering requires not just qualification but in fact *misstates the problem at hand.*

The difference between the two international "signature" projects that were to
bring international recognition to Arup brings this implicit conflict to the very
fore of both the architectural and governmental debate. Controversies over
the exponential costs rising from the entirely superfluous but defining "sails" of
the Sydney Opera House were to result in the very resignation of the project's
architect. The Centre Pompidou would realize in its decorative functionalism
the radical inversion of financial policy within the French Socialist Party. Both
these projects were government sponsored, and their respective developments
speak directly to fates of not only the character of postwar interventionism but
also the different visions of globalization nestled within them.

Writing in 1973, in a chapter titled "The Market System and the Arts" in a
book devoted to the role of government in delivering economic goods, John
Kenneth Galbraith sketched out from the economist's viewpoint an inherent
incompatibility between the idiosyncrasy of the "artist" and the behavioral trac-
tability assumed in *homo economicus*, while nonetheless acquiescing to the artist
as a special kind of entrepreneur and producer of value:

> The artist is, by nature, an independent entrepreneur. He
> embraces an entire task of creation; unlike the engineer or the
> production-model scientist he does not contribute specialized
> knowledge of some part of a task to the work of a team. Because
> he is sufficient to himself, he does not submit readily to the goals

of organization. . . . Not needing the goals of organization and
not being able or allowed to accept the goals of organization, the
artist fits badly into organization. . . . A few industries—the motion
picture firms, television networks, the large advertizing agencies—
must, by their nature, associate artists with rather complex
organization. All have a well-reported record of dissonance and
conflict between the artists and the rest of the organization.[44]

Had Galbraith glanced over his shoulder toward the field of architecture
at that time, he would have noticed an international cause célèbre that could
have offered him further substance for his argument. Architect Jørn Utzon's
histrionic resignation from the Sydney Opera House commission in 1966 was
the consequence of a long series of disputes over the respective professional provinces and competencies of its various authors, a process complicated
by exponential increases in budget, ideological shifts stemming from electoral
changes in the party in government, compounded by a general mismatch in
expertise and professional attitude between Utzon and the company headed
by his self-selected fellow Dane, Ove Arup. In the long run, spiraling costs from
Utzon's dithering over formal and technological resolution precisely instanti-
ated for the New South Wales government the caricature of the irrefragable
and intractable artist sketched by Galbraith. Their desperate turn to Arup for
professional assistance—producing a conflict of interest in that Arup was now
employed by both architect and client—added grist to the already paranoid
Utzon office that Utzon's technological resolutions were "not wanted in the
building project . . . [they merely want to] retain us as aesthetic consultants."[45]
The incidents left a bitter taste in the mouth even two decades later for Jack
Zunz, one of Arup's key engineers on the Sydney site, and point once again
to the perceived distance between aesthetic conception and technological and
managerial competence that Arup in many ways would make it its special voca-
tion to overcome. Zunz wrote:

> [The] Sydney Opera House was designed by Jørn Utzon, or
> so the guide who conducts thousands of visitors to the complex
> will have you believe. No one else is mentioned in the hour-long
> tour. The fact that what is now standing in Sydney Harbour was
> built without a single drawing or instruction from Utzon is beside
> the point. Our society likes its instant pop images—if they require
> some fabrication that's alright provided the paying customers are
> satisfied. And so everyone knows that the Lloyd's building in Lon-
> don was built by Richard Rogers and that (for those old enough to
> remember) the Festival of Britain Skylon in 1951 was designed by

Powell and Moya. I am a great admirer of Utzon, of Rogers, and of Powell and Moya, and have on many occasions waxed lyrical about their talents. But to imply that they individually created these artifacts is like suggesting that Botham won the Ashes single-handed.[46]

Arup's commission for the Sydney Opera House is also significant because it offers us the earliest precedent for today's transnationally produced "signature" architecture. The iconic sails that so define its silhouette for so many around the world comprise an entirely separate structure, large pieces of sculpture hiding the standard bootlike functional typology of operas and concert halls. Its form was explicitly recognized by its commissioners as the exercise of an architect's artistic "vision" in its power to create a powerful symbol for Sydney at the water's edge on Bennelong Point. This idiosyncratic shape, despite its horticultural allusions, diverged significantly from the long tradition of organicism, as pointed out caustically by Frank Lloyd Wright. "God help us all," he wrote, calling it a "disrupted, circus tent, blown open and apart by the wind . . . [a] non-constructive, inorganic fantasy [concocted by a] novice. . . . The absurd efflorescence of this opus [only] show[ed] the folly of these now too-popular competitions," none of which in Wright's view had produced a single good building, or ever would in the future.[47]

By contrast, in a retrospective account, Zunz, Arup's "man on the ground," was frank: "the engineering aspects of the Opera House . . . have no value in themselves. They are of interest in the context of the services they render to whatever they serve. . . . By itself the structure of [the] Sydney Opera House may have some virtuoso-like qualities—it may even be an engineering cadenza —but in itself it serves no purpose."[48] In his account Ove himself rationalized the building's "caprice" only on the grounds of the architect's special, *classical* license as the author of an unverifiable craft or genius, to create "masterpieces." Given its early extragovernmental inception in the hands of a colonial Bloomsbury-type clique—a derivative Australian Arts Council—but with no Keynes-like figure at its helm, both expertise and accountability in the Opera House's amateur-run executive committee was lacking, with members offering only vague estimates of what they required the architect to provide, leading to multiple confusions even on the number of seats to be provided for in the design. This bumbling also led to the bogus budget of 3.6 million Australian dollars, drafted by an unfortunate quantity surveyor at the competition venue under the overbearing influence of Eero Saarinen—the competition juror who saw in the Opera House a continuation of his own legacy—who provided him rough estimates from his own experience with MIT's Kresge Auditorium, on the basis of which the project was awarded to Utzon in the first place.

Compounding the puttering of the clients was the deceptive simplicity or, as Ove somewhat generously put it, the "unsuspected complexity" of Utzon's original sketches, a simplicity that could have been perceived as a mere gestural abstraction and equally well a sign of the architect's relative inexperience—having realized only a group of low-cost patio houses in Denmark—but wasn't. On his first meeting with Utzon, Ove recognized that the drawings were more or less "freehand sketches without geometric definition. Utzon certainly thought that he had found a solution which was structurally reasonable. He was therefore very disappointed when I told him at our first interview that the shape was not very suitable, structurally, for he was particularly keen on the idea of an ideal marriage between Architecture and Structure."[49]

Subsequent logistical complexity came from the architect's desire to realize his "perfect" vision, leading to a tendency on the one hand to inordinately long periods of reflection when drawing out the requisite details of each stage, and on the other hand to obsessively micromanage inputs from all contending forms of expertise, contriving to keep them apart under his authoritative command. As the melee of discordant inputs accumulated—from clients uncertain about their requirements to a clearly inept architectural office with inadequate quantity and quality of staff to substandard contractors—costs spiraled to more than sevenfold the first estimate by 1965 to approximately twenty-four million Australian dollars (and less than a quarter of the eventual total cost). With Labor's removal in that year, the new conservative minister of public works leveraged public outcry to push Utzon toward greater accountability and better schedules of deliverability.

Under pressure, Utzon increasingly began to suspect, all evidence to the contrary, Arup of conspiring to wrest the project for his own firm. This perception grew out of a peculiar arrangement decided upon by the Department of Public Works, which was to employ Arup as directly responsible to it instead of Utzon, a common practice in Britain, despite the fact that Utzon had recommended Arup in the first place. The rancor on Utzon's part escalated sharply by late 1965, which now saw both the New South Wales government and Arup as conniving in robbing the architect of "control" over the project. The following text is testimony to Utzon's growing paranoia: "After the Minister for Public Works took over as the Construction Authority, I wanted to make it quite clear that *I should be in complete control* of every detail. I therefore asked the last Premier to give me confirmation of this, but I have never received such confirmation, as you can see from our correspondence. It is absolutely vital that, in order to prevent the building being destroyed, *I must remain in full command* of every detail that comes in to the building, including furniture, decoration, etc."[50]

For governments everywhere the Sydney Opera House saga encompassed the eclipse of two prominent assumptions: the magisterial competence of architects as singular authors of public projects and the support of the arts as an element of welfarism. If the former was an assumption of the modernizing thrust of postwar Labor governments and the like, the latter was a leitmotif of the dirigiste state. It is important for our purposes to notice that the waning of these assumptions also carried with them the demise of the presumed organic relationship between skin and structure, as corporations of high expertise such as Arup increasingly intervened to disabuse architects of this innocence. Thus what Charles Jencks in 1977 announced as the end of modernism was in fact the unraveling of a certain *organicism*, that architecture had to be "worked from the inside out."

In a manner of speaking, both the Sydney fracas and ensuing stagflation experienced in global markets in the 1970s would significantly concretize in operational terms for Arup what was generally being experienced in architectural culture as a turn from modernism, both in its socializing and aesthetic element. On the other hand, the slow traversal to the financial icons of the fin de siècle in Arup's history can also be described in terms of its increased entanglement with the very operations of governments themselves—the flip side of the Sydney Opera House coin—and their constituencies.

The international lesson from the Sydney project was imbibed even more deeply by Arup's continuing frustration with the government at home: both the architects' bias toward modernism and the Tories' antagonism toward fiscal antagonism militated against any comparable public commissions like the Australian example in the realm of culture or along the stimulatory lines that Keynes had envisioned. (The brief exception here being Jennie Lee, Harold Wilson's minister of state for the arts—the UK's first—who commissioned both the Open University project and the new arts center on the South Bank, both commissions for Arup.) Under the circumstances there is no irony that the one built residue of the "angry young" generation of British architects would simply have to be realized abroad: the Centre Pompidou, an architectural trigger for Mitterand's subsequent Grands Projets in Paris, many of them—the La Defense buildings, the Louvre pyramid—designed by Arup.[51]

In citing a long history of socialist monuments (the Parc de la Villette), the Projets were in fact emblems of the ideological defeat of the Mitterand Socialists at the hands of large-scale capital flight. The new monuments were explicitly commissioned to foreign architects to convey an impression of being receptive to foreign investment and capital. Indeed, it is conceivable that no government on the right could have had the wherewithal to effect the relaxation of capital controls that the Mitterand government put into effect; what a "conservative government had feared to do, a Socialist government accomplished."[52] The increasing

economic openness of the state was thus providentially portrayed as a cosmo-
politan openness to culture, with the "glass state" happily hewing to an image of
the Socialists' continuing dedication to Revolutionary "institutions," complete with
visual reference to the Russian Constructivists.[53] The dynamic that had produced
Keynes's South Bank response to the Soviet rallies had found a postmodern resolution *within* the liberal consensus. (Elsewhere, Arup would use a highly visible
commission from a major investment body in one of Britain's last colonial bridge-
heads, the Hong Kong & Shanghai Bank, to project itself into Deng's new China.)

In Britain itself the situation would have to wait for one more purge. The
British government's long-term tacit encouragement of financial movements
beyond the grasp of formal regulation found its formal culmination in Thatcher's "Big Bang" Financial Services Act of 1986, a deregulatory move intended
to bolster London's position as the premier international financial center, or,
more accurately, legalized global money-laundering operation and tax-shelter
hub.[54] Within a year the City of London had become the route for a full quarter of American foreign investment in the services sector, making London the
world's premier financial entrepôt.[55] Despite this radical financial policy, Thatcher's petit-bourgeois consensus on the home front allowed no such grandiose
expressions of monumental culture, or for that matter, an equally intrepid fiscal policy. The Thatcher regime adopted the rhetoric of cutting government
spending, including in the arts, but in its structural approach to cultural policy
it only continued the interventional pattern set by earlier Labor governments
while turning it to other uses. In architecture, the spigot for significant public
building was turned off in marked contrast to the Wilson years; the government
devolved this to the commercial sector and the real estate industry, thus producing the clientele for Arup's buildings for Embankment Place, Canary Wharf,
and Lloyd's of London. The Tory's urban planning initiative significantly played
to a consensus forged between the preservationist elements of the old rentier
class and the enclavist energies of the new entrepreneurial factions. The planning profession declared itself more or less to be in "crisis," while architects
found themselves grappling with Prince Charles's comments on "glass stumps
and classic carbuncles."[56]

What is less evident in the cultural commentary on the period is the commensurate crisis on a front that cultural commentators were less likely to notice. Since its ascendance to a form of cultural heroism—one exemplified in the
work of Gideon and Banham—the profession of engineering had resolutely
looked to the state as the principal generator of the large scale; its counterpart
in the private sector was the manufacturing industries. The Tories' domestic
policy of evacuating the public sector put paid to the former aspiration; the
financial revolution moved manufacturing away from the regions of socialized

welfare to more pliant, cheaper labor pools. On the home front the crisis engendered by this double evacuation was immediately felt in the migration of young students from seeking careers in engineering to managerial or financial careers; at the same time, the stock market saw the "demise of great British manufacturing companies and the emergence of high technology international companies" whose ambitions were less technological than managerial.[57]

The crisis posed by this radical shift within a generation to the engineering profession may appear counterintuitive; certainly it is hard to sift any such sentiment from the utterances of the time from the engineers themselves. And yet basically the shift in the mode of governmentality eviscerated the very profession of the engineer. The despondence is evident in a number of articles in the *Arup Journal* of that time, particularly in the writing of Zunz, Ove's able lieutenant on the Sydney Opera House project: "Governments come and go, inducted and evicted by quotable slogans, none of which have any bearing on the training and education, or lack of it, of our [engineering] community—unless you count Harold Wilson's 1963 speech to the Labour Party Conference when he said: 'We are redefining and restating our socialism in terms of the scientific revolution. The Britain that is going to be forged in the white heat of this revolution will be no place for restrictive practices etc., etc. . . ' The 'white hot revolution' turned out more like a long cold winter, discontent and all."[58]

In a subsequent series of articles, Zunz's distemper is more than visible, as he tackles the many worries facing the profession, including fragmentation, "the cult of professional managers," and the shortage of engineers. "The 10 top construction companies in the United Kingdom have 124 listed directors," he wrote. "Of these 12 have an engineering qualification."[59] It is in the angst-ridden throes of a disappearing generation—replete with an exhortation to engineers to "stop whining" and to take more active charge of their own public self-image—that we find the implosive context for the harangue against Utzon quoted earlier in this chapter. It might be added that Arup experienced an actual downturn in profits in the early 1990s, owing to external conditions of "demand uncertainty" experienced during this period. The growing frustration was fueled also by more immediate, political provocation. In the early 1990s, accompanied by economic downturn, Arup's proposal for the nearby Paternoster Square was a key target of attack by Prince Charles, leading to its abandonment, in addition to a number of other master planning proposals by some of Britain's key architects.[60] In many ways this conservative resistance mirrored Winston Churchill's vengeful clearance of the Festival of Britain buildings after his return to power in October 1951.[61] Indeed, the intransigence of Tory politicians and Tory-identified architects and writers against modernism had for decades the effect of having the entire modernist faction in British culture to be resolutely

Labour-identified: from Berthold Lubetkin and Ove Arup to Leslie Martin, from the New Brutalists and the "New Empiricists" to the "neophiliacs" and the "Angry Young Men" of Britain's postwar generation, including Cedric Price and his early devotee Richard Rogers.[62]

Thus when the various propositions for the South Bank were broached in the early 1990s—by Arup, commissioned by the Tory government in 1995, and another by Richard Rogers and Labor's shadow minister for the arts and media, Mark Fisher—there is no presentiment of the institutional bodies that would come to occupy this site in the aftermath of the institution of the National Lottery in the 1990s. Quite to the contrary, both reports are significantly framed through infrastructural and logistical demands, pious calls to better housing, offices, civic spaces, and so on.

The Arup report, surprisingly given the firm's towering status as an engineering firm, consequently timidly kowtows to a "townscape" line, with contingent, localized specifications for river views, plantings, pedestrian-bicycle segregation and protection, riverside paths, control of building heights, distinctions to be made between public and private spaces, lighting, and so on.[63] The Rogers and Fisher report is a report on London in general but devotes special attention to the Thames as a key focus for urban reorientation of the city. As compared with the Arup report, hampered by the fact of being published literally under the shadow of John Major's government in 1992, its proposals tortuously work around the possibility that the kind of urban planning envisaged in the report may be seen as "strong-arm" interventions by the state, while simultaneously criticizing the specter of a city held hostage to developers' speculative trends and frenzies. Thus, quite in contrast to his own continental contributions, Rogers's report significantly rules out Grands Projets–like monuments as desirable for this site: "The most telling criticism of the Grands Projets is that they are imposed from on high and are parachuted in to sites . . . [thus making them] . . . primarily of interest to tourists." The model forwarded is that of Barcelona, the report thus going on to emphasize "community building," pedestrian walks and civic spaces, and visual outlooks as the basis for changes.[64] As for Fisher, upon his appointment as minister of the arts under the Blair government of 1997, this advice would not stop him from the immediate commissioning of tourist-friendly monuments such as the Tate, the Millennium Bridge, and City Hall. By 2001 one commentator could proudly remark that "London in the early twenty-first century is a city of *grands projets*."[65] Clearly this is an architectural *tournant* within the space of a few years; that it was able to gain such swift traction against the older baggage within so little time owed significantly to the clientele-public created by the National Lottery.

Again, it can be strongly argued that this turn drew less from a sudden

shift in urban or architectural sensibilities as their place within political constituency building involving the uses and prerogatives of the state. Just as shifts in
working-class attitude, long considered the mainstay of Labour, were critical
to Thatcher's triple election dominance, the "new" factor in the New Labour
victory of 1997 was the very class of service professionals that eighteen years
of continuous Conservative rule and the frenetic throes of the "Big Bang" had
fostered. The Blairite agenda did little subsequently to undo the monetary paradigms, the privatizing ethos, or the commercial mechanisms that earlier governments had put into place, in fact driving an economizing ideology into the very
operations of government itself. If under the Tories, welfarism was allowed to
become dysfunctional, the Blairites set about making it "cost-efficient," thus
enthusiastically assuaging the new financial and managerial class that the meager
revenues drawn from them were not being frittered away. In this transformed
context, the global organizational exercise carried out by Arup in 1995, ponder-
ously called the "Reformation," would also see a thrust toward the cultivation
of "signature" architects that came to embody a key element of Arup's expertise in the public eye, which was explicitly part of its new marketing approach.
(The so-called Reformation was an exercise that "flattened" out its technological units into a more managerially led consulting network of fifty independent
units reporting to a rotational main board.)[66]

At the same time, the new "signature" projects of the South Bank—now
integrally connected with the financial and service industries based in the City of
London through Arup's Millennium Bridge—was therefore literally conceived
as a territorial wedge driven between the new Blairite constituencies and their
potential alliance with the rentier classes ensconced in the dreary Georgian
neighborhoods of Mayfair and Belgravia. Lit late into the night for young traders
to entertain themselves after the "animal energies" had been released at work,
it effectively concretized a political faction through the catalysis of leisure, complete with Arup's building for the newly created mayor's office for Greater London—with appropriately radical incumbent "Red Ken" voting down the heritage factions at every turn—sited well at a distance from the old locations of
power and *their* ceremonial Lord Mayor of the City of London. Even as Blair
ejected scores of hereditary peers from the House of Lords, Richard Rogers
was raised Baron of Riverside.

The emancipatory aura of the new South Bank icons elided the rise of New
Labour itself as a *footnote* to the *fundamental restructuring* of the British state
under Margaret Thatcher. As a brochure cataloging the burst of architectural
projects in London puts it: "Thankfully, following the economic collapse of the
early 1990's after John Major's withdrawal from the European Exchange Rate
Mechanism, the architectural scene was rescued and reinvigorated by the intro-

duction of the National Lottery in 1994."[67] The arts were the key instrument to forge this catalysis. The rhetorical recourse taken was that of redescribing the shift from manufacturing to service industries as the growth of "creative industry," with significant implications for the organization of the National Lottery.

In 1998, Chris Smith, secretary of state for culture, media, and sport—the newfangled and integrated ministry created by the Blairite government to disburse goods from the lottery—laid out the key facets through which cultural policy drawing on the National Lottery would be critical to the economic policies of the government. Coming on the heels of the creation of the Creative Industries Taskforce, such areas as film, theater, music, fashion, television, and the visual arts are now redescribed as crucial to the integration of "culture, business and society." Encompassed under these areas are not only the "artistic" talents involved (actors, directors, and such) but also "scientific" and "technical" tasks (involving digital and electronic engineers and so on). The architectural outcome of this displaced state apparatus was tremendous, with about two thousand awards made in excess of one billion pounds in England alone over six years to upgrade or create new facilities and structures for the arts: dance and music centers and studios, galleries and museums, concert halls, waterside developments.[68] Much of this money was distributed through the Arts Council —Keynes's Art Council—now conveniently reinvigorated after the doldrums of the Thatcher years.

Arup lithely adapted itself to harness this new "public"—from providing designs for non-Euclidean geometric shapes to lighting services to designing iconic installations to acoustic services for a string of the new arts buildings. By the turn of the millennium, it became equally clear that instead of describing itself primarily as an engineering firm, Arup may be said to be increasingly embracing the definition of "creative industry." Arup's cultivation of the arts, embodied in the creation of the Advanced Geometry Unit at this time, oriented exclusively to the study and realization of complex forms, is of a piece with this new governmental approach as much as it pays lip service to Ove's Kantian notion of aesthetic autonomy.

It is clear, however, that for Blairite mandarins, this aestheticism of the state is in service of an economic goal: the policy mandate was not to see the "arts" as merely involved in the creation of better cultural consciousness and enthusiasm—although copious exhortations to the same are hardly foregone—but as "enhanc[ing] mainstream Exchequer support," in other words as an indirect support of private industry.[69] The London Olympics of 2012—complete with scenario-building by Arup—would be the swansong of that arc, a Potemkin ex-urbanism of inflated demand. "It has become clear that we . . . need to look at the benefits the creative approaches of the arts can in turn bring to business."[70] By a tortuous circle of events, Keynes's intuition on the arts as instinctual driver of demand had now chiasmically been worked into a *supply-side* motor. Maynard would have smiled.

Notes

Epigraph: Ove Nyquist Arup, *Doodles and Doggerels* (Aylesbury: Ove Arup Partnership, 1990), 27.

1. See Rawi Abdelal, *Capital Rules: The Construction of Global Finance* (Cambridge: Harvard University Press, 2007).

2. I am grateful to Andrea Johnson, graduate student at Columbia's School of Architecture, Preservation, and Planning, in providing me this information in the graduate paper she wrote for my class.

3. Rem Koolhaas, "Post-modern Engineering?" in *Content*, by AMO, OMA, Rem Koolhaas, Simon Brown, and Jon Link (Cologne: Taschen, 2004), 514–15.

4. Norman Engleback, "South Bank Arts Centre Architecture," *Arup Journal* 1, no. 5 (July 1967): 20–23.

5. Arup, *Thames Strategy: A Study of the Thames Prepared for the Government Office for London: Strategic Planning and Design Guidance from Hampton Court to Greenwich* (London: HMSO, 1995).

6. John Maynard Keynes, "Art and the State," *Listener*, August 26, 1936, in John Maynard Keynes, *The Collected Writings*, vol. 28, *Social, Political, and Literary Writings* (New York: Cambridge University Press, 1982), 348.

7. At that time Keynes would be drawn in against his wishes into these discussions, which he considered premature for the time, by Reginald Rowe, president of the National Federation of Housing Societies and Edwin Lutyens. John Maynard Keynes, letter to Reginald Rowe, November 20, 1942, John Maynard Keynes Papers, King's College Library, Cambridge (henceforth JMKP), file no. PP/84/1. Also see files in box no. PP/75: "Correspondence concerning the Royal Academy Planning Committee, including references to the reconstitution of the Fine Art Commission, 1942, 1940-2."

8. Robert Skidelsky, *John Maynard Keynes: The Economist as Savior, 1920–1937* (New York: Penguin Books, 1992), 536.

9. JMKP, file no. PP/80/4/8.

10. For my analysis of the relationship of Keynes and Robinson, see Arindam Dutta, "*Sui Generis*, Historically: On Prabhat Patnaik's *The Value of Money*," *Social Scientist* 37, nos. 3–4 (March–April 2009): 33–45.

11. Antonio Negri, "Keynes and the Capitalist Theory of the State post-1929," in *Revolution Retrieved: Selected Writings on Marx, Keynes, Capitalist Crisis, and New Social Subjects, 1967–1983*, vol. 1 of the *Red Notes Italian Archive* (London: Red Notes, 1988).

12. See Andrew Cox, *Adversary Politics and Land: The Conflict over Land and Property Policy in Post-War Britain* (Cambridge: Cambridge University Press, 1984).

13. John Maynard Keynes, "The End of Laissez-Faire" (1962), in his *Essays in Persuasion* (New York: W. W. Norton, 1963), 317–18.

14. John Maynard Keynes, "A Short View of Russia" (1925), in his *Essays in Persuasion*, 297–311, 300.

15. John Maynard Keynes, *The General Theory of Employment, Interest, and Money* (New York: Harcourt Brace Jovanovich, 1964), 162.

16. Keynes, *General Theory of Employment, Interest, and Money*, 129.

17. See E. G. Winslow, "Keynes and Freud: Psychoanalysis and Keynes's Account of the 'Animal Spirits of Capitalism,'" *Social Research* 53, no. 4 (1986): 549–78.

18. See David Glasner, "A Reinterpretation of Classical Monetary Theory," *Southern Economic Journal* 52, no. 1 (July 1985): 46–67.

19. Keynes, "Art and the State," 345–46.

20. Keynes, "The Arts in Wartime," in Keynes, *The Collected Writings*, vol. 28, *Social, Political, and Literary Writings*, 361.

21. Keynes as quoted in Skidelsky, *John Maynard Keynes*, xxviii. Italics added.

22. Piero Mini has hinted at the inception of these ideas in the Bloomsbury avant-gardist sensibility against the hereditary mavens of British cultural society. See Piero Mini, *Keynes, Bloomsbury, and the General Theory* (London: Palgrave Macmillan, 1991), 96–97.

23. Kevin Cahill, *Who Owns Britain: The Hidden Facts behind Landownership in the UK and Ireland* (Edinburgh: Canongate, 2001), 27.

24. See Cox, *Adversary Politics and Land*.

25. See, for instance, the proposal made by A. E. Richardson on behalf of the Royal Fine Arts Commission—found among Keynes's papers—where the polarity between the landed stewardship of existing urban heritage and the chaotic effects wrought by "architectural speculation" is made patent. A. E. Richardson, "The Reconstruction of London as an Architectural Entity," in JMKP, file no. PP/75/4-10. Also see A. E. Richardson, "The Reconstitution of London," *Journal of the London Society*, no. 268 (June 1941): 11–13.

26. Karl Marx, "The Eighteenth Brumaire of Louis Bonaparte," translated by Ben Fowkes in his *Surveys from Exile, Political Writings, Volume 2*, edited by David Fernbach (New York: Penguin, 1973, 1992): 143–249, 174.

27. Arthur Korn, Maxwell Fry, and Dennis Sharp, "The M.A.R.S. Plan for London," *Perspecta* 13 (1971): 243–67.

28. Roger Fry, "Art and Socialism," excerpted from Fry's *The Great State* (1912), reprinted in his *Vision and Design* (Cleveland, Ohio: Meridien Books, 1956), 73, 75.

29. John S. Harris, "Decision-Makers in Government Programs of Arts Patronage: The Arts Council of Great Britain," *Western Political Quarterly* 22, no. 2 (June 1969): 253–64.

30. See Peter Scott, *The Property Masters: A History of the British Commercial Property Sector* (London: E and FN Spon, 1996).

31. Ove Arup as quoted in Peter Jones, *Ove Arup: Master Builder* (New Haven: Yale University Press, 2006), 56, 95–96, 123.

32. The York Minster project occasioned a long historical dissertation in the *Arup Journal*, as unique for a house publication as for an engineering firm. See David Mitchell, "York Minster," Part 1: York, and Part 2: The Minster, *Arup Journal* 3, nos. 3 and 4 (May and July 1968): 50–58, 70–82.

33. On the Shah's monuments, see Peter Ayres, "The Geometry of Shahyad Ariamehr," *Arup Journal* 5, no. 1 (March 1970): 29–34.

34. See Robert Skidelsky, ed., *Thatcherism* (London: Chatto and Windus, 1988).

35. Ove Arup, "Modern Architecture: The Structural Fallacy," *Listener*, July 7, 1955, republished in the Ove Arup special issue in *Arup Journal* 20, no. 1 (Spring 1985): 19–21, 19.

36. Ove Arup, "An Engineer Looks at Architecture," *Arup Journal* 5, no. 3 (September 1970): 2–3, 2.

37. Arup, "An Engineer Looks at Architecture," 2–3, 2.

38. Arup as quoted in Jones, *Ove Arup*, 165.

39. Arup, "An Engineer Looks at Architecture," 2.

40. I would argue that this play of metaphors in relationship to a certain economic use—of words and precedents as much as of building materials and resources—may be better examined against the background of a peculiar post-Keynesian theoretical discourse crisscrossing the economics, engineering, and developmental fields between 1949 and 1974, almost exactly spanning the first phase of Arup's growth, in what was described as the "engineering production function" debate. For reasons of space, this must be left to a more elaborated version of this chapter. See Arindam Dutta, *Ancestralities: Architecture, Nature, and the Debt* (forthcoming).

41. See "Mammoths, Inc.," in Dutta, *Ancestralities*. Also see Jean-Joseph Goux, *Symbolic Economies: After Marx and Freud*, translated by Jennifer Curtis Gage (Ithaca: Cornell University Press, 1990); and Gayatri Chakravorty Spivak, "Scattered Speculations on the Question of Value," in her *In Other Worlds: Essays in Cultural Politics* (New York: Methuen, 1987), 154–78.

42. Philip Mirowski, *More Heat Than Light: Economics as Social Physics, Physics as Nature's Economies* (Cambridge: Cambridge University Press, 1989), 329.

43. It would be important to add that the advent of computation into engineering processes does not significantly alter this epistemological framework; it only subjects the multiple determinants, by way of a systems approach, into less mathematically cumbersome models, thus allowing for more atypical solutions.

44. John Kenneth Galbraith, "The Market System and the Arts," in his *Economics and the Public Purpose: How We Can Head Off the Mounting Economic Crisis* (Boston: New American Library, 1973), 59–68, 59–60.

45. Letter from Mogens Prip-Buus, Utzon's chief assistant, to his partners, Sydney, March 13, 1966, from *Letters from Sydney: The Sydney Opera House Seen through the Eyes of Utzon's Chief Assistant Mogens Prip-Buus* (Hellerup: Edition Bløndal, 2000), 108. Research on the Sydney Opera House affair was conducted at State Records New South Wales, Department of Public Works, Sydney Opera House Records (henceforth SRNSW: DPW), file name COD 531B—Public Works, Sydney Opera House.

46. Jack Nunz, "Mirror Mirror on the Wall . . . How Fair Is the Engineer's Image," *Arup Journal* 28, no. 2 (February 1993): 8–11, 11.

47. Frank Lloyd Wright, as quoted in David Messent, *Opera House: Act One* (Sydney: David Messent Photography, 1997), 113.

48. Jack Zunz, "Sydney Revisited," *Arup Journal* 23, no. 1 (Spring 1988): 2–11, 4.

49. Arup, "Sydney Opera House," 32.

50. Utzon to Hughes, July 12, 1976, SRNSW: DPW 4/7893.

51. Stanley Mathews, *From Agit-Prop to Free Space: The Architecture of Cedric Price* (London: Black Dog Publishing, 2007).

52. See Rawi Abdelal, "The Paris Consensus: European Unification and the Freedom of Capital," in Abdelal, *Capital Rules*, 58–64, 61.

53. Annette Fiero's book on the Grands Projets subscribes to this line with little query. See Annette Fiero, *The Glass State: The Technology of the State, Paris 1981–1998* (Cambridge: MIT Press, 2003).

54. Jonathan Brown, "Britain's Big Bang," *Multinational Monitor* 7, no. 1, and 8, no. 1

(December–January 1986–87); also see Nicholas Shaxson, *Treasure Islands: Tax Havens and the Men Who Stole the World* (London: The Bodley Head, 2011).

55. See Murray Fraser and Joe Kerr, *Architecture and the "Special Relationship": The American Influence on Post-War British Architecture* (London: Routledge, 2007), 421.

56. A number of studies appeared at this time describing the factors that underlay this "crisis." See Andy Thornley, ed., *The Crisis of London* (London: Routledge, 1992); Nicholas Deakin and John Edwards, *The Enterprise Culture and the Inner City* (London: Routledge, 1993); and also Thornley, *Urban Planning under Thatcherism* (London: Routledge, 1991).

57. Robert Hawley, "Engineering, the City, and the Arts: Who Needs to Change?" *Royal Institution of Great Britain Paper*, November 29, 2002, online at http://www.rigb.org/events/transcripts.jsp (link no longer available).

58. Jack Zunz, "Continuing Education and Training: Where Do We Go from Here?" *Arup Journal* 24, no. 1 (Spring 1989): 2–5, 3.

59. Jack Zunz, "Matters of Concern," *Arup Journal* 24, no. 3 (Autumn 1989): 22–23.

60. See the special issue of the *Architectural Review* (83, no. 1091 [January 1988] on "Unbuilt London" for documentation of these projects.

61. See Adrian Forty, "Festival Politics," in *A Tonic to the Nation: The Festival of Britain 1951*, edited by Mary Banham and Bevis Hillier (London: Thames and Hudson, 1977). Also see Alan Powers, *Britain* (London: Reaktion Books, 2007).

62. Christopher Booker, *The Neophiliacs* (Boston: Gambit, 1970); Bryan Appleyard, *The Pleasures of Peace: Art and Imagination in Post-war Britain* (London: Faber and Faber, 1989); Claude Lichtenstein and Thomas Schregenberger, *As Found, the Discovery of the Ordinary: British Architecture and Art of the 1950s* (Zurich: Lars Müller, 2001); and Stanley Mathews, *From Agit-Prop to Free Space: The Architecture of Cedric Price* (London: Black Dog Publishing, 2007). For the Tory-Labour conflict over architecture in the 1980s, see Murray Fraser and Joe Kerr, "Culture and Monumentality," chapter 6 in *Architecture and the "Special Relationship": The American Influence on Post-War British Architecture* (London: Routledge, 2007), 341–412.

63. [Ove Arup Partnership], *Thames Strategy: A Study of the Thames Prepared for the Government Office for London* (London: Government Office for London, 1995).

64. Richard Rogers and Mark Fisher, *A New London* (London: Penguin Books, 1992), 61, 76. In 1999, Rogers was commissioned by the deputy prime minister's office to make another report. See the Urban Task Force (chair Richard Rogers), *Towards an Urban Renaissance* (London: E & F N Spon, 1999).

65. Kenneth Powell, *New London Architecture* (London: Merrell, 2001), 23; also see Kenneth Powell, *City Reborn: Architecture and Regeneration in London, from Bankside to Dulwich* (London: Merrell, 2004).

66. See Evelyn M. Fenton and Andrew M. Pettigrew, "Integrating a Global Professional Services Organization: The Case of Ove Arup Partnership," in *The Innovating Organization* (London: Sage Publications, 2000), 47–81.

67. Marianne Butler, *London Architecture* (London: Metro Publications, 2004), viii.

68. Arts Council England, *Pride of Place: How the Lottery Contributed £1 Billion to the Arts in England* (London: Arts Council and August, 2002).

69. Chris Smith, *Creative Britain* (London: Faber and Faber, 1998), 53, italics added.

70. Smith, *Creative Britain*, 53.

Selected Bibliography

Arup. *Review of the Publicity Requirements for Planning Applications.* London: HMSO, 2004.

Cahill, Kevin. *Who Owns Britain: The Hidden Facts behind Landownership in the UK and Ireland.* Edinburgh: Canongate, 2001.

Maynard Keynes, John. "Art and the State." From *The Listener,* August 26, 1936. In John Maynard Keynes, *The Collected Writings.* Volume 28, *Social, Political, and Literary Writings.* New York: Cambridge University Press, 1982.

———. *The General Theory of Employment, Interest, and Money.* New York: Harcourt Brace Jovanovich, 1964.

Mini, Piero V. *Keynes, Bloomsbury, and* The General Theory. New York: St. Martin's Press, 1991.

Contributors

Aggregate

The authors of *Governing by Design* are ten scholars who five years ago commenced a collaborative discussion on the topics and the methods of architectural history. In workshops and in a formal colloquium, the members of Aggregate (as the group identified itself) presented research and debated our disciplinary aims and concerns. The group helped one another to frame our subjects, present our findings, coordinate our questions, and rethink our results. Two points of consensus—that the discipline of architectural history must engage with historical situations more broadly and that it must also address an audience beyond its affiliated professions of architecture and urbanism—prompted the writing of *Governing by Design*. Aggregate continues as a working group dedicated to questions of methodology. Although its membership remains housed within institutions of architecture and art history, the group commitment is to enriching architectural history by engaging with other fields and disciplines.

Daniel M. Abramson is associate professor of art history and director of architectural studies at Tufts University. He is the author of *Building the Bank of England: Architecture, Money, Society, 1694–1942* (Yale University Press, 2005) and *Skyscraper Rivals: The AIG Building and the Architecture of Wall Street* (Princeton Architectural Press, 2001). His current work is on obsolescence in twentieth-century architecture and urbanism.

Lucia Allais is assistant professor of architectural history and theory at Princeton University. She specializes in the intellectual and political history of architecture, urbanism, and preservation since 1900, with a particular focus on international institutions and global practices. She has published a number of essays, including "International Style Heritage" in *Volume* 20 (2009); "The Real and the Theoretical 1968" in *Perspecta 32* (2010); and a translation of Superstudio's *Salvage of Historic City Centers* in *Log 22* (2011). She is working on a book about the international preservation movement and the history of destruction in the twentieth century.

Arindam Dutta is associate professor of architectural history at MIT's Department of Architecture. He directs the Master of Science in Architecture Studies program. He is the author of *The Bureaucracy of Beauty: Design in the Age of Its Global Reproducibility* (Routledge, 2007) and is editor of the forthcoming volume *A Second Modernity: MIT, Architecture, and the "Techno-Social" Moment.* He is currently at work on a book examining the convergences of financial and aesthetic theory, provisionally entitled *Ancestralities: Architecture, Nature, and the Debt.*

John Harwood is associate professor of modern and contemporary architectural history in the Department of Art at Oberlin College. His forthcoming book project, to be published by the University of Minnesota Press, is *The Interface: IBM and the Transformation of Corporate Design, 1945–1976.*

Timothy Hyde is associate professor of architecture at the Harvard University Graduate School of Design, where he teaches courses in history and theory and serves as area coordinator for the history and philosophy of design concentration of the Master of Design Studies degree. Hyde's research on entanglements between architecture and law includes his essay "Some Evidence of Libel, Criticism, and Publicity in the Architectural Career of Sir John Soane," published in *Perspecta,* and his forthcoming book, *A Constitutional Modernism: Architecture and Civil Society in Republican Cuba,* to be published by the University of Minnesota Press.

Pamela Karimi is assistant professor of art history at the University of Massachusetts–Dartmouth. Her articles, interviews, and reviews have appeared in *Persica, Perspecta, International Journal of Middle Eastern Studies, Art Journal, Bidoun, Arab Studies Journal, Thresholds,* and the *Encyclopedia of Women and Islamic Cultures.* Currently she is completing her first monograph, *Domesticity and Consumer Culture in Iran: Interior Revolutions of the Modern Era* (Routledge, 2013). Her coedited volume (with Christiane Gruber), *Images of the Child and Childhood in Modern Muslim Contexts,* will be published by Duke University Press.

Jonathan Massey is an architect and historian of modern architecture with degrees from UCLA and Princeton as well as experience practicing and teaching in Los Angeles and New York. He is associate professor in the School of Architecture at Syracuse University, where he has chaired the bachelor of architecture program and the University Senate, cofounded the Transdisciplinary Media Studio, and helped create the LGBT studies program. Massey's research examines the ways architecture mediates power by giving form to civil society, shaping social relationships, and regulating consumption. His book *Crystal and Arabesque* reconstructed the techniques through which American modernists engaged the new media, audiences, and problems of mass society. Building on several articles examining Buckminster Fuller and the roots of sustainable design, Massey is currently researching the ways architecture manages our consumption of resources, ranging from energy and water to time, credit, and risk.

M. Ijlal Muzaffar is an assistant professor of modern architectural history at the Rhode Island School of Design. In addition, he has also taught at Columbia University, Indiana University–Bloomington, and MIT. He received his PhD from MIT in 2007 in the history, theory, and criticism of architecture and art. He holds a master of architecture degree from Princeton and a BA in mathematics and physics from the University of Punjab in Lahore, Pakistan. He is currently working on a book titled, *The Periphery Within: Modern Architecture and the Making of the Third World.* This work, based on his dissertation, looks at how modern architects and planners played a critical role in shaping the discourse on Third World development and its associated structures of power and intervention in the postwar era.

Michael Osman is assistant professor of critical studies in the Department of Architecture and Urban Design at the University of California in Los Angeles. His writings have appeared in *Log, Grey Room, Perspecta,* and *Thresholds.* In his forthcoming book, *Regulation, Architecture, Modernism,* he investigates the dependence of organizational, political, and technological systems on architecture to control the environment and the economy.

Meredith TenHoor is doctoral candidate in architecture at Princeton University and teaches architectural and urban theory in the Graduate Architecture and Urban Design program at Pratt Institute. Her research focuses on the political economy of modern architecture. She is writing a history of food, architecture, and biopolitics in postwar Paris. Other recent projects have included *Street Value: Shopping, Planning, and Politics at Fulton Mall* (Princeton Architectural Press, 2010, with Rosten Woo), a history of architects' designs for improving the food supply; "The Architect's Farm" in *Above the Pavement, the Farm* (Princeton Architectural Press, 2010); and a series of performances imagining everyday life in New Towns of the 1970s.